The Dow Jones-Irwin Guide to
Stock Index Futures and Options

The Dow Jones-Irwin Guide to
Stock Index Futures and Options

William E. Nix and Susan W. Nix

DOW JONES-IRWIN

Homewood, Illinois   60430

ISBN 0-87094-482-7

Library of Congress Catalog Card No. 83–73716

Printed in the United States of America

3 4 5 6 7 8 9 0 MP 1 0 9 8 7 6

This book is dedicated to our parents for whom we have the deepest love and respect—

Donald and Pauline Nix
John and Ruth Wilkinson

Preface

This book is the first major presentation of the new stock index futures and options markets. Our purpose in writing this book is to present the reader with the necessary terminology, conceptual understanding, and tools of analysis in developing a successful trading and investment program.

This guide is written for new and experienced commodity dealers and traders, as well as securities and options investors who wish to diversify their investments. Securities and commodities brokers will find this book a valuable source of information on these new contract markets. Financial executives and institutional money managers will find this book helpful in explaining alternative risk-management strategies using stock index futures and options contracts to hedge against both systematic and unsystematic risks of the stock market as well as enhance yields on a portfolio through an aggressive index option writing program.

The authors believe that the roles of the computer-assisted trading methods and management information systems (MIS) will expand greatly as the investing public buys personal computers and financial software to help them analyze their investments. A chapter on how to use a personal computer and computer-assisted trading techniques has been included as means of integrating the diverse fields of data processing technology and investments.

The chapters are structured to provide reference information on the basic concepts and mechanics of commodity futures and options trading, put and call trading strategies, methods of price forecasting and the current interpretation of the tax treatment of commodity and securities transactions for commercial and speculative trading accounts. Practical advice is also included on how to select a broker or brokerage firm and how to utilize commodity and securities research services available through a broker.

A general knowledge of the commodity futures and securities markets would be helpful before an investor begins trading stock index and option contracts. We integrate substantial material about futures and options markets to facilitate the understanding of the prospective stock index trader. As the reader will soon realize, several of the potentially most profitable trading strategies involve combinations of index futures and options contracts.

Trading in stock index futures and options is not for everyone. A prospective investor must analyze his orientation toward financial leverage and the risks associated with it. Many investors do not like to leverage their investments because of the possibility of margin calls and of taking large losses in relationship to their investment capital. As is true of the commodity futures and securities markets, there are two types of traders: the speculative trader who seeks substantial profits in return for taking substantial risks and commercial traders (portfolio managers) who desire to reduce risks associated with holding a portfolio of securities. Commercial and speculative traders each play essential roles in vitality and effectiveness of the capital and risk-transfer markets.

Although the motives of the speculator and commercial trader (hedger) differ, the trading objectives are the same—to make money! In actuality, there is much common ground between the speculator and commercial trader. Each must be familiar with the idiosyncrasies of the market; a workable trading program must be developed and employed; performance criteria for evaluating results must be established; and most important, each must develop a methodology for controlling risks and managing risk capital. These are not easy tasks, but neither are they insurmountable. Careful planning, thorough study, the assistance of a good broker, and the development of a trading strategy for controlling risks and evaluating performance are the essential ingredients of successful trading and investment.

William E. Nix
Susan W. Nix

Acknowledgments

The authors wish to acknowledge the following people and organizations that assisted us in compiling and reviewing information for the book:

Warren Shore and Elliott Mirman of the Chicago Institute of Financial Studies, Chicago, Illinois.

Rudy Gallat, Sam Kahan, Luke Moretti, John Helms, Jim Florsheim, and Linda Allen of the Heinold Research Department. Marvin Koehler of the Data Processing and Communications Department, Heinold Commodities, Chicago, Illinois. We owe special thanks to Messrs. Harold Heinold and John Wuethrich.

We owe special thanks to Joseph P. Tyrrell of Coopers & Lybrand, Chicago, Illinois, for his assistance and contributions to Chapter 15 on the tax treatment of index futures and options contracts.

The Staff of the Chicago and New York Federal Reserve, especially Ms. Mindy Silverman.

Jerry Traver and Reiner Triltsch of Traver Management Trust Company, Fort Worth, Texas.

Robert Bunn, independent trader on the Mid-America Exchange, for assistance on technical analysis.

The Public Relations and research staff of the following commodities and securities exchanges:

    American Stock Exchange—Julie Goodman
    Chicago Board of Trade—Jim Meisner

Chicago Board Options Exchange—Deborah Clayworth
Chicago Mercantile Exchange—Barbara Richards and
Dr. Mike Assay
New York Stock Exchange—Stan West
Pacific Stock Exchange—Robert Case Jennings
Toronto Stock Exchange—Andrew G. Clademenos

Mr. and Mrs. Harvey Tillis, Tillis Studios, Chicago, Illinois, for producing the photographs.

W. E. N.
S. W. N.

Trademarks

The following is a list of trademarks used throughout the publication.

Standard & Poor's, S&P, S&P 500, S&P 100, S&P Integrated International Oil Index, and S&P Computer and Business Equipment Index are trademarks of Standard & Poor's Corporation.

Value Line, Value Line Index, and Value Line Investment Survey are trademarks of Value Line, Inc.

NYSE, NYSE Composite, and NYSE Index are trademarks of the New York Stock Exchange.

AMEX, Major Market Index, Market Value Index, AMEX Oil and Gas Index, and AMEX Computer Technology Index are trademarks of the American Stock Exchange.

Dow Jones Averages, Dow Jones Industrials, Dow Jones Transportation, and Dow Jones Utilities are trademarks of Dow Jones and Company.

MARKETWATCH is a trademark of Heinold Commodities, Inc.

Contents

Management of Risk. The Capital Asset Pricing Model.
Optimization of Portfolio Risks and Returns. Formula for
Adjusting the Beta Factor of a Portfolio.

The Federal Reserve's Monetary Policies. Federal Reserve
Regulations Governing Securities Transactions. Interpreting
the Federal Reserve's Actions. The Structure of the Federal
Reserve. The Impact of the Federal Reserve's Open-Market
Operations. Inflation versus Disinflation. The Effects of Federal
Reserve Policies on the Business Cycle. The Effects of Federal
Reserve Policies on Stock Index Prices.

Methods of Forecasting Stock Index Prices. What Is Technical
Analysis? Types of Technical Market Indicators. How to
Determine the Trend. Support and Resistance Areas. Trend
Channels. Triangles and Flag Formations. Double and Triple
Top and Bottom Formations. Retracements. The Thrust Rule.
Head and Shoulders Top and Bottom Formations. Key Reversal
Patterns. Gaps. How to Interpret Volume and Open Interest
Indicators. Basis Graphs. Point and Figure Charts. Moving
Averages. Contrary Opinion. Analysis of Cycles of the Index
Markets. Chart Patterns and Formations. The Dow Theory
of Stock Market Activity. Correlation of Dow Jones Averages
with Other Indexes. Methods for Evaluating Index Option
Prices. Differences among the Types of Option Markets:
1. *Volatility of the Index Price.* 2. *Time to Expiration of the
Option.* 3. *Strike Price of the Option.* 4. *Prevailing Risk-
Free Rate.* 5. *Current Spot Index or Index Futures Price.* The
Black and Scholes Model for Valuation of Option Premiums.
Option Deltas and Hedge Ratios.

What Is a Business Cycle? Business Cycle Indicators: *Reference
Dates. Coincident Indicators. Lagging Indicators. Leading
Indicators. Composite Indexes.* Components of a Time Series
and Seasonal Adjustment. How to Use the Economic Indicators
for Trading the Stock Indexes. Monetary and Financial
Variables of the Monetary Cycle. The Value of the U.S. Dollar.
Fundamental Analysis and Valuation of the Stock Indexes. How

Contracts. Taxation of Index Options. Bona Fide Hedging
Transactions. Trading Activities of Broker/Dealers and
Market-Makers. Tax Treatment of Hedging Transactions on
a Portfolio of Securities. Tax-Exempt Investments. Tax
Treatment of Speculative Transactions: *Tax Treatment of Long
and Short Futures Transactions. Tax Treatment of Futures-
Options Purchases. Tax Treatment of Written Put and Call
Futures-Options.* Spreads and Straddles: *Spreads. Straddles.*
Long-Term versus Short-Term Capital Gains Treatment.
Deductions Relating to Trading Activities. Conclusions.

1

Introduction

Dow Jones Averages Breaks through the 1200 Mark for the First Time in History, April 22, 1983

It is estimated that over 30 million Americans own securities and that a sizeable number of them buy and sell securities on a regular basis. Individuals and institutions can own securities in many ways: (1) the outright purchase through a broker, (2) mutual funds, (3) pension and retirement plans, (4) employee stock purchase plans, (5) variable annuities, and (6) inheritance and gifts. Until the arrival of the new stock index futures and options markets, there had not been an efficient, cost-effective way of "buying or selling the market." The decade of the 1980s promises to be a period of strong capital investment and broad ownership of common stocks as both private and institutional investors switch funds from fixed-income investments to growth-oriented securities.

Since August 1982, the volume of shares traded on the New York and American Stock Exchanges (NYSE and AMEX) has risen dramatically. Daily volume exceeding 80 million shares for the NYSE is now commonplace. Similarly, the Standard & Poor's (S&P) 500 Index futures contract has traded over 45,000 contracts daily. The Standard & Poor's (S&P) 100 Index options contract has traded over 80,000 contracts daily within the first few months of trading at the Chicago Board Options Exchange (CBOE). These markets are expected to grow considerably over the next 10 years. Their huge trading volumes demonstrate the popularity and appeal to the equity-oriented investor and speculator.

This book is about the new stock index futures and options markets that began trading during 1982–83. Its purpose is to describe and explain the numerous trading and investment strategies that these

1

new financial products offer the investing public. Several of these new contracts are traded on commodity futures exchanges, while others are traded on securities and options exchanges. This situation tends to confuse both new and experienced investors who are not familiar with the different regulations, order-execution, and margining procedures governing futures and securities markets. The authors have tried to clarify these differences as they are presented in the book.

The authors designed a questionnaire to administer to both private and institutional investors to receive their valuable comments and opinions on how to trade these new markets. This questionnaire became a research tool in analyzing the perceived effectiveness of these new markets. The authors greatly appreciate the input from the contributors. In addition, the authors are indebted to the staff of the Chicago Institute of Financial Studies, Chicago, Illinois, for their assistance and guidance. The material for this book is the result of a series of seminars and lectures given at the institute.

The authors believe that this book will be a useful reference guide to stock and stock option investors as well as commodity traders. Professional and institutional investors may find this book useful in designing investment strategies for optimizing their established programs. Financial executives and fiduciaries who choose to ignore these new risk-management tools run the risk of criticism from their shareholders or clientele for not achieving optimum performance when compared to industry standards. It is estimated that pension funds alone control over $700 billion in securities. This represents a large pool of assets that requires price protection and yield enhancement. The field of financial planning and management is highly competitive and requires the full resources and skills of trained professionals who study and implement new concepts of investment management.

Chapter 4 is devoted to the discussion of the Federal Reserve and the impact its monetary policies and open-market operations have on the stock market. An understanding of the administration of Federal Reserve policies and open-market operations are helpful in forecasting major changes in the U.S. business cycle and stock index prices.

Chapters 5 and 6 describe and explain technical and fundamental tools of analysis for forecasting index futures prices and for the evaluation of option premiums. Various approaches to trading the stock index markets are presented so that readers can develop their own trading techniques. Chapter 16 provides sources of information and computer data bases to further research trading methods.

Chapter 15 presents the current Internal Revenue Code (IRC) rulings regarding taxation of index and options transactions for speculators and portfolio managers. The authors strongly advise that readers consult with a qualified tax attorney or certified public accountant with respect to the tax treatment of these instruments, since IRS rulings can change and may vary with individual situations.

The authors also discuss the importance of the role of computer technology in modern-day investment planning and portfolio management. In a period of a few years, the personal computer has become part of the home and office environments as a tool to manage time and information resources. We believe that the role of the personal computer will undoubtedly expand as younger generations of investors and business executives become familiarized with its applications. Well-designed computer programs and data bases can be important tools in designing and managing investment programs. A personal computer along with appropriate software can be an invaluable tool for organizing and managing time and information resources.

The authors have provided numerous examples to illustrate the various investment and trading strategies available. Tables, charts, and graphs are excellent tools for conveying information. We have strived to make these examples clear and concise for the reader regardless of his or her level of sophistication.

A stock index is a method of reflecting in a single number the market values of many different common stocks. Data on the stock indexes are compiled and published daily by various sources, including commodities and securities exchanges. An index may be designed to be representative of the stock market as a whole, of a broad market sector, or of a particular industry. An index may be based on the prices of all, or only a sample, of the stocks whose value it is intended to represent. There are numerous stock indexes available for study. This book will deal specifically with index futures and options contracts on the Standard & Poor's 500 and 100 Indexes, value line 1700, New York Futures Exchange Composite Index, Market Value Index, Major Market Index, and other industry indexes such as the Oil and Gas, Computer Technology, S&P Integrated International Oil, and S&P Computer and Business Equipment Indexes.

Other indexes, such as the Dow Jones 65 and their corresponding subindexes, will be discussed as they relate to the contract markets. It is possible in the near future that non–U.S. securities exchanges will offer index contracts based on their securities markets. This would open up possibilities for arbitrage trading between, for example, the New York Stock Exchange and the Toronto Stock Exchange (TSE).

A stock index, like a cost-of-living index, is ordinarily expressed in relation to a "base" established when the index was originated. Some stock indexes are "price weighted," while others are "market weighted."

A stock index can serve many purposes such as listed below:

To use as statistical reporting tools by Government and trade associations to measure changes in economic and business cycles over time.

To compare the performance of industry indexes such as the AMEX Oil and Gas Index versus the Market Value Index composite.

To compare the relative levels of stock prices as an economic barometer among other countries with securities markets. Stock index prices are leading indicators of economic and business activity.

To compare the performance of a portfolio manager against a representative index.

To use as a hedging tool by private and institutional investors against adverse changes in securities prices.

To increase the yield on a portfolio of securities by writing index options.

To guide speculators who want to buy or sell the "stock market" with relatively small capital outlay and assume the risk of stock market fluctuations.

Stock Indexes versus Common Stocks

Stock index futures and options contracts are not meant to compete with the selection and purchase of quality common stocks. When an investor buys shares of common stock, he is buying corporate assets in the form of management, earnings, products, services, and technology that a company possesses. An investor expects his shares to appreciate in price over the years and pay dividends as a return on capital. Corporate shares are perpetual assets unless a company ceases its business, whereas stock indexes are risk transfer instruments that allow investors to hedge risk associated with common stock ownership. Futures and options contracts are nonperpetual and do not represent the business assets that corporate shares do. Stock index futures contracts represent the broader fundamental and technical aspects of the securities market.

Some investors are good at picking individual stocks that appreciate in price, while others are better at analyzing the major trend of the entire market. Trading stock index futures and options contracts is an excellent way of "buying or selling the market" with small capital outlay. An investor should analyze and understand his own strengths and weaknesses in this area before deciding whether to trade the stock indexes.

Index Options versus Options on Individual Stocks

Index options can be traded on a composite of common stocks, such as the S&P 500, or on specific industry groups, such as the S&P International Oil Index. Index futures-options can be offset for cash settlement or exercised into a futures contract. In contrast, index options can only be offset or exercised by cash settlement.

Put and call options are listed on over 358 securities on four options exchanges. Prices and other relevant data are reported daily in *The Wall Street Journal.* Options on individual stocks such as IBM can be offset for cash or exercised requiring delivery of 100 shares of stock per option. For example, if an investor buys one IBM call option, he may exercise that call for 100 shares of IBM if it is profitable to do so. Similarly, if an investor sells a call option on IBM, he must deliver 100 shares of IBM if it is exercised.

Securities exchanges find it is more economical to list an index industry option than to offer options on the stocks within an industry group. For example, it is much less expensive to list a single index on the S&P International Oil Index than to offer options on the six oil companies that it is comprised of. Space limitations on the trading floor and budget constraints limit the number of individual option contracts an exchange can offer the public.

For the trader and investor, index options offer several advantages over options on individual stocks because (1) they have cash settlement, (2) they represent a broader segment of the securities markets, and (3) no actual deliveries of securities are required. Specific examples of the benefits of trading index options over options on individual stocks are presented in Chapter 13.

Figure 1-1: Stock Indexes of Foreign Markets

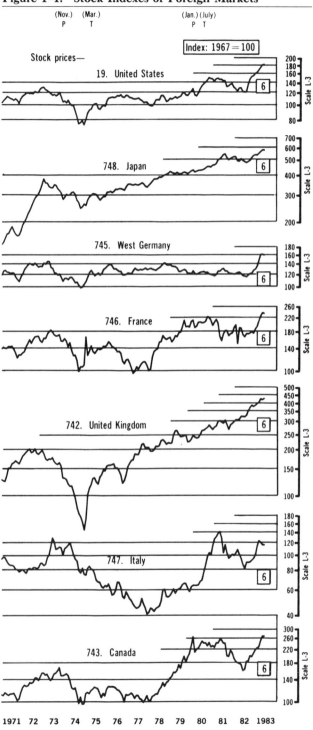

Source: *Business Conditions Digest,* June 1983.

United States and Foreign Stock Exchange Indexes

The S&P 500 Index is used as the "yardstick" for measuring the common stock prices listed on the U.S. markets against the composite indexes of foreign securities exchanges (See Figure 1–1). The S&P 500 Index is listed as one of the 12 leading economic indicators for measuring business and economic activity in the United States. Table 1–1 compares the S&P 500 against other foreign stock exchange indexes as of September 30, 1983.

Table 1–1

Country	Index	Closing Prices
United States	S&P 500	166.07
United Kingdom	Financial Times Index	702.60
West Germany	Commerzbank	939.00
Japan	Nikkei Dow Jones	9,402.59
France	CAC General	163.76

The objectives of this book are to provide the reader with the basic background and trading tools for investing in the stock index futures and options markets. The reader will have the burden of choosing which methods and strategies are appropriate for his situation. The authors genuinely hope that investors will find this book a valuable source of information and advice.

2

The Role of Stock Index Futures and Options Markets

How to Get Started Trading the Stock Index Futures and Options Markets

In way of review, some background material should be covered before getting into the more interesting aspects of trading the stock index futures and options markets. There are three distinct types of contracts for trading:

1. Futures contracts on a spot index such as the Standard & Poor's 500 Index. These contracts are traded on commodity exchanges.
2. Put and call options on index futures contracts. These are futures-options contracts and are traded on commodity exchanges.
3. Put and call options on stock indexes. These are traded on securities exchanges such as the Major Market Index (MMI) listed on the American Stock Exchange (AMEX).

Even though the underlying concepts and principles of trading are similar for these different markets, futures, futures-options, and securities-options differ significantly with respect to procedures for margining, order execution, exercise, tax treatment, pricing, sales practices, and accounting. Table 2–1 lists some general information on the various types of contract markets available.

All of these contracts have one aspect in common: they require a cash settlement upon expiration, or offset, of the contract. The cash settlement feature differs from other types of commodity and securities contracts. For example, if one were to buy a COMEX June gold futures contract, a person would take delivery of 100 ounces of gold bullion upon expiration. Or if one were to buy a July 110 call option on IBM, a person would receive 100 shares of IBM if the option were exercised.

9

Table 2–1

Futures Index and Option	Contract Size	Minimum Tick	Value of 100-Point Move
Value Line	500	5 points	$500.00
Mini-Value Line	100	5	100.00
S&P 500	500	5	500.00
S&P 100	200	5	200.00
NYSE Composite	500	5	500.00

Index on $1.00 Option	Contract Size	Minimum Tick	Value of $1.00 Move
Major Market Index	100	$\frac{1}{16}$	$100.00
AMEX Market Value Index	100	$\frac{1}{16}$	100.00
Oil and Gas Index	100	$\frac{1}{16}$	100.00
Computer Technology Index	100	$\frac{1}{16}$	100.00
S&P 500	100	$\frac{1}{16}$	100.00
S&P 100	100	$\frac{1}{16}$	100.00
NYSE 1500 Index	100	$\frac{1}{16}$	100.00

Cash settlement of index futures and options contracts was probably the single most important feature that delayed federal regulatory approval of these markets. Opponents to these contracts argued that Cash settlement was "dangerously similar to legalized gambling" since a person could bet on the stock market without taking delivery of actual securities.

Cash settlement was the only practical method that permitted these contracts to function smoothly as a legitimate hedging tool because of the near impossibility of making or taking delivery of securities on a composite index. Imagine a speculator who buys one contract of the S&P 500. Upon expiration, he would be liable for taking delivery of a large number of odd-lot shares at different prices and quantities. This possibility would have killed interest in trading these contracts for both speculators and hedgers. Also the buyers of futures and call option contracts would have been penalized since sellers and call option writers would have delivered only "poor performing stocks" against their contracts.

Registered commodity brokers are licensed to sell futures and futures-options contracts. The Commodity Futures Trading Commission (CFTC) assumes responsibility for regulating the futures and futures-options brokers and markets. The National Futures Association (NFA) plays an important role in regulating the sales practices of futures brokers and their associated persons with respect to the public.

Registered securities broker/dealers are licensed to sell index option contracts. The Securities and Exchange Commission (SEC) regulates securities and stock option brokers and markets. The National Association of Securities Dealers (NASD) was formed in 1939 to regulate sales and audit practices of securities broker/dealers. Unlike futures brokers, securities broker/dealers are required to be licensed by the state in which they are conducting business.

What Is a Stock Index Futures Contract?

A stock index futures contract is a transferable agreement between an anonymous buyer and seller to make a cash settlement upon the expiration or offset of the contract based upon the futures price at that time. Both parties are obligated to post initial margins and any required variation margins with a broker to maintain their contracts.

For example, a person buys June New York Composite Index futures at 92.50 from another party who sold it at that price. Both parties deposit $3,000 each with their respective brokers as initial margin. The total value of the contract is $500 \times 92.50 = \$46,250$. The initial margin represents 6.5 percent of total value of the contract. If the price of the index moves significantly up or down, the broker will call the losing party for more money—known as *variation margin call*. If the losing party cannot meet the margin call on time, the broker is obligated to liquidate his position. This is necessary to prevent customer debits and to preserve the financial integrity of the futures broker and the clearing house.

What Is an Index Futures-Option?

An option is the right but not the obligation to take or make delivery of a long or short index futures contract. An index futures-option is priced against its corresponding futures price and not against the spot index. An option buyer has a predefined financial obligation with respect to the contract. His maximum loss is limited to the premium paid for an option. Option premiums are determined by various factors of the market. These will be explained in Chapter 5. An option buyer has no fear of having to meet variation calls if an index price moves against him. Only licensed futures brokers can sell futures-options. Prospective customers must read and sign a disclosure document that describes risks associated with options trading.

An option writer (grantor) sells a put or call option to the buyer for a premium. The writer of an option has an obligation to post initial margins and variation margins with his broker. An option writer receives a premium credit in his account for assuming this risk. A broker is obligated to liquidate a writer's position if he cannot meet a variation call. In this respect, the obligations of an option writer are similar to that of a futures trader.

For example, a person buys a June S&P 500 160 call for a premium of 4.00 ($2,000) from an option writer as a fully paid premium. The call buyer deposits $2,000 with his broker. The call option writer deposits $6,500 in initial margins and receives a premium credit of $2,000. The account balance of the option writer has increased to $8,500 by this transaction. The option writer may sell an uncovered call, or he may buy a June futures contract to protect himself against a rising index price. Both the call buyer and writer break even in this transaction if the June S&P 500 futures close at 164.00.

What Are the Index Options Listed on Stock Exchanges?

Index options listed on stock exchanges are different than index futures-options in the following respects:

1. They are priced against a spot index price and not a futures price.
2. They cannot be exercised into an underlying futures or securities position. They have a cash settlement upon expiration, close out, or exercise.
3. Initial and maintenance margin requirements are different than futures-options for option writers.
4. Order handling and execution procedures are different than futures-options.
5. They can be offered only through securities brokers. An Options Clearing Corporation (OCC) Prospectus must accompany the first transaction.
6. Option contracts are standardized to represent a 100 shares which corresponds to regular stock options such as puts and calls on IBM. Prices are quoted as fractional numbers such as 2¼, 3½, or 5¾.

For example, a person buys a July Major Market Index (MMI) 115 call option for a premium of 5½ ($550). The call buyer must pay $550 to his securities broker. The option writer must deposit approximately $1,150 as an initial margin with his broker. The option writer may sell an uncovered call, or he may sell a call against a portfolio of securities held in his account.

Comparison of Different Investment Vehicles

With the arrival of the index futures and options markets, an investor has several choices available to him for committing risk capital. This section will compare the alternative methods for investing in the securities and futures markets using simplified examples.

Assume that you believe that the stock market will rise by 10 percent over the next 90 days. You have $70,000 in risk capital to invest. What choices do you have available?

Example 1: You buy $70,000 of "blue-chip" stocks that follow the S&P 500 Index for cash. You deposit $70,000 with your stock broker to pay for these securities.

Example 2: You buy $70,000 of the same stocks as in Example 1 except that you buy on 50 percent margin instead of fully paying for them. You deposit $35,000 with your stock broker and put the balance in an insured money market fund to meet maintenance calls should they arise.

Example 3: You buy a June S&P 500 futures contract at 140.00. This price equals a market value of $70,000 (140.00 × 500 = $70,000). You deposit $6,500 in initial margins with your futures broker and put the balance in a money market fund to meet variation calls should the futures price decline.

Example 4: You buy a June S&P 500 140 call option for a premium of 5.00. You deposit $2,500 (5.00 × 500 = $2,500) with your futures broker and put the balance in a money market fund. Since the call option is fully paid for, you would not have to meet margin calls should the S&P price decline.

Using these four examples, let us analyze the net results assuming that the stock market, as measured by the S&P 500 Index, rose from 140 to 154—a 10 percent gain. The portfolio of stocks valued at $70,000 would have appreciated to $77,000 assuming that these stock followed the S&P 500 Index. These examples do not reflect differences in financing costs, dividend distributions, or transaction costs that may significantly alter results.

Example 1:   The net gain for the portfolio of stocks is $77,000 − $70,000 = $7,000.

$$\text{Return on invested capital} = \frac{\$7,000}{\$70,000} \times 100 = 10\ \%$$

Example 2:   The net gain is also $7,000.

$$\text{Return on invested capital} = \frac{\$7,000}{\$35,000} \times 100 = 20\ \%$$

Example 3:   The next gain is 154 − 140 = 14 × 500 = $7,000.

$$\text{Return on invested capital} = \frac{\$7,000}{\$6,500} \times 100 = 108\ \%$$

Example 4:   The net gain is 14 × 500 = $7,000 − $2,500 = $4,500.

$$\text{Return on invested capital} = \frac{\$4,500}{\$2,500} \times 100 = 180\ \%$$

The authors have presented these examples for illustration purposes only and do not make a judgment as to which method is the most suitable for individual investors since there are many factors to be considered in making investment decisions. An investor should understand his attitudes toward leverage—taking profits and losses—before deciding which approach is appropriate for him. Many times this only comes with experience and may change over time as a person learns more about his attitudes toward risk.

Where and How Are Index Futures and Options Prices Quoted?

Newspapers with large circulations usually provide daily quotations on the index futures and options markets. *The Wall Street Journal* gives the most complete listing of daily prices. *Barron's* gives a weekly range of prices as well as a listing of indexes for foreign stock markets. Brokerage firms will provide price quotes to their customers when they call in. Large volume traders can have quotation equipment installed in their place of business that will give up-to-the-minute quotes on transactions. These quotations services can cost from $250 to $700 per month plus installation fees.

Futures index and option prices are quoted as cents or dollars per unit size depending on the contract size. Prices for indexes on options are quoted as fractional numbers such as 1½, 2¾, which is the convention for stock options.

How to Develop a Trading Plan for the Index Futures and Options Markets

Before one develops a plan for trading the stock index futures and options contracts, one should ask: Do I want to speculate or hedge using these markets? What is my attitude toward risk—am I a risk preferrer, risk neutral, or risk avoider? How much trading capital do I want to commit to a trading program? Do I have time to follow the markets to make my own decisions, or must I rely on a broker's recommendations? Am I a market fundamentalist or a technician? What stock advisory services should I subscribe to for information? How do I select an account executive and brokerage firm to handle my account?

The material covered in this book is presented to help both inexperienced and experienced traders formulate their trading plans. There are many different approaches to market timing, market analysis, and risk-capital management. The structure of a trading plan must include the following elements:

1. A procedure for signaling entry into the market, that is, initiating new positions in the index markets.
2. A procedure for signaling exit from the market position, that is, liquidation of market positions.
3. A procedure for allocating and management of risk capital to minimize risk and yet optimize profit opportunities.
4. Satisfactory performance criteria for measuring the success (profitability) of a trading plan.
5. Procedures for obtaining reliable sources of market information, price quotes, necessary fundamental and technical information, and trading recommendations derived from research of the index futures and options markets.

What Is the Systems Approach to Trading the Index Futures and Options Markets?

Investment funds, especially large speculative and commercial accounts, can be managed using a computerized systems approach. Fundamental and technical trading systems using computer technology have been developed for timing entry and exits from the markets as well as managing risks associated with index futures and options positions. A systems approach to trading the stock index markets, even though not guaranteed to be profitable, has distinct advantages over other trading methods. Computerized trading systems can detect price trends, give unemotional buy or sell signals, manage account equity so that risk capital is diversified and not concentrated in too few positions, and eliminate much of the market myopia caused by emotions, rumors, and unverified beliefs.

The primary advantages of a computerized trading system approach is that the validity and reliability of its performance can be measured and tested on historical price data and then cross-validated using current market price data to confirm the validity of its design. The profitability of a particular system can be tested on a simulated basis to determine its reliability and validity.

Selection of an Account Executive and Brokerage Firm

Before opening an account to trade the index futures and options markets, a prospective customer should discern the following information:

1. How reputable is the brokerage firm in handling customers' funds?
2. How committed is the brokerage firm to commodity research, broker training and licensing, and providing good customer service?
3. How experienced and knowledgeable is the account executive managing index futures and options accounts?

There are a number of reputable brokerage firms that will meet their financial and moral obligations to their customers. Recent legislation should create a less favorable climate for nonreputable brokers, but it is still imperative that prospective customers assure themselves that the brokerage firm they select is reputable and has the customers' interests in mind.

The Commodity Futures Trading Commission (CFTC) passed new legislation in August 1983 regarding categories of futures brokers. The Commission recognizes four different entities that are registered to handle commodity futures and options business in the United States. They are described as follows:

Futures Commission Merchant (FCM), clearing member of the exchange: The firm or individual is registered by the CFTC and NFA and is authorized to sell futures and hire associated persons to sell. There is a minimum capital requirement of $300,000, depending upon the exchange it is registered to do business on.

Futures Commission Merchant (FCM), nonclearing: Similar to the FCM clearing member but not a member of an exchange and not subject to all exchange financial and other requirements. Clears trades through a clearing FCM. Minimum capital requirement is $75,000.

Introducing Broker (IB): New category of firm or individual registered by the CFTC. Authorized to sell futures and/or hire Associated Persons (APs) to sell but cannot handle customer funds. Must clear trades through FCM. Minimum capitalization is $20,000 for a nonguaranteed status.

Associated Person (AP): Retail salesman also known as an account executive or registered representative. Must work for either an IB or FCM. Paid on commission, usually a percentage of rate charged to client. Registration fee, $50.

If in doubt about the reputation or business practices of a brokerage firm, a person can obtain information from the local Better Business Bureau, National Futures Association (NFA), Securities and Exchange Commission (SEC), or the Commodity Futures Trading Commission (CFTC). Before opening an account with a brokerage firm, a person should thoroughly check the firm's reputation, business practices, and the amount of experience their account representatives have had in handling customer accounts. A reputable firm will provide full disclosure of its commission costs, mail written confirmations to its customers, be registered with the CFTC and the NFA, and have licensed and well-trained account executives.

Market research is a very important subject for the prospective trader of the index futures and options markets. Good fundamental and technical research reports with trading recommendations provided by a brokerage firm could substantially increase performance. Fundamental research is needed for developing longer-term perspective of the overall market potential to move in a trend during a period of time. Technical research is needed for timing the entry and exit from the market once the move has begun or ended.

Cyclical research is the study of patterns of recurring events within identifiable time periods. The study of cycles assists in providing a "time window" for the recurrence of events that can signal the beginning or end of a price trend. For example, we might observe that the S&P Index tends to make intermediate lows every 8 to 10 weeks on the price charts. If we were looking to initiate a long position in the June S&P futures, we would time our purchase to occur somewhere within the 8- to 10-week time period of the cyclical low. Of course, we would not probably buy at the lowest price. Our objective is to buy the S&P futures at price with a reduced risk. We should set a stop-loss order to limit our losses in case the timing of our purchase is wrong.

Cyclical research can be a very useful tool of analysis when combined with sound fundamental and technical research. These approaches to market analysis complement each other and are not in opposition for making profitable trading decisions. Many brokerage firms committed to research provide excellent fundamental market reports and technical recommendations for both speculative and commercial clients.

How Much Risk Capital Should I Invest in Trading the Index Futures and Options Markets?

The novice speculator is advised not to put more than 10 percent of his or her net worth into a trading program as a rule of thumb. The net worth figure should be exclusive of home, car, and other personal assets. For example, if John Q. Public, a prospective trader, had an estimated net worth of $100,000 composed of stocks, bonds, and real estate, he should probably not invest more than $10,000 in a trading program.

Another rule of thumb for speculative trading is to set a predetermined loss figure to terminate an account. As an example, John Q. Public, a speculative trader, would terminate his program if he incurred $5,000 in losses out of his original $10,000 investment. Of course, these trading rules for risk-capital management apply to the speculator, not to the commercial trader who uses the index futures and options markets for price insurance for a portfolio of securities.

How Do I Open an Account?

A prospective trader must first determine if he wants to trade index futures and futures-options contracts or if he wants to trade the index options contracts. Registered commodity brokers are licensed to solicit accounts for futures and futures-options, whereas securities representatives are licensed for the index options contracts. Many brokerage firms have account executives who are dually licensed to solicit orders for all types of contracts—futures, futures-options, or index options.

Most brokerage firms have minimum financial requirements for their customers to prevent an undercapitalized person from suffering disastrous financial consequences in the markets. These financial requirements differ among firms; however, they are instituted for the protection of customer's and the firm's assets.

Opening an account with a brokerage firm involves filling out a *Customer Account Form,* signing several forms required by the exchanges, and making an initial deposit of funds. The broker will ask for the usual personal information, including references (personal and credit), type of trading account (speculative or commercial), instructions on sending notice statements, and any special requests the customer may have regarding the account; for example, setting up a limited or general power of attorney.

The type of account opened depends upon the client's situation and trading objectives. The different types of accounts are *Speculative, Commercial, Sole Ownership, Partnership,* and *Corporate.* Commercial accounts are designated differently from speculative accounts. A commercial client must sign a *Commodity Hedge Agreement Form* to qualify for hedge margins and commissions. A broker is obligated to explain the risks and pitfalls of trading the index futures and options markets to a prospective customer before opening an account in order to be certain that the customer understands and appreciates the risks and mechanics of trading before placing an order.

Precise communication between broker and customer is essential for maintaining a long-lasting broker-customer relationship. Broker-customer communication should result in clear instructions for placing an order. Ambiguous instructions can only result in the broker placing a discretionary order, which generally spells trouble and costly mistakes for both broker and customer. Discretionary orders are usually undesirable and should be avoided.

How Orders Are Executed on the Exchanges

When a customer gives an order to the broker, the broker then transmits it to the exchange trading in that particular contract (see Figure 2-1). Orders are sent to a specified exchange for execution depending upon the customer's preference and the particular commodity. Once on the exchange floor, the floor broker attempts to fill the order by open outcry. If other floor brokers are willing to do business, the transaction is completed, and notification of the

Figure 2–1

Index Option Order-Execution Process

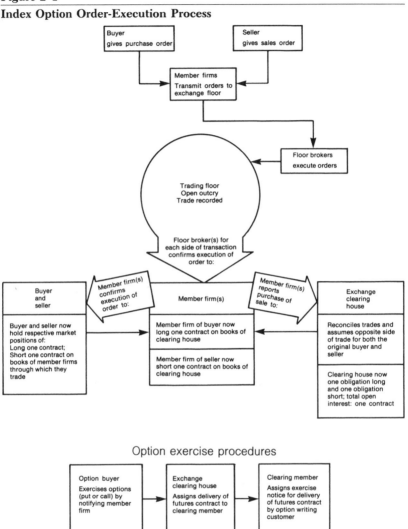

Option exercise procedures

order is transmitted to the initiating broker. The broker then communicates the confirmation of the trade to the customer by phone, followed by a written confirmation from the brokerage firm. The entire process of entering an order and receiving notification of its execution might not take longer than 5 to 10 minutes if the order can be filled immediately. The following are sample orders that might be placed by a customer:

Buy 1 June S&P futures at the Market	Market
Buy 1 June Major Market Index 120 calls at 4½	Limit
Sell 1 December Value Line futures at 195.30 stop	Stop
Buy 1 June S&P futures/sell 1 December S&P futures at December 70 points premium	Basis

The open outcry method of executing orders is probably one of the best methods of filling customer orders because orders from a multitude of buyers and sellers are shouted out on the exchange floor to be filled at a free-market price.

Where Can I Find Information on Trading the Index Futures and Options Markets?

There are many excellent sources of information for educating oneself about the index futures and options markets. Brokerage firms will provide free literature to prospective customers. Public relations departments of commodity and securities exchanges will mail free literature as well as movies, slide presentations, and other educational materials upon request. Local public and university libraries are sources of reference information. The U.S. Government Printing Office has general booklets, pamphlets, and statistical reports on the commodity and securities markets. The Federal Reserve has information available regarding the status of the U.S. and global economies.

Chapter 16 goes into further detail with regard to obtaining information, statistical data, computer software, and other specialized services a trader might need. The Bibliography at the end of the book lists some of the primary and secondary sources of information to help the reader get started in researching topics of interest.

Market and Broker Terminology

Before prospective traders begin trading, they should have a grasp of the following market terms so that they understand what they want or what their brokers want them to do. Improper understanding and communication between customer and broker can only result in hard feelings and financial losses.

The role of clear communication between broker and customer cannot be overemphasized. Even experienced brokers become confused on occasion as to what a customer wants to do. This miscommunication results in errors and unnecessary financial losses.

Margin Requirements for Trading the Index Futures and Options Contracts

Margins are the amount of customer funds deposited with a brokerage firm to maintain index futures and options contracts. Margin requirements represent only a percentage of the total value of an index futures contract. For example, if a Value Line Index futures is bought at 190, a customer might post $6,500—whether he be long or short the contract. The futures index represents $95,000 of actual stock value (500 × 190 = 95,000). The margin deposit of $6,500 is then 7 percent of the total value of the index price.

For Futures Commission Merchants (FCM), minimum margin requirements are established by the exchange on which the contract is traded for speculative and commercial customers. FCMs require less margin deposits for commercial clients because of their higher creditworthiness and hedging operations. In some instances, margin funds may be kept in the form of government securities in order to earn higher yields.

Only written futures-option contracts are marginable. Purchased options must be paid for in full. This ruling may change in the future to allow margining of purchased options, in order that they will track the underlying futures contract more closely.

Margin requirements for index options (securities options) are set by the Federal Reserve—Regulation T. Margin requirements pertain only to written options since purchased options must be fully paid for. For example, if an S&P 100 165 call is quoted at 2½, an option buyer would have to pay $250 to buy a call.

Margin requirements are related to the amount of leverage allowed by the regulatory exchanges and the brokerage firms. Higher leverage is equated to increased risk and higher potential profits for the active trader. During times of easier credit, the margin requirements permit higher leverage. During times of tight credit, higher margin requirements may discourage trading activity because of the lower leverage.

Finally, futures contracts can generate additional equity (if the trader is right the market) that can be used to put on additional positions. Options do not generate additional buying equity until they are offset or exercised. Other chapters will go into more depth with regards to margin requirements and their effects on trading activity.

The Broker Loan Rate

The *broker loan rate* is the interest charged by brokerage firms on margin accounts for securities transactions. It is related to the prime rate charged by major commercial banks. Commercial banks extend loans backed by securities to brokerage firms. Only securities transactions done on margin are charged interest on debit balances. Futures transactions, also done on margin, are not subject to the broker loan rate. This difference gives index futures a competitive edge over equivalent securities transactions.

For example, if an investor were to buy $80,000 of securities on margin, he would deposit 50 percent of the transaction value in cash, or $40,000. The brokerage firm would then finance the balance of $40,000 at the broker loan rate. Assuming the broker loan rate is 10 percent, the customer would be responsible for paying $4,000 per year in interest if the debit balance does not increase.

The S&P 500 Index futures contract priced at 160 has an equivalent value of $80,000 of securities. A customer deposits $6,500 with a futures broker as a "good faith deposit." The debit balance is $73,500 ($80,000 − $6,500). A customer does not pay interest on the debit balance of $73,500. However, he is responsible for maintaining proper margins with the broker. As these examples demonstrate, buying index futures is a cost-effective way of purchasing an equivalent value of securities when compared to buying securities on margin.

Types of Orders

Brokers can enter many types of orders for their customers. Our discussion will be limited to the more commonly used orders. They will be defined so that readers will have a general knowledge of how to use them. Both the customer and his account executive should have it clear in mind what their objective is in placing an order. This extra thought can prevent miscommunication and costly errors for customer and broker.

MARKET ORDER—Buy or sell orders filled at the prevailing market price; used to initiate or close out positions.

LIMIT ORDER—Buy or sell orders filled at specific price or better; that is, buy orders filled at limit price (or lower) and sell orders filled at limit price (or higher).

STOP ORDER—Buy or sell orders become MARKET orders when a specific price is reached or penetrated; stop orders can be used to prevent excessive losses as a stop-loss order or can be used to initiate new positions.

DAY ORDER—The order is entered for one day only; it is canceled, if not filled, at the close of the market.

GOOD-TIL-CANCELED-ORDER—The GTC order remains a valid order until it is filled or canceled.

MARKET-IF-TOUCHED ORDER—The MIT order becomes a market order if a trade occurs at the specified price. For example, buy one June S&P 100 at 167.50 MIT.

FILL-OR-KILL ORDER—This order must be filled immediately or it is canceled by the floor broker.

STOP-LIMIT ORDER—This order is executed when the market price reaches the stop price. However, the floor broker has a price limit at which he can fill the order. Unlike the regular STOP order, which becomes a MARKET order when executed, the STOP-LIMIT order places a price limit on the order. For example, sell one Mini-Value Line at 193.50 stop-limit 193.00.

BASIS ORDER—This order is entered as a price differential between two futures or options contract series; used for executing a spread or straddle order at a given basis; for example, buy one June Value Line and sell one December Value Line with December 100 points over June (100 points is the basis between June and December Value Line).

Definitions and Terminology

The following is a list of important definitions and market terms that are essential for understanding index futures and options trading. The Glossary at the end of the book is provided to help clarify other concepts and terms presented throughout.

CALL OPTION—The right but not the obligation to buy. Call buyers anticipate a rise in market prices.

PUT OPTION—The right but not the obligation to sell. Put buyers anticipate a decline in market prices.

EXERCISE—Put and call options can be converted (exercised) to a futures contract at a given strike price prior to the expiration date of the option. Call options can be converted to long futures position. Put options can be converted to a short futures position.

INDEX FUTURES CONTRACT—An agreement to buy or sell a specific stock index at a given price at some future date. Futures contracts can be bought and sold at any time up to the last trading date specified by the commodity exchange on which it is traded. All stock index futures and index options contracts specify cash settlement upon expiration, thus eliminating any problems with actual delivery of shares of stock comprising the index. Most futures contracts require less than a 10 percent margin deposit of the initial value of the stock index.

EXPIRATION DATE—(Also referred to as declaration date.) The date on which a put or call option expires worthless. Put and call futures-options may be offset, or exercised to a futures contract, at any time prior to the expiration date by the option holder. Index options can be exercised or offset for cash using the spot index price as the settlement price.

PREMIUM—The monetary consideration, minus intrinsic value of the option, for buying or writing an option. Option buyers pay the consideration to the option writer. Option premiums are paid in full to the option writer and, therefore, are not marginable as futures contracts are.

STRIKE PRICE—(Also referred to as the exercise price.) The predetermined price at which an option can be exercised into a spot index or a futures contract. Strike prices are listed at fixed intervals for each contract series.

COMMISSION—The fee charged by the brokerage firm for executing and processing customer's orders.

STRADDLE—The combination of a put and call option. Straddle buyers would buy a put and call on the same contract series. Straddle writers would write (sell) a put and call on a contract series.

OPTION CONTRACT SERIES—The designation of the type of option, the contract month, and the strike price. For example, June 160 S&P calls, December 180 Value Line puts.

SPREAD—The combination of buying and selling either puts or calls of a different contract series. Not to be confused with a straddle that is a combination of a put and a call. Buy June 165 S&P calls and sell June 170 calls for a debit of 200 points as an example.

SPECULATOR—A trader who seeks optimum risk in return for optimum profit opportunities in the market.

COMMERCIAL TRADER—(Usually referred to as a hedger.) Person who trades stock index futures or options contracts as a means of price protection against actual securities comprising a portfolio. A commercial trader may be a private investor, corporate financial officer, bank trust officer, or pension fund manager as examples.

HEDGE—The process of buying or selling futures and/or options contracts against a portfolio of securities, correlated in price and related in value to a specific stock index such as the Value Line Index or S&P 500.

CONFIRMATION—The written communication between broker and customer notifying the customer of a transaction. The confirmation usually includes the quantity, price, contract month, and the name of the securities or commodity exchange as details of the customer's transaction.

EXCHANGE—The physical location of a contract market (either a commodity or securities exchange) where customer's orders are transmitted for execution on the floor of the exchange by open outcry. Many different index futures and options contracts may be traded at an exchange. Orders are executed by floor brokers who are members of the exchange.

ORDER—The written or verbal communication between customer and broker to buy or sell a futures or options contract. An order must specify the quantity, type of commodity, contract month, commodity exchange, price, and time period that the order is to be kept in force. An example would be "Buy five December S&P 100 calls at 2.00—day order."

MARGIN DEPOSIT—The amount of funds required by a brokerage firm to initiate and maintain an index futures or written option position. Margin deposits are usually no more than 5 to 10 percent of the market value of the stock index bought or sold. Brokerage firms may require additional margin deposits if a customer position goes against him. All margin calls should be met immediately by the customer.

OPTION WRITER—A trader who sells (writes) puts or calls for a consideration (premium) that obliges the trader to deliver a long or short futures position to the option holder up to the expiration date of the option. Written options are marginable, and therefore an option writer must post initial margins with the clearing corporation.

INTRINSIC VALUE—The option price minus the premium; if the option price for out-of-the-money puts and calls equals the premium, the intrinsic value equals zero; a call has intrinsic value only if the index futures price is above the option strike price; a put option has intrinsic value only if the index price is below the strike price.

IN-THE-MONEY OPTION—A call is in the money when the futures price, or spot index in the case of index options, is above the strike price; a put is in the money when the futures price, or spot index, is below the strike price.

OUT-OF-THE-MONEY OPTION—A call is out of the money when the futures price, or spot index in the case of index options, is below the strike price; a put is out of the money when the futures price, or spot index, is above the strike price.

OFFSET—A closing-out transaction of selling a put, call, a long futures position, or buying back a written option, or short futures position.

OPTION PRICE—The price quote of the put or call that includes option premium and intrinsic value (if any). Option premium is often used interchangeably with option price but is not the same since an option premium never includes intrinsic value of the option.

SPOT INDEX PRICE—The current price of the total value of the securities comprising the actual index as computed and reported by an authorized service of the exchange. Spot index prices are calculated and disseminated throughout the trading day and may be found on market information systems along with futures and option prices.

COMPOSITE INDEX—The actual securities making up the total market value of an index such as the S&P 500, Value Line 1700, or the New York Stock Exchange 1500 Indexes.

SUBINDEX—The grouping of stocks comprising a part of a composite index. For example, the 40 utilities, 20 transportation companies, and 40 financial institutions are classified as subindexes of the S&P 500 Index.

INDUSTRY GROUP INDEX—The grouping of stocks comprising a specific industry group such as the Oil and Gas and Computer technology Indexes listed on the American Stock Exchange (AMEX).

Examples of Daily Listing of Prices, Volume, and Open Interest Data

The following is a listing of daily information on prices, trading volume, and open interest for the Value Line futures contract, S&P 500 futures-options, and the NYSE Index options.

KC Value Line Futures as of October 11, 1983

500 times index

Index closed at 200.98

Month	Open	High	Low	Settlement	Volume
December	204.30	204.70	201.60	201.65	3,136
March 84	205.50	206.20	203.00	203.00	319
June	—	—	—	204.50	2
September	—	—	—	206.00	6

Estimated volume	3,511
Estimated Open Interest	3,463

Source: *The Wall Street Journal.*

S&P 500 Futures-Options as of October 11, 1983

500 times premium

Index closed at 170.34

Strike Price	Calls-Last December	March	Puts-Last December	March
160	12.15	14.50	.65	1.60
165	7.90	11.00	1.35	2.75
170	4.50	8.00	2.90	4.60
175	2.05	5.50	5.45	—

Total call volume	262
Total put volume	291
Total call open interest	6,316
Total put open interest	1,772

Source: *The Wall Street Journal.*

NYSE Index Options as of October 11, 1983

100 times premium

Index closed at 98.39

Strike Price	Calls-Last November	February	Puts-Last November	February
90	9⅝	10½	⅛	—
95	4⅛	6½	⅝	1⅝
100	1¹⁄₁₆	3⅛	2⅞	3½
105	⅛	1⅜	6⅝	6⅝

Total call volume	2,894
Total put volume	2,062
Total call open interest	15,750
Total put open interest	14,383

Source: *The Wall Street Journal.*

3

The Role of Stock Index Futures and Options Markets in Portfolio Management

This chapter presents the applications of the stock index futures and options markets in risk management of investor-owned portfolios of securities. Modern Portfolio Theory (MPT) provides a conceptual framework for the quantitative approach to evaluating portfolio risks and expected returns. The *Capital Asset Pricing Model* (CAPM) describes the mathematical relationships between systematic risks and returns in a diversified portfolio of securities. Chapter 13 describes specific trading strategies with examples for portfolio managers and financial executives who control sizable investment funds.

Proponents of the stock index contracts experienced extensive criticism from many segments of the investment community—including the regulatory authorities who oversee these markets. The idea of trading a stock index was an abstract concept that had no precedent or regulatory history. Opponents of these markets called them a form of legalized gambling since no physical securities were exchanged, or deliverable, at contract expiration. They were concerned that the index markets would compete with and undermine the traditional function of securities markets—capital formation.

Others argued that there was no need for these markets because there were other (more acceptable) methods for hedging stock market risks. Nevertheless, the Kansas City Board of Trade (KCBT) broke tradition when it introduced the Value Line Futures Index, which began trading on February 24, 1982, despite all arguments and objections against it. Since that time, other futures and securities exchanges have begun trading indexes and petitioned the regulatory agencies for additional index futures and options contracts.

Securities markets provide a diversified media for the pooling of capital and investment funds. The process of capital formation from private sources is essential to the free-world economies. Investors have an incentive to contribute portions of their wealth and discretionary income in hopes of making further gains in the future. The securities of profitable corporations may pay generous dividends from earnings, and the price of their shares appreciate over time.

The investment of funds is not without risk. There are no guarantees that a corporation will be profitable or survive the possibility of bankruptcy. In fact, the track record for many new businesses is quite dismal in this respect. Many new as well as established companies declare bankruptcy each year for a variety of reasons. An investor assumes this risk when he or she invests in common stocks. The exchanges proposed contracts on index futures, futures-options, and index options on composite indexes, their subindexes, and industry indexes. They offer investors instruments for transferring risk of ownership of securities to speculators. An observer may ask: Why are there some many different type of index contracts available when it would appear that only a few would be necessary? This is a valid question to which we do not have all the answers. The reasoning is that the marketplace will determine which index contracts will survive. Unpopular contracts will cease to be traded after a test period. The authors believe that we will see the arrival of many new financial contracts over the next five years and the disappearance of ones that fail to attract investor and speculative interest. Until a contract has been trading for a number of months, no one can predict how successful it will be in attracting new traders.

Composite, Subindexes, and Industry Indexes

A composite index is composed of several subindexes. For example, the S&P 500 Composite is comprised of 400 industrials, 40 utilities, 20 transportation companies, and 40 financial institutions. Each of the subindexes represents an important segment of the securities markets. The subindexes can move in the same direction, or in opposite directions in relationship to each other, or in relationship to the composite index. Technical and fundamental variables can affect the prices of each of the subindexes in different ways. For example, the utility and financial subindexes are especially sensitive to changes in interest rates since their effects on corporate earnings can be evaluated immediately, whereas the transportation subindex responds quickly to major changes in fuel prices. Rising fuel costs have a negative impact on corporate profits of airline, trucking, and railroad companies.

According to the Dow Theory, described in further detail in Chapter 5, the trend of the subindexes can be used to confirm the primary trend of the composite index. A divergence in the trends may signal a reversal in the primary trend. For example, if the primary trend of the Dow Jones Average (DJA) has been up, and if the Dow Transportation Index fails to make new highs after the Industrial Index has, the lack of confirmation between the Industrial and Transportation subindexes could signal a major trend reversal in Dow Averages.

Industry indexes pertain to classifications of companies that comprise 100 industry groups as listed by the *Standard & Poor's Industry Survey*. Examples of industry groups are Aerospace, Chemicals, Drugs, and Publishing to list only a few. An industry index consists of the leading companies of a specific industry. For example, the CBOE S&P Integrated International Oil Index is a group of six international oil companies: Exxon, Gulf, Mobil, Royal Dutch, Standard Oil of California, and Texaco. The authors believe that the exchanges will introduce many new industry index markets because of their appeal to public investors and portfolio managers.

Fund managers structure their portfolios using securities included in a well-recognized index such as the Dow Jones, Standard & Poor's, or Value Line. In this way, they can compare their performance against an index when they report results to clients. Index futures and options contracts provide these managers with cost-effective methods for hedging themselves against adverse price moves without expensive restructuring of their portfolios. Some fund managers may concentrate their holdings in oil and gas companies; others may take positions in computer technology stocks. Industry indexes provide fund managers with specific hedging instruments tailored to their needs.

The Structure of U.S. Securities Markets

The structure of U.S. securities markets is divided into four general categories:

1. *Securities of closely held corporations.* These shares are owned by a relatively few number of persons and are not publicly traded, for example, corporation owned by three family members.

2. *Securities of nonprofit corporations.* These shares are owned by people who seek to create an organization for purposes other than making a profit. These shares are not publicly traded, for example, shares of Blue Cross/Blue Shield Insurance Company.

3. *Over-the-counter (OTC) securities.* These shares are publicly owned but are not broadly traded. Securities dealers make a market in these stocks via the NASDAQ system. The NASDAQ system is a nationally network of securities broker/dealers who are linked by a computerized marketing making system. As an example, shares of medium-sized commercial banks are traded in this market.

4. *Exchange-traded securities and options.* These shares are publicly owned and traded on national securities exchanges such as the New York and American Stock Exchanges. Options on securities are traded on the New York Stock Exchange (NYSE), Chicago Board Options Exchange (CBOE), the American Stock Exchange (AMEX), Philadelphia Stock Exchange (PHLX), and the Pacific Stock Exchange (PSE). These securities and options represent well-capitalized companies with a history of earnings and management. Shares of International Business Machines (IBM) are broadly owned and traded daily on the NYSE.

The stock index futures and options markets pertain to the third and fourth categories. Exchange-traded and over-the-counter (OTC) securities represent the bulk of capital owned by private and institutional investors.

A stock index is a method of reflecting in a single number the market values of many different common stocks. Other types of securities such as preferred issues, convertible preferreds, warrants, and rights are not included in the composition of an index.

Stock indexes are calculated and disseminated regularly by market information services, including commodities and securities exchanges. An index may be designed to be representative of the stock market as a whole, of a broad market sector, or of a particular industry. An index may be based on the prices of all, or only a sample, of the stocks whose value it is intended to represent. There are numerous stock indexes available for study. This book will deal specifically with index futures and options contracts traded on the futures and securities exchanges. Other indexes such as the Dow Jones Composite and the various subindexes will be discussed as they relate to the contract markets.

A stock index, like a cost-of-living index, is ordinarily expressed in relation to a "base" established when the index was originated.

Some stock indexes are *price weighted,* while others are *market weighted.* A price-weighted index gives equal value to all securities comprising the index. In contrast, a market-weighted index gives greater proportional value to those securities with the larger number of shares outstanding.

A stock index can serve many purposes in managing a portfolio of securities such as listed below:

1. Substitute purchase of securities comprising an index.
2. Substitute sale of securities comprising an index.
3. To protect portfolio against an adverse price decline by selling index futures.
4. To enhance yields on portfolio by writing put and call options against the index.
5. Dividend capture to increase yields by writing deep in-the-money call options on a quarterly basis.

In all types of equity ownership, there are benefits and risks. Prices of common stocks change, and whether individually or institutionally managed, shares of stock or portfolios are subject to the risks of adverse price moves. An understanding of the special uses of stock index futures and options requires some analysis of the nature of stock market risks. The risks associated with a stock position (whether long or short securities) can be divided into two types: *unsystematic* and *systematic.*

Unsystematic risk relates to factors that affect common stock prices of a (1) particular company or (2) an industry group. For example, if the price of sugar increased 200 percent, baking companies that have to buy sugar would be hurt by the increased costs. Rising sugar costs would not have a broad effect on stock market prices but would affect the earnings and stock prices of those companies that produce or use sugar products. Unsystematic risk can be reduced through portfolio diversification. Rising sugar prices has a favorable impact on earnings of companies that produce sugar but a negative effect on earnings of companies that use sugar in finished products.

An investor can reduce unsystematic risk by owning shares of companies that both produce sugar and consume sugar products. In this way, the impact of rising sugar prices should not have a significant effect on the overall portfolio. In addition, he can sell covered call options against specific stocks that have listed options.

Unsystematic risk declines rapidly as the portfolio increases in the number of issues from 1 to 18 or so, but it is never completely eliminated. Refer to Figure 3–1 for a graph illustrating the reduction of unsystematic risk through diversification.

Systemic Risk (also known as market risk) pertains to global factors that affect stock prices in general; for example, the level of interest rates, inflation rate, government and Federal Reserve Board policies, and changes in the tax laws affecting capital gains or dividends. Research studies show that systematic risk accounts for about 34 percent, on the average, of the price variability of common stocks. However, for a large number of issues, this risk category can account for 50 to 70 percent. The index futures and options markets can be useful tools in managing systematic risk. The S&P 500 Index is used as the barometer for comparing systematic risk since it represents a diversified portfolio of common stocks.

Index futures and options markets offer investors protection against systematic risk that is both innovative and cost efficient. The application of these markets can be combined with other risk-management strategies to reduce the costs of hedging stock market risks as well as yielding possible tax benefits for investors.

Figure 3–1

Reduction of Unsystematic Risk of Holding Common Stocks in Relation to the Number of Different Securities Held in a Portfolio (illustrates the reduction of unsystematic risk by diversification of common stocks in a portfolio)

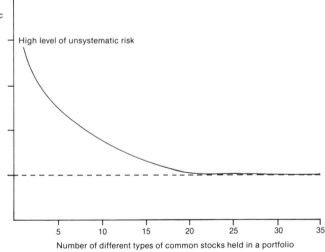

Note: Dotted line indicates the level of systematic risk as measured by a broad-based market index such as the S&P 500. Represents the degree of market risk due to price variability of common stocks in broad-based common stock portfolio.

Before an investor decides to use the index futures and options markets to hedge the price risks of his stocks, he must consider the following items:

1. Are my stock holdings large enough to assume a hedgeable position in the index markets?
2. Which spot index does my portfolio correlate the closest to in terms of price fluctuation—Value Line, Standard & Poor's or Major Market Index?
3. Which approach—fundamental or technical—should I use in making my decision to buy or sell contracts?
4. What percentage of my total portfolio value do I want to hedge at any one time—25 percent, 50 percent, or 75 percent?
5. Should I use index futures or options contracts as the hedging vehicle? What are the advantages and disadvantages of each?
6. How much trading capital should I commit to a hedging program?
7. Which types of trading strategies should I experiment with in my hedging program?
8. What kinds of advisory services and market research do I need to assist me in making risk-management decisions?
9. What are the betas of each of the securities in the portfolio? And what is the average beta of the entire portfolio?
10. Should I use fundamental or technical analysis, or a combination of both in making trading decisions?
11. What is the expected return on the portfolio if I were to leave it alone (unhedged)?

Modern Portfolio Theory and the Management of Risk

Investments in the stock market entail uncertainty of outcomes with respect to (1) estimated risk of capital and (2) expected return on capital. Modern Portfolio Theory (MPT) addresses itself to these problems. MPT is a theory of portfolio optimization that accepts the risk/reward trade-off for total portfolio return as a crucial criterion. MPT is a quantitative approach to portfolio management problems derived from statistical decision and optimization theorems. Dr. Harry M. Markowitz has been given credit for pioneering the application of statistical decision theory to investment problems. Readers are referred to Andrew Rudd and Henry K. Clasing, Jr., *Modern Portfolio Theory: The Principles of Investment Management*, for an in-depth presentation of this subject.

MPT provides the conceptual framework for mathematical models for evaluating portfolio organization, estimated risks, and expected total returns. *Index futures and index options are risk-transfer instruments that can be applied to implement the objectives of modern portfolio management.* The authors wish to describe the salient features of MPT and the Capital Asset Pricing Model (CAPM) and its implications for the index futures and options markets. To further understand the role of MPT in analyzing securities portfolio, certain concepts must be explained.

RISK-FREE RETURN (risk-free rate) is the nominal return promised by certain riskless investments. In practice, it is the rate of return guaranteed by short-term U.S. Treasury bills. Investments with a risk-free return are considered to have a beta of zero. The risk-free rate does not take into account inflation risk.

EXPECTED RETURN is the average investment return. It is the mean of the probability of investment return.

TOTAL RETURN is the combination of dividends, price appreciation, and other distributions of value from a portfolio of securities over time.

RISK is the uncertainty of investment outcomes. The term *risk* is used to define all uncertainty about the mean outcome, including both upside and downside possibilities. An intuitive definition of risk is the standard deviation of the distribution. Risk also refers to the probability of incurring loss from market action. Variance, the square of the standard deviation, must be used in comparing independent elements of risk.

BETA is the systematic risk coefficient that compares an individual security against the S&P 500 Index. Betas are derived from regression analysis in comparing the fluctuations of a security against a "market portfolio," such as the S&P 500. The S&P 500 Index is assumed to have a beta of 1.00. Data on a stock's beta is published in *Value Line Investment Survey.*

SYSTEMATIC RISK is the degree of the variance of the S&P 500 Index, which is used as a diversified portfolio of securities representative of the stock market.

RESIDUAL RETURN is the component of return that is uncorrelated with the return on the market portfolio. Residual return is referred to an unsystematic return.

RESIDUAL RISK is the component of risk associated with residual return. Residual risk is composed of extra-market covariance and specific risk.

S&P 500 is an index of 500 common stocks maintained by the Standard & Poor's Corporation. The index is used as the accepted "market portfolio" for comparison against other stock indexes both domestic and foreign. It is assumed to have a beta of 1.00.

COEFFICIENT OF DETERMINATION *(R²)* is an estimate of the proportion of return variability explained by the market factor. R^2 is a pure number that can vary from 0 to 1.00.

STANDARD DEVIATION is a statistical term that measures the degree of variability of a probability distribution of stock prices or portfolio values. It is the square root of the variance. A risk-free investment has a standard deviation and variance of zero. Approximately 99 percent of all outcomes fall within ±2.5 standard deviations.

CAPITAL ASSET PRICING MODEL (CAPM) is a model that implies that the total return on any security is equal to the risk-free return, plus the security's beta, times the expected market excess.

COVARIANCE is the tendency of different investment returns to have similar outcomes, or to covary. Covariance is positive if the outcomes are positively related.

RATE OF RETURN is the change of value of the investment, which includes capital appreciation or (loss) plus cash yield, divided by the initial value. Rate of return is usually expressed as a percentage annual rate. It may also be expressed as a decimal fraction (e.g., .10 for a 10 percent return).

INFLATION RISK is associated with the loss of real purchasing power of the dollar.

The Capital Asset Pricing Model

The Capital Asset Pricing Model (CAPM) implies that an investor should earn an expected return commensurate with the market risk he assumes above the risk-free rate. The expected return should be correlated (over a three- to five-year period) to the systematic risk of a diversified portfolio plus the risk-free rate. The systematic risk of a portfolio is equal to the average systematic risk of its component securities, weighted by their proportionate value of the portfolio.

Let us assume that an portfolio manager has sizable funds to invest. He has a choice of:

1. Investing funds in 90-day Treasury bills at a risk-free rate of 10 percent.
2. Investing in one of three diversified portfolios of common stocks.

If he invests all funds in Treasury bills, his portfolio would have no market risk and would have a beta of zero, since the return of principal would be guaranteed upon maturity. Portfolios invested 100 percent in Treasury bills can incur inflation risk due to the depreciation of the dollar and loss of real purchasing power of physical assets and services. Fears of inflation risk motivate investors to purchase common stocks if the estimated risks justify the expected returns.

Let us now assume that a portfolio manager has a choice of investing funds in one of three diversified portfolios. He compared the relative risks of the different portfolios using the S&P 500 Index as the indicator of general market risk and expected return (see Table 3–1).

Table 3–1

Sample Portfolios of Common Stocks

PORTFOLIO A—CONSERVATIVE APPROACH   Average beta = .73

Stock Name	Symbol	Price	Beta	Estimated Yield
Beatrice Foods	BRY	$30	.80	5.5
Blue Bell	BBL	36	.80	5.0
Commonwealth Edison	CWE	27	.70	11.1
Duke Power	DUK	24	.65	9.8
Procter & Gamble	PG	57	.70	4.4

PORTFOLIO B—BALANCED APPROACH   Average beta = 1.01

Stock Name	Symbol	Price	Beta	Estimated Yield
Abbott Labs	ABT	49	1.05	2.2
Avon Corp.	AVP	25	1.00	8.0
Cont'l Ill. Corp.	CIL	25	.95	8.0
MCA Corp.	MCA	35	1.00	2.6
Polaroid Corp.	PRD	29	1.05	3.4

PORTFOLIO C—AGGRESSIVE APPROACH   Average beta = 1.40

Stock Name	Symbol	Price	Beta	Estimated Yield
Amdahl Corp.	AMH	19	1.60	1.1
Hewlett-Packard	HWP	45	1.20	.4
US Air Group	U	30	1.40	.4
Tandy Corp.	TAN	44	1.40	Nil
Valero Energy	VLO	30	1.40	1.4

Source: *Value Line Investment Survey*, September 30, 1983.

1. Portfolio A is a conservative portfolio, which is assumed to have a low risk relative to the S&P 500 Index. Beta = .73.
2. Portfolio B is a balanced portfolio, which is assumed to have equal risk relative to the S&P 500 Index. Beta = 1.01.
3. Portfolio C is an aggressive portfolio, which is assumed to have greater risk than the S&P 500 Index. Beta = 1.40.

Optimization of Portfolio Risks and Returns

The scientific approach to portfolio management seeks to optimize the parameters of risk and reward to the benefit of the investor. Optimization is the best solution among all solutions available for consideration. Portfolio theory provides the mathematical constructs for optimizing expected risks and returns. The index futures and options markets supply the financial tools for adjusting portfolio risks to achieve optimal returns. These statements are best clarified by examples.

Portfolios composed of low-beta stocks (e.g., Portfolio A) yield an expected return greater than the risk-free rate but less than a portfolio that tracks the market. Such portfolios are described as conservative since their values tend to resist market declines. Conservative fund managers show good results in preserving investors' capital in bear markets. However, in bull markets, conservative portfolios lack performance which disenchants investors. They feel as if they are being cheated by not participating in rapidly rising stock prices. Consequently, they withdraw their funds and reinvest them in more aggressive funds. Investors believe they are incurring inflation risk because the real purchasing power is losing ground relative to the return on their investments.

Aggressive portfolios, such as Portfolio C, achieve outstanding appreciation in bull markets since they significantly outperform the market. Theoretically, a portfolio with a beta of 1.40 should appreciate 40 percent more than the S&P 500 Index. However, in bear markets, aggressive portfolios can lose significant value since they will tend to decrease by a greater percentage relative to the market. When this happens, investors want to park their monies in more conservatively managed portfolios. They believe they are taking too much risk relative to their expected returns. (See Figures 3–2 and 3–3.)

For these reasons, many portfolios are structured to follow the market with respect to both estimated risks and expected returns. Many fund managers prefer a balanced approach to structuring their portfolios to avoid the pitfalls of being labeled "too conservative"

Figure 3–2

Graph of Distribution of Returns for Sample Stock Portfolios

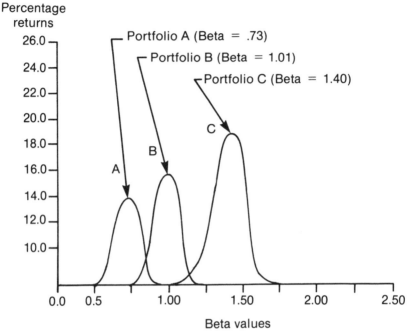

Percentage
returns

Portfolio A (Beta = .73)

Portfolio B (Beta = 1.01)

Portfolio C (Beta = 1.40)

Beta values

or "too aggressive." *Index funds* tend to follow a particular market
index such as the Dow Jones Industrial Averages (DJIA), Value Line
Composite, or S&P 500. Fund managers rely upon fundamental
analysis for stock selection and technical analysis to improve market
timing for buying and selling securities to achieve better performance than the index.

Prior to the introduction of index futures and options markets,
portfolio managers did not have a cost-effective way of adjusting
their portfolios to different market conditions. "Fear of second-guess-
ing the market" and high commission costs discouraged fund
managers from actively managing their portfolios in times of high
volatility and rapidly changing fundamentals. Also fund managers
invest substantial time and financial resources into fundamental and
technical research in selecting securities that meet the criteria of
their management philosophy. Subsequently, they do not desire to
disturb their portfolio by actively trading securities in it. Index futures and options contracts become surrogates for the trading of
the underlying securities themselves at a lower cost. Many managers
have acquired the attitude of buying quality stocks and holding
them until they go up—regardless of how long it takes.

Figure 3–3

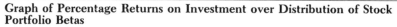

Graph of Percentage Returns on Investment over Distribution of Stock Portfolio Betas

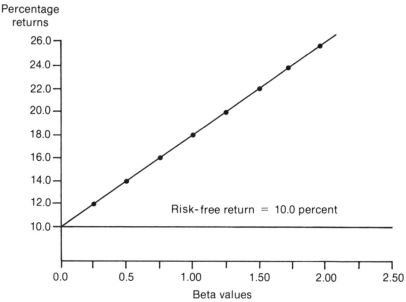

Formula for Adjusting the Beta Factor of a Portfolio

Index futures and options allow investors the flexibility of fine-tuning their portfolio risks and expected returns at low transaction costs without disturbing the underlying securities of a portfolio. For example, a conservative portfolio (beta less than .85) can be adjusted to raise the beta factor to greater than 1.00 in bull markets. Similarly, an aggressive portfolio (beta greater than 1.15) can be adjusted to reduce the beta factor to 1.00 or less. The following formula provides an example of one method for adjusting the beta factor of a portfolio using S&P 500 Index futures contracts:

$$\frac{PV(B1 - B2)}{CV} = N$$

Where:

PV = Total dollar value of securities in portfolio
$B1$ = Desired beta factor of portfolio
$B2$ = Current beta factor of portfolio

CV = Current value of one futures contract
N = Number of futures contracts need to be bought or sold for the adjustment

Let us assume the following values for the variables in the formula:

PV = \$3,000,000
$B1$ = 1.00
$B2$ = 1.40
CV = \$80,000 (S&P 500 = 160.00 × 500)

$$\frac{\$3,000,000(1.00 - 1.40)}{\$80,000} = 15 \text{ S\&P 500 contracts}$$

The sale of 15 S&P 500 contracts at a price of 160.00 will adjust the beta factor of the portfolio from 1.40 to 1.00. A portfolio manager would effect this type of strategy to reduce his exposure in anticipation of a general market decline.

The authors have presented the applications of the index markets for adjusting securities risks and returns within the framework of protfolio theory and the Capital Asset Pricing Model. Chapters 5 and 6 describe fundamental and technical methods of analysis for assisting both investors and speculators in deciding when and in what manner to trade the index markets.

4

The Role of Federal Reserve

An investor in the stock index futures and options markets should have a basic understanding of the role of the Federal Reserve System and its monetary policies. The purpose of this chapter is to provide a fundamental and conceptual framework in which to evaluate the impact of Federal Reserve's credit and monetary policies on stock index prices. The Federal Reserve System controls the supply of money to commercial banks and thus directly affects short-term interest rates. Short-term rates include federal funds, U.S. Treasury bills, prime, broker loan and commercial paper rates, certificates of deposit, and bank repurchase agreements.

Long-term interest rates are influenced by Federal Reserve policies along with the policies of Congress and the general level of business activity. Long-term rates are reflected in yields on U.S. Treasury notes and bonds, corporate bonds and debentures, and municipal bond offerings.

The Federal Open Market Committee (FOMC) meets approximately once a month to review policies and recommend changes in the course of action for the upcoming months. The FOMC advises the Board of Governors with respect to changes in monetary and credit policies that should be effected to alter the system's current status.

The Federal Reserve Board of Governors issues regular reports on the state of national and global economies. The information contained in these reports provides the basis for Federal Reserve action—whether to ease credit by increasing the supply of money, or to restrict credit by draining reserves from the commercial banking system or by putting constraints on the capability of financial institutions to extend credit.

The Federal Reserve System can only directly affect the supply of credit, which can influence the demand for it. The overall status

43

of the domestic and international business community creates the demand for credit and the longer-term growth in money supply.

The Federal Reserve's policies and open-market operations play an intricate role in adding liquidity to the banking system during times when there is a need for business expansion. Similarly, the Fed will reduce liquidity during times when there is a need for economic slowdown in order to curb corporate and consumer borrowings that put a strain on the banking system.

The Federal Reserve's Monetary Policies

The Federal Reserve has been entrusted by Congress with responsibility for making monetary policy. The Federal Reserve is responsible for monitoring money and credit conditions in the country and for providing enough money and credit so that the economy can attain the economic goals of the administration; for instance, full employment with steady growth and stable prices. At the same time, the Fed has the responsibility not to add too much money since rapid rise in the money supply could upset the economy's balance and generate inflationary expectations.

The Fed has a variety of instruments available to control the supply of credit and the growth of monetary aggregates as measured by M1, M2, and M3 (see Figure 4–1). M1 is the sum of currency held by the public, plus traveler's checks, demand deposits, and other checkable deposits. M2 includes M1 plus savings accounts and shares in money market mutual funds. M3 includes M1 and M2, plus large-denomination time deposits at all depository institutions, large-denomination repurchase agreements, and shares in money market mutual funds restricted to institutional investors.

The Federal Reserve relies on three principal tools to implement monetary policy: (1) reserve requirements, (2) the discount rate, and (3) open-market operations. Changes in the business cycle are correlated with the growth and contraction of these monetary aggregates. See Table 4–1 for a listing of economic and financial indicators.

Federal Reserve Regulations Governing Securities Transactions

The financial jolts to U.S. banking system caused by the stock market crash in 1929 and the ensuing wave of bank failures in the 1930s provided justification for new legislation to regulate the supply

Figure 4–1: Money Stock with Target Growth Ranges (monthly; seasonally adjusted)

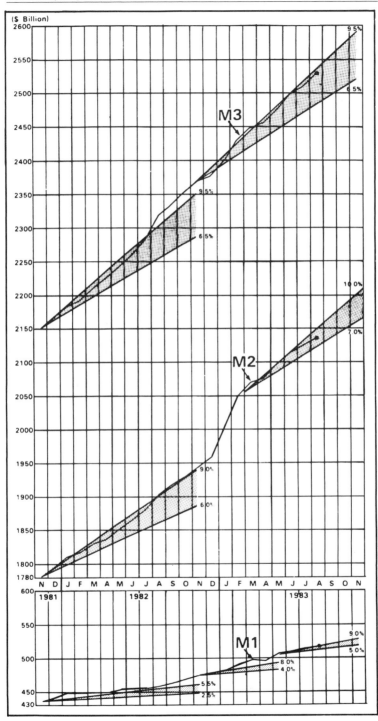

Source: Federal Reserve Board, August 1983.

Table 4-1

Table of Economic and Financial Indicators

	Latest Period	Preceding Period	Year Ago
Federal Reserve Condition Report, Mil $, Sept. 7:			
Loans and securities, total	671,483	r670,860	643,705
U.S. Treasury securities, total	52,692	r51,400	38,973
Other Securities, total	84,740	r84,421	81,669
Other loans, gross	507,556	r507,292	494,713
Commercial & Industrial	214,098	r214,063	213,645
Real estate	137,246	r137,078	132,462
Financial institutions, total	41,635	r41,046	43,177
Nonbank brokers & dealers	8,941	r9,421	7,165
Total Assets	919,640	r915,593	878,518
Demand deposits, total	181,746	r177,392	177,682
Domestic commercial banks	21,297	r20,049	21,376
Savings deposits, total	174,705	r172,771	83,272
Time deposits, total	245,567	r246,250	322,148
Total Liabilities	858,113	r854,221	821,107
Federal Reserve Bank Changes, Mil $, Sept. 21:			
Gov't. securities bought outright	145,805	144,732	131,319
Federal agency issues bought outright	8,737	8,740	8,949
Borrowings from Fed	2,109	1,148	810
Seasonal Borrowings	186	185	100
Extended credit	520	501	118
Float	877	r1,640	2,282
Total reserve bank credit	169,028	r164,005	153,823
Treasury gold stock-z	11,128	11,128	11,148
Currency in circulation	161,542	162,678	148,425
Treasury deposits with banks	7,175	3,438	3,611
Reserves with Fed banks	21,829	r19,561	24,543
Total reserves including cash	38,341	r37,133	40,254
Required reserves	38,096	36,711	40,004
Net borrowings from Fed	1,403	462	592
Excess reserves	245	r422	250
Free reserves	−1,158	r−40	−342
Money Supply (M1) Bil $, sa, Sept. 14:	515.4	518.5	460.6
Monetary Base, Bil $, Sept. 21	183.20	r183.09	172.11
Federal Reserve Interest Rates, % Sept. 21:			
Federal Funds	9.48	9.54	10.31
Treasury bill (90 day)	9.02	9.10	7.75
Commercial paper (dealer, 90 day)	9.28	9.29	10.52
Certfs of Deposit (resale, 90 day)	9.42	9.43	10.84
Eurodollar (90 days)	9.85	9.91	11.93
Money Market Funds, Bil $, Sept. 21:			
Total Assets	164.5	164.1	225.8
Mutual Funds Liquidity asset ratio, % July:			
Equity and Balanced Funds	9.1	9.7	11.0
Treasury Statement, Bil $, Sept. 19:			
Gross Federal Debt	1,354.7	1,355.3	1,106.7
Statutory Debt Limit	1,389.0	1,389.0	1,143.1

p—Preliminary. r—Revised. sa—Seasonally Adjusted. z—Actual.
Source: *Barron's*, September 14, 1983.

of credit in this area. The Federal Reserve System directly adminis-
ters the extension of credit for securities transactions through
Regulations X, G, T, and U.

Regulation U (Reg U) establishes the credit relationship between
the bank and broker or dealer—specifically loans made by the
bank to the broker or dealer against securities pledged as collat-
eral.

Regulation T (Reg T) establishes the credit relationship between
the broker or dealer and the customer. Reg T sets the initial
minimum margin requirements for purchasing securities. Reg
T applies to both listed and unlisted securities—cash and margin
accounts.

Regulation X (Reg X) pertains to borrowers who obtain securities
credit.

Regulation G (Reg G) pertains to securities credit by persons
other than banks, brokers, or dealers.

In contrast to the securities exchanges, there are no Federal Reserve regulations governing the extension of credit and margin
requirements for commodity exchanges and commodity futures contracts. Policies and regulations regarding margins and credit are
determined by the Board of Governors of each commodity exchange
subject to approval by the Commodity Futures Trading Commission
(CFTC).

Interpreting the Federal Reserve's Actions

Fed Watchers are economists who specialize in evaluating the
Fed's policies and translating them into an investment strategy for
the firm's clients. At best, Fed Watchers make educated guesses
at what course of action the system will take in easing or restricting
the growth of money and credit.

The Structure of the Federal Reserve

The Federal Reserve System is the nation's central bank, which
is a quasi-independent organization that reports to Congress. It provides essential services to the banking community, and it functions
as a bank for the federal government. In emergencies, the Federal

Reserve can act as the "lender of last resort" if a financial institution borders on collapse.

The President appoints seven persons, who serve as members of the Board of Governors, by and with the consent of the Senate, for 14-year terms. The Federal Reserve Board makes policy decisions that do not have to be ratified by the President or one of his appointees in the executive branch of the government. However, the Fed is sensitive to the policies of Congress and the President.

The nation's central bank sets policies and procedures that impact a broad spectrum of investment decisions. The fundamental responsibility of the Fed is to regulate the growth of the nation's money supply and the expansion of credit extended through the commercial banking system. Most of the major commercial banks are members of the Federal Reserve System, which allows it to regulate interest rates and credit.

The Federal Reserve System was established in 1913 when President Woodrow Wilson signed the Federal Reserve Act. The original purpose of the system was to give the country an elastic currency, provide facilities for discounting commercial paper, and improve the supervision of banking. From its inception, it was recognized that the policies of the system were in fact aspects of broader economic and financial objectives. Over the years, the primary objectives of the Federal Reserve have been to foster economic stability and growth, a high level of employment, stability in the purchasing power of the dollar, and a reasonable balance in transactions with foreign countries.

Prior to 1980, access to Federal Reserve services was restricted, with limited exceptions, to commercial banks that were members of the system. Member banks maintained reserve accounts and received Fed services at no charge. The Monetary Control Act of 1980 changed all that. This act extended reserve requirements to all depository institutions, opened Fed services to all depository institutions, and required the Federal Reserve to charge fees for specified services.

The Federal Reserve is headquartered in Washington, D.C. It oversees the activities of the 12 Federal Reserve banks. These Reserve banks are located in major cities throughout the United States. Each bank serves one of the nation's Federal Reserve Districts. They act as borrowers and lenders to over 5,800 member banks. In addition, the Federal Reserve can act as a "lender of last resort" for depository institutions that face emergency situations. Should a depository institution experience a short-term, unexpected drain on its funds, the Fed can extend a temporary loan to that institution.

The Impact of the Federal Reserve's Open-Market Operations

The Federal Reserve holds a large portfolio of U.S. government securities and engages in open-market trading with approximately 36 major securities dealers. The trading desk at the New York Federal Reserve Bank, through which open-market purchases and sales of government securities are made, maintains direct telephone communication with the dealers. A "foreign desk" at the New York Federal Reserve Bank conducts transactions in the foreign exchange market.

When it wishes to restrain money supply growth, the Fed sells U.S. government securities on the open market. Securities dealers then pay the Fed from deposits held at their banks, and the Fed simply deducts an equivalent amount from the bank's reserve accounts. As a result, the banks have fewer lendable funds, and they are not able to make as many new loans. They might even have to sell some of their investments. This could in turn lead to a contraction throughout the banking system, and the total volume of checking account money would decline. The federal funds rate rises thus raising short-term interest rates.

The Federal Reserve Account Manager, who is located at the New York Federal Reserve District Bank, can add and drain reserves from the commercial banking system by repurchasing and selling from his portfolio of government securities. Depending on his actions, he can add either temporary or permanent reserves to the banking system. Likewise, he can drain reserves on either a temporary or permanent basis.

The Fed can add reserves by repurchasing securities—known as repurchase agreements (or REPOS)—and can drain reserves by performing matched sale-purchase agreements. When the Federal Reserve makes a matched sale-purchase agreement, it sells a security outright for immediate delivery to a dealer or foreign central bank, with an agreement to buy the security back on a specific date (usually within seven days) at the same price. Matched sale-purchase agreements are the reverse of repurchase agreements and allow the Federal Reserve to withdraw reserves on a temporary basis.

The act of adding or draining reserves serves to regulate the cost of funds. Adding reserves temporarily increases the supply of money and thus lowers interest rates, whereas draining reserves tightens up the availability of money and thus raises rates.

Federal Reserve actions can affect the value of the U.S. dollar against other currencies. When U.S. interest rates are high relative to other countries such as Germany or the United Kingdom, foreign investors will buy U.S. dollars to invest in dollar-denominated securities. When U.S. rates are low relative to other countries, investors will sell dollars and liquidate their dollar-denominated securities. A strong dollar attracts foreign funds into U.S. capital markets, which are bullish for securities prices. A weak dollar is bearish for securities prices since investors will sell U.S. securities in order to buy securities of stronger currencies.

The stock market began a major rise (over 480 points) since August 1982, when the Fed lowered the discount rate from 11 to 8.5 percent. Prior to that tremendous rise, high U.S. rates discouraged the purchase of common stocks but strengthened the dollar. Investors had invested their monies in money market funds, which earned a high rate of interest. When interest rates dropped in sympathy with the Fed's cut in the discount rate, investors moved funds from money markets to the stock market, thus fueling a major bull market. A strong dollar encouraged foreign buyers to invest in U.S. securities as a flight to quality against further devaluation of their own currencies.

As the nation's central bank, the Federal Reserve Board tries to respond to national and international events in ways that preserve political and economic stability in the free-world countries. Inappropriate Federal Reserve policies can destabilize national and (indirectly) foreign economies. For example, tight credit policies can cause high unemployment, declining business activity, large federal budget deficits, and a large balance-of-trade deficit due to a uncompetitive foreign exchange rate.

Similarly, loose credit policies can produce an equally bad situation by creating an environment of spiraling price inflation in which the U.S. dollar loses purchasing power and the respect of both American and foreign investors. The energy crisis caused by the rising cost of oil and gas prices helped depreciate the U.S. dollar over a 10-year period. Both domestic and foreign investors lost confidence in the dollar as a reserve currency. Investors shifted their funds from dollar-denominated securities to hard assets such as precious metals and commodities in response to fears that inflation would soon make paper currencies worthless.

The Federal Reserve attempts to balance monetary expansion while keeping price inflation in check. This appears to be a contradiction, and in many ways it is. Compromise is in order since the Fed attempts to regulate credit to allow a reasonable growth in monetary aggregates while tolerating a moderate rate of price inflation. In recent years, the Fed, under the direction of Federal Reserve Chairman Paul Volcker, has tried to target the growth of monetary aggregates within predefined band (see Figure 4–1). If the money supply exceeded the upper limits of this band, thus signaling the danger of inflation, the Fed would tighten credit by exercising a number of alternatives such as restricting the availability of reserves and then raising the discount rate. The Fed would lower the discount rate when the money supply figures dipped below the lower end of the target band. In this way, the Fed would hope to achieve a moderate growth in money supply to "grease the wheels of the economy" while tolerating a limited degree of price inflation.

Inflation versus Disinflation

Inflation is misunderstood by most people. Essentially, it is a phenomenon that occurs when prices of products and services increase at a faster rate than the level of real productivity necessary to produce them. Inflation is measured by various indexes such as the consumer and producer price indexes (CPI and PPI) or in relationship to the gross national product (GNP).

Inflation has been with mankind since governments began issuing paper money. Some economists and politicians believe that any inflation is evil and could be removed from the economy by returning to a commodity-backed currency redeemable in gold or silver. Gold and silver represent tangible assets with intrinsic value that cannot be debased, only enhanced, by the government's printing presses. There are merits to this line of reasoning. However, a currency based on gold or silver is impractical for many reasons and may not be in the national interest. A gold-backed currency does not ensure stable prices or guarantee economic growth. Economists opposed to gold-backed currency argue that a government could arbitrarily set the price of gold and silver in response to its need to monetize its debt.

The authors believe that a moderate rate of inflation (in a band between 2 to 4 percent per year) is part of the normal process of economic and business growth as the supply of credit grows and contracts to changing demands of business and government. Excessive inflation can distort the decision-making process of businessmen and labor. Businessmen accumulate and hoard inventories that create shortages in fear that prices of raw and finished goods will rise still further. Labor leaders and workers demand higher wages and benefits to offset the decline in real purchasing power. Excessive inflation creates an environment in which everyone loses. People lose faith in their national leaders and their system of government as inflation strips them of their means to support themselves.

The Federal Reserve System can add liquidity to the banking system in response to the need for increased credit by businesses. The Fed wants to foster business expansion especially after a recessionary period.

Disinflation occurs when prices fall dramatically as measured by the consumer and producer price indexes. In some ways, disinflation can be as harmful as excessive inflation. Prior to a deflationary period, businessmen have adapted their decision making and planning to rising prices and an increased demand for their products or services. It appears they cannot keep up with the robust demand for their goods and services. Near the end of a long inflationary period characterized by rapid business expansion, the demand for goods and services accelerates rapidly as do prices for raw materials, labor costs, and administrative expenses.

In order to meet the accelerating demand for their products and services, businesses borrow money at high interest rates to expand capacity and production. The increased borrowings push interest rates up even higher to a point where businesses assume tremendous debt service. At this point the Federal Reserve System decides that inflation is out of hand and that it must take corrective measures to curb the growth in the money supply. Depending upon the seriousness of the situation, the Fed can take any number of actions to curb inflation. The following list includes possible actions to reduce liquidity in the economy (i.e., shrink the growth of the supply money and thus reduce inflation). See Figures 4–2, 4–3, and 4–4 for the relationship between the inflation rate and (a) interest rates, (b) economic activity, and (c) unemployment.

1. Raise the discount rate.
2. Raise reserve requirements for depository institutions.
3. Conduct matched sale-purchase agreements of Treasury securities via open-market operations.
4. Raise the federal funds rate.

If the Fed wants to increase liquidity in the banking system and the overall economy, it can:

1. Lower the discount rate.
2. Lower fractional reserve requirements for depository institutions.
3. Repurchase agreements of Treasury securities via open-market operations.
4. Lower the federal funds rate.

Figure 4–2

Inflation and Interest Rates (quarterly)

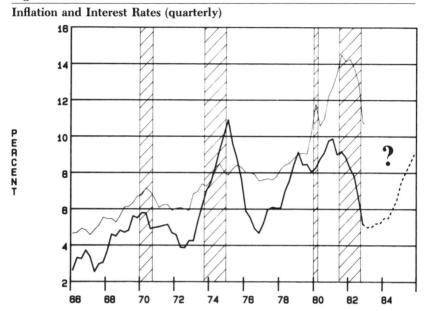

Source: *Heinold Marketwatch*, June 1983.
Thick line = Inflation rate, measured by four-quarter average of GNP price defla-
tor. Thin line = 20-year U.S. bond yield. Shaded areas = U.S. recessions.

The Effects of Federal Reserve Policies on the Business Cycle

A business cycle describes the time series of events during which
the level of economic and business activity expands and contracts.
The peak of a business cycle is characterized by robust activity,
low unemployment, rising prices, high plant utilization, and rising
corporate borrowings and interest rates. The trough of a business
cycle is depicted by depressed economic activity, high unemployment, declining prices, low plant utilization, and declining corporate
borrowings and interest rates. The events of a business cycle are
affected by total spending from government, corporate, and consumer sectors.

The events of a business cycle are related causally to the Federal
Reserve's expansionary and restrictive credit and monetary policies.
The Fed's policies are modified in response to changes in the business
cycle in order to maintain the primary objectives of the Federal
Reserve System: (1) stable prices, (2) strong U.S. dollar, and (3) mod-

Figure 4-3

Economic Activity and Inflation (quarterly)

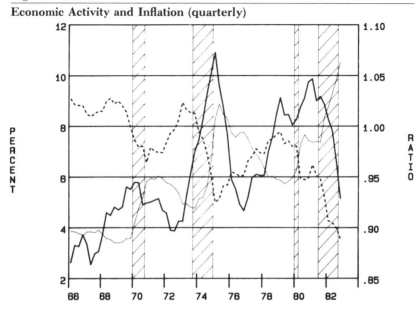

Source: *Heinold Marketwatch*, May 1983.
Thick line = Inflation rate, measured by four-quarter average of GNP price defla-
tor. Thin line = unemployment. Dotted line = Ratio of real GNP to potential GNP.

erate rate of growth in the money stock. The Fed takes decisive
action to restore balance whenever their major objectives are threat-
ened by excessive robustness in business activity or a steep recession.

Thus the Fed's monetary policies and open-market operations
indirectly affect investor expectations about corporate earnings and
profitability by imposing Fed control over the availability of credit
and funds from the banking system to consumers and businesss.

Expansion in business activity after the trough of a business cycle
has been observed is positively correlated with rising stock index
prices. At or near the trough of a business cycle, the Federal Reserve
eases credit and increases the liquidity of the banking system to
stimulate economic activity and the subsequent demand for goods
and services.

Investors buy securities on the anticipation of increased earnings
and profits at or near the bottom of the business cycle. Rising stock
index prices are positively correlated with an easing of credit and
an expanding money supply near the bottom of a business cycle.

Figure 4–4

Inflation and Unemployment Rates (monthly)

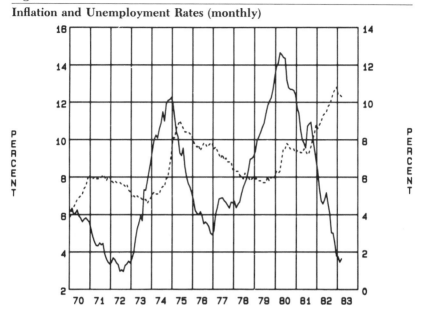

Source: *Heinold Marketwatch*, March 1983.
Solid line = Inflation (left scale).
Dotted line = Unemployment (right scale).

Thus, stock indexes prices are leading economic indicators of an eventual turn in the business cycle.

The Effects of Federal Reserve Policies on Stock Index Prices

One of the problems in analyzing the effects of Fed's policies on stock index prices is the lead-lag variables that exist in the time series of events. The correlations between specific changes in the Fed's policies and stock prices are distorted by these relationships.

Stock index prices are affected by investors' expectations regarding inflation, interest rates, credit conditions, taxation of capital gains, and the capability of corporations to earn profits and pay dividends. Common stocks and equivalent securities are compared by investors to alternative investments with respect to total expected return on capital and the risk assumed by the investor.

Table 4–2 summarizes the factors that are bullish and bearish to stock index prices.

Table 4–2

Bullish and Bearish Factors

Factor	Bullish	Bearish
Discount rate	Raise	Lower
Broker loan rate	Raise	Lower
Rate of inflation	Low	High
Money supply growth	Higher	Lower
Reserve requirements	Lower	Raise
Open-market operations	Repurchase agreements	Matched sale
Reg T and Reg U	Lower	Raise

In conclusion, actions by the Federal Reserve affect investors' expectations of corporate earnings performance and are ultimately reflected in the behavior of the stock indexes. An investor who is aware of the Federal Reserve's actions and how to interpret them within a framework of appropriate investment strategies can apply this knowledge to forecast the direction of stock index prices.

5

The Tools of Technical Analysis for Trading

Methods of Forecasting Stock Index Prices

Methods of forecasting stock index prices range from astrological predictions to sophisticated computer trend following models. Because of the great diversity of techniques available, we will restrict our discussion to fundamental and technical analysis of stock index prices. The tools of fundamental and technical analysis can be used to complement each other in formulating short-term and longer-term price forecasts of stock index prices—which can be translated into investment decisions. The large number of interacting variables that influence stock index prices causes the apparent uncertainty and randomness of price behavior. At any point in time, stock index prices appear to be either *(a)* rising, *(b)* staying unchanged, *(c)* declining, *(d)* following an identifiable trend, or *(e)* fluctuating randomly without an apparent direction—random walk.

Level of business activity, interest rates, rate of inflation of consumer and producer prices, investor expectations regarding corporate earnings and dividends, capital gains taxation, Federal Reserve Board policies, U.S. Treasury and congressional policies, and the status of the global economy are only a few of factors that impact stock market prices. Investors translate their beliefs and feelings about these events into buying or selling behavior. If their feelings are generally good about corporate earnings, they buy stocks. Similarly, if their psychology is pessimistic about the ability of corporations to earn profits, they liquidate holdings and buy other investments such as gold, real estate, or government securities.

The question that a trader asks is: How can I profit from the volatile price action of the stock market? There are many different factors that push stock prices higher or make them fall. How can traders profit from these price gyrations under conditions of uncertainty? The partial answer to this question is the formulation of a long-term price forecast based upon a fundamental approach to the stock market. Fundamental analysis attempts to answer the questions: Is the price of this index expected to rise or fall over the next three to six months? How much is it expected to rise or fall during that period? The fundamental approach to the market uses methodology for valuing stock index prices based upon current and historical date. The price of a stock index reflects the expected values of corporate earnings, profits, and dividends in relationship to the prices of the securities comprising the index.

What is the expected market value of the stocks comprising the S&P 500 Index? Should the total value of the stocks in the composite index be valued at 165.00 ($82,500) or 170.00 ($85,000)? These are difficult questions to answer. However there are statistical valuation methods that can be applied to give estimates for these values. Chapter 6 covers these methods in more detail.

What Is Technical Analysis?

Technical analysis attempts to answer the following questions: What is the current price trend of the stock index—up, down, or sideways? At which price should I buy, sell, or close out my positions? Thus, fundamental analysis tells the trader what the long-term perspectives and expectations of stock index prices are, based upon valuations of corporate profits, earnings, and dividends. Technical analysis tells the trader when to initiate or close out positions in the market. Stated another way, fundamental analysis provides a rationale for either buying or selling a particular index, and technical analysis assists the trader in telling him when and at what price to do it.

Before proceeding further, several points of clarification might assist the reader. Price forecasting models make the implicit assumption that knowledge of past events can be utilized with sufficient reliability in making inferences about future events. This is a reasonable assumption, and the best one considering the degrees of uncertainty of the stock market. We would like to emphasize that future stock index price changes are not necessarily related to past price patterns. Price forecasting models cannot predict the future value of the stock index but can only make inferences and probability statements about future price expectations with certain limits of reliability. Drastic changes in global economics, governmental policies, Federal Reserve policies, and Internal Revenue Code (IRC) rulings regarding the treatment of capital gains can bring about fundamental reappraisals of stock index valuations.

The study of technical analysis is a fascinating subject even though strict fundamentalists may accuse technicans of trying to "read tea leaves or tarot cards." The purpose of this chapter is to provide readers with some of the basic tools for analyzing price behavior and for formulating appropriate trading strategies. It is beyond the scope of this book to present a comprehensive review of technical analysis since the subject could cover several volumes by itself. There are several excellent books available on this subject that explains it in greater detail. *Technical Analysis of Stock Trends* by Edwards and Magee remains a primary source for serious students of this subject. Readers are referred to the Bibliography at the end of the book for additional references.

Technical analysis of stock indexes involves the study of price behavior irrespective of any fundamental valuation of securities prices. An important assumption of technical analysis is that all relevant factors of the index price are reflected in price variability, open interest, and volume of trading. Technical traders look for "signs" to give them indications when a major price move—up or down—is about to begin or when a reversal has occurred in a previous price trend. Technical signs may take many forms depending upon the orientation of the trader. Technical trading systems are derived from the formal principles of technical analysis. The technical approach to trading has the following advantages:

1. Data on index prices, volume, and open interest is available to the public. There is no "insider information."
2. Many technical systems give precise buy or sell decision signals at specified prices that can be tested for reliability and validity with historical data.
3. Technical trading systems can be integrated with risk-management techniques that can "cut losses and let profits ride."
4. Certain technical models can be used to forecast the extent of price moves by using geometric projections; for example, the Fibonacci number series for estimating price retracements.
5. Many technical systems are simple to understand and update for trading, usually by keeping graphs, charts, and worksheets. Graphical displays of technical data allow the trader to visualize past and current price trends as well as levels of price support and resistance.

6. Many technical systems lend themselves readily to computerization to manage data files and generate trading parameters. The use of personal computers can be instrumental in generating graphs and charts from a data base of stock index prices. And finally, the principles of technical analysis apply to a broad spectum of situations—from trading pork bellies contracts to shares of General Motors.

The more frequently used methods of technical analysis are (1) bar-graph charting, (2) point-and-figure charting, (3) moving averages, (4) relative strength indicators, (5) momentum oscillators, (6) support and resistance areas, (7) volume and open interest indicators, (8) cycle analysis, (9) basis graphs, (10) chart pattern formations, and (11) pattern recognition—the use of multiple criteria in making a technical trading decision.

Types of Technical Market Indicators

Stock prices tend to move in random fashion about 70 percent of the time. By random, we mean that index prices form congestion patterns on the charts with no clear trend. Similarly, they tend to develop a price trend about 30 percent of the time. The task of technical analysis is to identify when a specific stock index is exhibiting *(a)* nondirectional or *(b)* directional movement. Once a trader has made this determination, he can select the appropriate technical trading techniques. The following is a list of technical trading indicators categorized by the type of price movement:

**Nondirectional Movement—
Random Price Behavior**
1. Relative strength indicator (RSI).
2. Momentum.
3. Volatility.
4. Reaction trend.
5. Swing index.
6. Cycle.
7. Basis trading.
8. Chart formations.

**Directional Movement—
Indentifiable Trend**
1. Moving averages.
2. Parabolic.
3. Chart formations.
4. Volatility.
5. Reaction trend.
6. Cycle.
7. Pattern recognition.

A technical analyst uses charts as his basic tools for developing a visual representation of past and current stock index price behavior. Charts may be constructed on arithmetic, logarithmic, or square root scale, or projected as "oscillators." Charts can delineate moving averages, trading volume, open interest, or an infinitude of other relations, ratios, and indexes. Usually, constructing a bar chart is the first step in technical analysis. Price movement is charted on a graph with price movement recorded on the vertical axis and time on the horizontal axis. In most cases, a market's price action is recorded a day at a time by drawing a line between the daily high and low, with the close denoted by a small vertical dash. In addition, many chartists keep weekly and monthly price continuation charts. Weekly and monthly charts provide a more accurate picture of major support and resistance areas. As the market's price action is plotted, certain patterns of movement can be seen. These patterns or "chart formations" often signal impending price action or at least permit a trader to adopt a reasonable trading strategy and limit his risk.

Percentage relations are important in trading stock index contracts. Arithmetic scales represent equal amounts in points, whereas semilogarithmic scales represent percentage changes. Using the Value Line Index as an example, the difference between 80 and 100 on the vertical scale is exactly the same as that from 180 to 200. On the logarithmic scale, the difference from 80 to 100, representing an increase of 20 percent, compared to a 10 percent increase, is the difference between 180 to 200.

Semilogarithmic graph paper permits direct comparison of high- and low-priced indexes and makes it easier to choose the one offering the greater percentage profit on the funds to be invested. In addition, it facilitates the placement of stop-loss orders. We recommend the use of semilogarithmic graph paper over arithmetic scales in constructing index price charts.

How to Determine the Trend

Charts are valuable tools for visualizing index price trends. Sometimes the major price trend may be disguised within a series of minor and intermediate trends that might be compatible or contrary to the major trend. Minor trends run less than 30 days and are the steepest of all trends. The next longest trend is called an intermediate trend. It may run from one to six months. It can be identified by comparing closing prices for each week. The longest trend, called the major trend, continues in the same pattern for six months or longer. Investment and trading decisions should be consistent with the major trend of the index market.

An uptrending market is characterized by index prices making higher highs and higher lows. A downtrending market is characterized by index prices making lower highs and lower lows. A trend can last for days, weeks, months, or years depending upon the fundamentals that cause the price trend. When a market is not in a trending phase, prices often swing within a definable range, and a "sideways" trading pattern results. A 45-degree angle drawn across major tops and under major bottoms can help a technician identify major changes in the trend. This is especially true on weekly price charts.

In an uptrending market (bull market), a trader wants to initiate long index futures positions or purchase call options to profit from expected higher index prices. In a downtrending market (bear market), a trend should initiate short futures positions or buy put options to profit from an anticipated price decline.

Support and Resistance Areas

Investors buy stocks at prices that they believe to be fairly valued in relation to corporate earnings. Price levels at which securities are bought establish the *support* areas of the market. Investors tend to accumulate securities at these levels. Support areas on the charts constitute the demand level for buying securities comprising a stock index.

Price levels at which investors sell securities are called *resistance* areas. Investors believe that securities are overvalued in relation to earnings and therefore distribute their stocks to others. The resistance areas on the charts constitute the supply level at which investors sell securities comprising an index.

In relation to a trend channel, index prices often find support along the trend line connecting previous market lows, and conversely index prices find resistance along the trend line connecting previous market highs. Traders often purchase price setbacks to the support line and sell rallies near the resistance lines. Protective stops can be placed outside of the trend channel. When a market exhibits no definite trend, prices sometimes fluctuate between readily observed support and resistance areas. If a market is in such "trading range," traders again purchase setbacks to support and sell rallies near resistance. Traders also use breakouts from trading ranges to adopt appropriate positions since a breakout sometimes signals the start of a new trend.

Traders can buy index futures contracts or purchase call options at the support levels with protective stops below the trend channel line. Conversely, they can sell index futures contracts or buy put options near the resistance levels with protective stops above the trend channel line.

Trend Channels

Within major and intermediate trends, minor waves are sufficiently regular to be defined at their other extremes by another line. The tops of rallies composing an intermediate advance sometimes develop along a line that is approximately parallel to the basic trendline projected along their bottoms. This parallel might be called the return line since it marks the zone where reactions (return moves against the prevailing trend) originate. The area between the basic trendline and return line is the trend channel. Channels may trend up, down, or sideways.

By drawing lines (usually parallel) connecting market highs and market lows, you can often determine a trend channel. A trend reversal is often indicated when a market changes direction and breaks out of its trend channel. Traders often take positions to follow this breakout or trend reversal, especially if the market closes outside the trend channel.

Once a market breaks out of the trend channel and reverses trend, traders often wait for the market to move back to the breakout point to establish positions. If the breakout occurs above the trend channel line, a trader can initiate a long position in the index futures or purchase a call option in expectation of the price going higher. Conversely, if a breakout occurs below the channel line, a trader can sell index futures or purchase a put option in anticipation of a further price decline. Protective stops can then be placed beneath the low point of the previous trend.

Triangles and Flag Formations

When a line is drawn across the highs of the corrective phase and also along the lows, a *triangle* is defined. Prices usually break out before the apex of the triangle is reached, in the direction of the main trend. Traders often wait for these corrective phases to run their course and then follow a breakout in the direction of the main trend.

The triangle formation also is called a coil because of the way prices squeeze tighter and tighter between the upper and lower lines of the triangle before penetrating the top or bottom side. The triangle formation becomes valid when index prices have moved at least two thirds into the triangle. At that point, watch for prices to rise above the upper triangle or decline below the lower triangle line. A breakout occurs when this happens. Once a trader observes a breakout signal, he can determine an objective for how far index prices may continue in the same direction. To find the objective, first measure the length of the left or third side of the triangle. Then add this distance to the breakout point for a triangle up or substract it for a triangle down. Some technicians prefer to use the apex (the point where the upper and lower lines meet) rather than the breakout point for measuring the objective. Using the apex will decrease the distance to the objective and thus increase the odds for reaching it. Whichever rule is used, a trader may want to place buy or sell orders at a point within 90 percent of your objective.

After a market establishes a trend, it seldom continues in a straight line to its ultimate price objective. Along the way, prices often move contrary to the main trend for a short period of time, or prices can trade in a sideways action in consolidation of a previous major price move. These consolidation or corrective moves can take many forms, including the following. A "flag" formation is identified by a well-defined trend channel that runs contrary to the main trend. Prices usually break out of the flag in the direction of the main trend. Sometimes in a corrective phase, a market can edge sideways, making successively small price swings.

Double and Triple Top and Bottom Formations

Whenever a market scores a low or a high at the same price two times *(double top or bottom)* or three times *(triple top or bottom)*, this is viewed as a signal that the trend may be changing. Traders often view a double (or triple) bottom as a good buying opportunity and conversely a double (or triple) top as a good selling opportunity. Protective stops can be placed above or below a top or bottom. Confirmation of a bottom is sometimes signaled when prices move through the rally high made in the middle of double bottom "W" (called the fulcrum). The reverse is true for a double top.

Double and triple bottoms often will hold a market from sliding further. Double and triple bottom formations present buying opportunities for initiating long index futures positions or buying call options.

Double and triple tops are just the opposite, occurring at market tops and keeping index prices from advancing further. Double and triple tops are good sell signals in which a trader can initiate a short index futures position or purchase a put option.

Retracements

After an index market makes a significant price move in one direction, it often becomes "overbought" or "oversold" and reverses direction, retracing part or sometimes all of the previous move. Many times a market retraces roughly 50 to 67 percent of the previous move, and traders look for the "countertrend" to stop approximately at the halfway back point. Other popular retracements values traders watch for are 25 and 75 percent. Many traders buy a 62 percent retracement of a downmove, looking for support or resistance to develop at those points.

Major retracements in a bull market offer traders an excellent opportunity to buy index futures or call options. Conversely, retracements in a bear market offer an opportunity to sell index futures or buy put options to profit from a continued decline in index prices.

The Thrust Rule

If a market, in reversing trend or breaking major support or resistance, makes a big one- or two-day price move, the market sometimes experiences a one-day reversal. Traders take the initial market move as a signal of the coming trend and use a one-day countermove as an opportunity to take appropriate positions. Protective stops can be placed beneath the low of the countertrend day.

Head and Shoulders Top and Bottom Formations

The *head and shoulders formations* are probably the one chart pattern even many nontechnicians have heard about. It receives its name because it looks a lot like the front profile of a person. The chart pattern consists of a right shoulder, a head, a left shoulder, and neckline.

Head and shoulders formations may be symmetrical or asymmetrical in appearance. These formations present traders with a reliable buying (head and shoulders bottom) or selling opportunity, in the case of a head and shoulder top, upon penetration of the neckline. The price objective can be computed by measuring the distance between the tip-point of the head and the neckline.

After an extended move, a market often develops a head and shoulders top or inverse head and shoulders bottom. This distinctive pattern appears as a major market high (in case of a top) sandwiched by two lower peaks. Many times a support zone (called the neckline) is evident at the same price level just after the first shoulder and just before the second shoulder is formed. Once the neckline is formed, a breakdown through that support indicates a major top has been completed. The ensuing downmove is sometimes equal to the distance from the high of the head and shoulders formations to the neckline. Traders often follow a breakdown of a head and shoulders formation by taking short positions. The reverse is true for an inverse head and shoulders formation.

Key Reversal Patterns

In an extended move, a market can reverse direction suddenly. In the case of an upmove, if prices have gapped to new contract highs and then close below the previous day's low, on high trading volume, a standard key reversal has been formed. Sometimes prices gap higher on heavy volume one day only to gap lower the next, leaving an *island reversal.* Both types of reversals often signal a major market top has been established. The reverse is true of a key reversal bottom.

Gaps

A *gap* on a bar chart is formed when one day's price action does not overlap the previous day's price action. For example, an upside gap is formed when the low of one day's trading range is above the high of the previous day. Large price gaps often occur after unexpected news items are released or when prices change trend abruptly or break through support and resistance areas.

An old trading rule states that all gaps are eventually filled, but in today's volatile markets that sometimes occurs years later. After a trading range has been violated, a price gap out of that range can signal a major move. This is called a *breakaway* gap. During a major move, a big price gap sometimes occurs roughly at the halfway point, permitting traders to approximately calculate the final top or bottom of the move. This is called a *measuring* gap. After an extended move, price movements often accelerate (either up or down in the direction of the main trend), accompanied by a series of gaps, finally leading to a major trend reversal. These are called *exhaustion* gaps. Good support can develop in or just above upside price gaps, and traders often establish long positions in anticipation of a resumption of the uptrend. The reverse is true of downside gaps.

How to Interpret Volume and Open Interest Indicators

Looking at the combination of *volume, open interest,* and price action can provide a technician with clues to how index prices may behave in the future. Technical analysts believe the study of volume and open interest statistics provide reliable indicators to future index price action. Volume is defined as the total number of contracts traded over a certain period of time. It is a way of measuring total market supply and demand for a given period of time. Figures for volume and open interest can be plotted against price at the base of a bar graph. This gives technicians a visual picture of the relative changes in each variable over time.

Open interest is defined as the number of total purchase or sale contracts outstanding. Each "buy" contract and opposing "sell" contract equals one open contract. Meaningful changes in volume and open interest can occur in a few days or over a month's time. Proper analysis requires comparing current changes with historical patterns. Historical changes in volume are not as significant as those changes that occur in open interest patterns.

The following rules apply to volume:

1. A sharp increase in volume generally occurs at market tops and bottoms or on breakouts from congestion areas.
2. During a major upward price movement, volume increases on rallies and decreases on setbacks.
3. The reverse is true of price declines: volume decreases on rallies and increases on setbacks.

Open interest changes can indicate the type of buying and selling that is affecting price movement. For instance:

1. When prices are in an uptrend and open interest increases as the market rises, the market is in a technically strong position; new short sales are replacing old short covering in the face of aggressive buying, thus setting the stage for further advances.
2. In a down market, when open interest increases as prices decline, the market is technically strong as new buyers are meeting the old long liquidation and aggressive selling, thus fueling further price declines.
3. A market is technically weak when, as prices trend in either direction, the open interest decreases. This signals traders are liquidating positions and the market may be running out of buying or selling power near a bottom or top.
4. Near a bottom or top, open interest can change drastically either up or down indicating a major change in trading sentiment.

Basis Graphs

Basis is defined as the difference between spot and the index futures prices:

Basis = Spot price − Index futures price

The spot price represents the actual price of the portfolio of securities as calculated by the authorized reporting service. Pricing of the index futures is the result of trading by open outcry on the exchange floor. Futures prices can trade at premium or discount to the spot index and between different contract months. The premiums and discounts in price represent differences in expectations about future index prices, spreading operations, arbitrage, and sometimes inefficient pricing on trading floor. Table 5–1 shows the fluctuation in basis values over time for the S&P 500 Index.

If a spot price develops a large premium over the futures price, hedgers will sell stocks and buy futures. Similarly, if the spot price is at a deep discount to the futures, hedgers will buy stocks and

Table 5–1

Basis	Spot Price	Futures Price	
+100	165.00	164.00	Premium basis
0	165.00	165.00	Zero basis
−100	165.00	166.00	Discount basis

sell the futures. This activity is called *basis trading* when traders buy and sell futures contracts in relationship to the premium or discount of the spot price. Basis trading serves to keep the futures prices in line with the spot price. Before using basis as a technical trading tool, historical analysis should be performed to determine the probability distributions and variance for each index. In other words, at what premium basis should I buy the index futures, or at which discount basis should I sell futures? Information about the basis coupled with other technical indicators can improve market timing for buying and selling index futures and options contracts.

Point and Figure Charts

Point and Figure (P&F) Charting is entirely different from bar charting. A P&F chart is constructed by keeping track of price movement continuously throughout the trading session, regardless of time. For example, in the case of the S&P 100, if prices are moving higher, a P&F chartist would mark an "X" in a column every time the market moved .05 (or one price tick) higher. If prices turn lower by a predetermined amount, then a new column of "0s" is started to chart the downmove. When shifting to a new column, start one box higher or lower. Thus, sucessive columns of alternating Xs and Os are charted to keep track of price movement. By changing the reversal size (number of squares needed to be reversed before a new column is started) and box size (size of move represented by one X or O), a chartist can alter the scope of his chart. A bigger reversal size can eliminate small back and forth moves on a P&F chart.

1. The same chart patterns that are seen on bar charts can be seen on P&F charts, too. Aside from generating the buying and selling opportunities previously discussed, P&F charts permit use of other trading strategies. A buy signal is generated when a new column of Xs moves above the high of the previous X column. A sell signal is generated when a new column of Os breaks the low of the previous column.
2. On P&F charts, major support and resistance often occur along 45-degree angle lines drawn from market highs and lows.
3. Price objectives can be measured using P&F charts. When a bottom is formed and the market breaks out on the upside, count the number of columns contained in the bottom. That number added to the breakout point indicates an upside price

objective. Measure the number of reversals in a top to determine an approximate downside objective.

Moving Averages

Another valuable trading method is the use of *moving averages.* Moving averages are often used to determine the trend of a market. Two moving averages are usually used in conjunction to signal a change in trend. For instance, to construct a 10-day moving average for any market, basis the closing price, take the sum of the previous 10 days' closes and divide by 10. This number can be plotted on a graph to illustrate the major trend. Traders often plot other moving averages for comparison. A 20-day moving average changes more slowly than the 10-day and "filters out" small, temporary market swings—as a short-term (10-day) average crosses the long-term (20-day) average and appropriate positions can be initiated. One other frequently used moving-average comparison is the 4-day versus the 9-day versus the 18-day. When the 4-day average crosses the 9-day and 18-day averages, a buy or sell signal is generated; if it crosses a downtrending 9- and 18-day average, a long position could be considered, and vice versa.

Contrary Opinion

Contrary opinion is a technical tool that can be used in conjunction with other technical indicators. This method inidcates the *Bullish Consensus* of the market in percentages. Bullish Consensus figures are available from several private services that calculate percentages based on opinions contained in the market letters of major brokerage firms. For example, 60 percent of the market analysts may be bullish on the S&P 500 Index, whereas the remaining 40 percent have bearish opinions. Thus, the Bullish Consensus is said to be 60.

Should a market become very one-sided, 80 percent bullish or 20 percent bullish, the market is probably overbought or oversold. At such extremes, the contrarian trader anticipates a change in market trend and takes a position contrary to the prevailing market opinion.

Analysis of Cycles of the Index Markets

The two most frequently asked questions of stock market analysts are: How high will stock index prices go? and How low will the index prices go? Price is what the traders and investors are most interested in because it is our nature to seek to buy stocks at the bottom of the market and to sell them at the top. In previous sections, we described tools that one can use to estimate these price objectives.

The study of stock market cycles involves research into the fundamentals that produce their recurrence. However, strict cycle theorists believe that price cycles behave as leading indicators to the fundamental factors that cause them. The authors can present only an overview of the subject due to space limitations. The Bibliography at the end of the book contains several references for readers who want to pursue this subject further.

While price is most critical to profitability, time is a more reliable variable in the analysis of the stock index markets. Time cycles help one to look for periods when index prices are most likely to bottom out and turn higher or to peak and turn lower. Cyclical analysis requires empirical measurement with regard to a time span or *period, reliability, synchronicity, harmonics, magnitude, persistance,* and *covariance with other indexes* independent from the fundamentals of the business and monetary cycles.

Cycles are measured in time—not price—usually from low to low because lows are more reliable. Weekly bar charts are useful in determining recurring lows. Highs are erratic and do not necessarily crest neatly midway between bottoms. Cycles indicate price direction only, not the extent of highs or lows. The fundamentals of business and monetary cycles and their affects on corporate earnings still determine investor demand for buying common stocks and hence the index prices.

The stock market exhibits primary, intermediate, and minor price cycles. An important cycle is the four-year business cycle. This cycle tends to bottom midway between U.S. presidential elections. Characteristics of the bottom include lower stock market and commodity prices, lower inflation and money supply, and higher interest rates. Cycle tops tend to come near presidential elections as economic conditions improve. Cyclical analysis can assist both speculators and hedgers in anticipating significant lows and highs in stock market prices. When used in conjunction with other technical tools, cyclical analysis can improve timing of initiating and exiting positions in the market.

Chart Patterns and Formations

Table 5–2 provides a guide for comparison of various chart formations and market sentiments. A bullish sentiment indicates a rising

Table 5-2

Chart Formation and Pattern	Market Opinion	Projected Price Trend
Double or triple top	Bearish	Down
Double or triple bottom	Bullish	Up
Head and shoulders top	Bearish	Down
Head and shoulders bottom	Bullish	Up
Triangle—up	Bullish	Up
Triangle—down	Bearish	Down
Flag—ascending	Bearish	Down
Flag—descending	Bullish	Up
Rounding top	Bearish	Down
Rounding bottom	Bullish	Up
Island bottom	Bullish	Up
Island top	Bearish	Down
Cycle low	Bullish	Up
Cycle high	Bearish	Down
Congestion phase	Neutral	Uncertain

index market. A bearish sentiment suggests a declining index market. Certain chart formations are more reliable than others. Refer to Chapters 11 and 12 for the appropriate trading strategies. A strategy can be devised once a trader has acquired an opinion of the market based upon chart formations.

These are some of the primary technical patterns that can assist in forecasting index prices. A *bullish market opinion* would indicate a trading strategy for being long the index market in expectation of a price rise—either by buying futures or purchasing call options. A *bearish market opinion* would suggest a strategy for being short the market in anticipation of a price decline—either by selling index futures or purchasing put options. *Readers are cautioned not to use these chart patterns blindly but to employ rules for equity management since these patterns are not fully reliable and may lead to trading losses.*

Chapters 11 and 12 describe specific trading strategies for index futures and options contracts. Chapter 11 discusses spreads and options combination strategies. Chapter 12 explains how to develop a net long or short position in the market using either futures or options contracts.

The Dow Theory of Stock Market Activity

The *Dow Theory* is named after Charles H. Dow (1851–1902), one of the founders of Dow Jones & Company, Inc., the financial reporting-publishing organization. He is credited with the invention of stock market averages. The Dow Theory is the Grandfather of all technical market studies. Dow believed that the stock market is a barometer of general business trends. Dow Theory is built upon and concerned with only the action of the stock market averages themselves, deriving nothing from business statistics or other fundamental data. Many popular advisory letters on the stock market base their recommendations on the basic tenets of the Dow Theory. Proponents of the Dow Theory constitute a significant force in the marketplace.

After Dow's death in 1902, William P. Hamilton, his successor as editor of *The Wall Street Journal*, organized and formulated the basic tenets of the Dow Theory as we know it today. The purpose of the theory is to signal major turns in the stock market and to forecast the business cycle, or longer movements of depression and prosperity—not to estimate the prices of individual securities. Followers of the Dow Theory use it to signal both the beginning and end of bull and bear markets.

Technicans criticize the Dow Theory on several counts: (1) many believe that the "buy and sell signals" given come too late—that major profit opportunities are missed; (2) that the theory has not been updated to deal with modern-day changes in the economic, business, and monetary interactions in the global economy; and (3) that the breadth, scope, and significance of the stocks comprising the Dow Averages do not accurately represent the diversified, more technologically oriented structure of the U.S. stock market. Nevertheless, an understanding of the Dow Theory may be helpful in interpreting the technical actions of the Dow Jones Industrial, Transportation, and Utility Averages, which are still widely used indexes of the stock market.

The Dow Jones Averages consist of 65 companies, composed of (1) 30 industrial companies, (2) 20 transportation companies, and (3) 15 utilities. *The Dow Jones Averages are price-weighted indexes.* The Dow Averages are widely reported by the news media as an indicator of stock market activity. Many money managers structure their investment portfolios using Dow stocks and compare their performance against the composite index. The Dow Averages have no corresponding stock index futures or options contracts even though several exchanges have tried to establish Dow Jones Index contracts.

The authors do not recommend using the Dow Theory as a trading tool for the stock indexes because of the large degree of risk one would have to assume. The Dow Theory can be useful for taking

Figure 5–1

The Dow Jones Averages

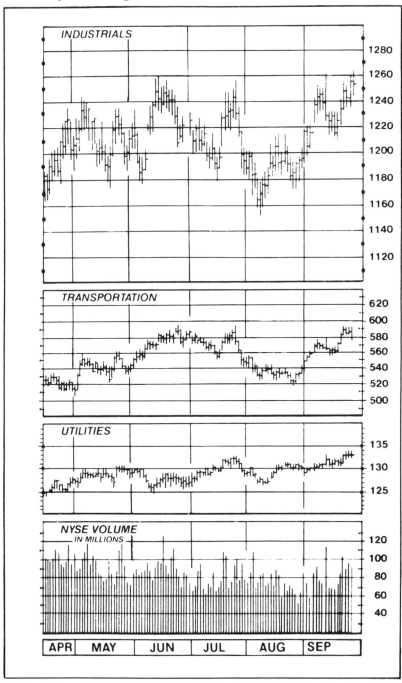

Source: *Barron's*, September 14, 1983.

Figure 5-1 *(continued)*

Components—Dow Jones 65 Stocks Averages

The Dow Jones Stock Averages are compiled daily by using the New York Stock Exchange only closing prices and adjusting by the then current appropriate average divisor. The divisors appear in the second column of the Market Laboratory page under the data for the yearly Dow Jones Stock Average. A list of the stocks on which these averages are based follows:

Industrials

Allied Corp.	General Electric	Owens-Illinois
Aluminum Co.	General Foods	Proc & Gamb
Amer Brands	General Motors	Sears Roebuck
Amer Can	Goodyear	Std Oil of Calif
Amer Express	Inco	Texaco
Amer Tel. & Tel.	IBM	Union Carbide
Bethlehem Steel	Inter Harvester	United Tech.
Du Pont	Inter Paper	US Steel
Eastman Kodak	Merck	Westinghouse
Exxon	Minnesota M&M	Woolworth

Transportation

AMR Corp.	Eastern Air Lns.	Southn Pac.
Burlington Nrth	Norfolk Southn	Transway Int'l
CSX Corp.	Northwest Air	Trans World
Canadian Pac	Overnite Trans	UAL Inc.
Carolina Frt.	Pan Am Wld Air	Union Pac
Consolid Frt.	Rio Grande Ind.	USAir Group
Delta Air Lns.	Sante Fe Ind.	

Utilities

Am Elec Power	Consol Nat Gas	Panhandle E Cp
Cleveland E Ill	Detroit Edison	Peoples Energy
Colum-Gas Sys	Houston Indust	Phila Elec
Comwlth Ed	Niag Mohawk P	Pub Serv E&G
Consol Ed	Pac Gas & El	Sou Cal Edison

a long-term view of the stock market for purchasing quality securities in a cash account. The use of margin accounts for Dow Theory investors could cause forced liquidation of a good long-term position in securities.

The financial leverage of the index futures markets can work against the long-term investor because of the volatile secondary and minor wave patterns within the primary trend of the market. A long-term investor would have to assume too much risk in holding onto a position that could seriously impair his risk capital.

The following represents only some of the major tenets of the Dow Theory (see Figure 5-1):

1. The Dow Averages discount everything except "Acts of God."
2. The stock market consists of three trends: (1) *primary*, (2) *secondary*, and (3) *minor waves*.
3. A *bull market* is defined as the primary trend being up. A *bear market* is in effect if the primary trend is down. Secondary trends occur as "significant corrections within the primary trend." Minor waves are considered to be insignificant within the primary trend.
4. Primary bull markets are characterized by the following investor actions: *(a)* the accumulation phase in which farsighted investors buy high-quality stocks for value, *(b)* stock prices advance due to the demand created by public investors and speculators associated with improving business conditions, and *(c)* rampant speculation occurs as stock prices advance because speculators buy securities with little or no investment value. All good news with regard to corporate profits and earnings becomes fully discounted at the termination of a bull market.
5. Primary bear markets are characterized by the following: *(a)* investors abandoning hopes on the market and selling securities purchased at inflated prices, *(b)* the panic phase associated with continued selling of securities upon deteriorating business and economic conditions, and *(c)* distress selling of quality securities despite their investment value, also known as the "washout phase"—all bad news becomes fully discounted at termination of the bear market.
6. The *Industrials* and *Transportation Averages* must confirm each other to establish the validity of the primary trend. That is the primary trends for both averages must be up to confirm a primary bull market, or down to confirm a primary bear market.
7. Volume goes with the trend. High relative volume tends to confirm the validity of the primary trend. Low or moderate volume may indicate secondary trends or corrections within the primary trend. Low or moderate volume may indicate secondary trends or corrections within the primary trend of the market.
8. The Dow Theory uses only closing prices and disregards the highs and lows of a trading session. Many other technical systems use a combination of the high, low, and closing prices, or an arithmetic average of the three.
9. A primary trend should be assumed to stay in effect until its reversal has been signaled. There is oftentimes a tendency for both novice and experienced investors to anticipate changes in the primary trend of the market too early and thus lose the opportunity for extended gains by buying or selling their securities too early before a true trend reversal has been confirmed.

Correlation of Dow Jones Averages with Other Indexes

The Dow Averages are composed of some of the largest capitalized companies of American business. As of this writing, the Dow Jones Indexes are not traded on any futures or securities exchanges. However, many of the same companies comprising the Dow Averages have large, proportional weightings in the S&P 500, S&P 100, Major Market Index, and the New York Stock Exchange Indexes (see Figure 5–2). These indexes could be used as surrogates for trading the Dow Averages if a speculator or hedger is so inclined. Appendix E (all appendixes are at the end of the book) lists the cross correlations between the various indexes to assist traders in choosing a surrogate index to the Dow Averages.

Methods for Evaluating Index Option Prices

Principles of technical analysis can be applied to trading index options and futures-options. However, there are significant differ-

Figure 5–2

Values of Selected Stock Indexes from 1968 to 1981

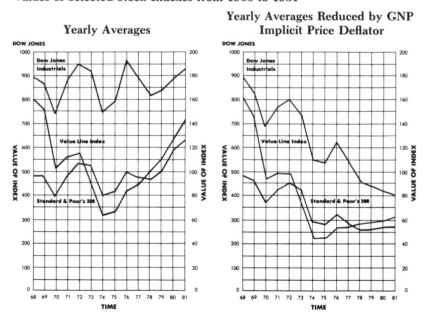

Source: *Chase Econometrics.*

ences between index futures and options contracts with regard to their fair market price. The price of a futures contract is determined by the bids and offers of floor traders on the exchange. Futures prices are determined by the open outcry method of trading on the exchanges. Naturally, the price of an index futures cannot deviate too far from the spot index. For example, if a trader wants to sell 1 S&P 500 futures contract at 168.00, and another trader is willing to buy 1 at 168.00, the price of the S&P futures is 168.00 at that moment.

Determining index option prices is not as straightforward as it is for futures contracts. Unlike futures contracts, options have a limited risk for the buyer and an unlimited risk obligation for the seller (writer). The buyer is willing to pay a consideration *(premium)* to the seller for this right. Subsequently, option contracts have *time value,* which is an important component of their price. An option is an unilateral contract since the buyer has no further obligations to the *option writer* upon payment of the premium. An option writer maintains an obligation to the buyer until an option expires, is offset, or exercised.

Developing a valid procedure for valuing option premiums lies at the heart of a profitable speculative or hedging program. In option trading, it is possible for a trader to "be right the market" but still lose money because he paid too high a premium for an option. Therefore, successful option trader must be skillful in determining the (1) trend of the market and (2) paying a fair price for the option. Naturally, option buyers want option prices to be undervalued in relationship to their *Expected Return on Investment* (EROI). Option writers (sellers) want option prices to be overvalued in relation to their risks of holding the underlying index futures.

Differences among the Types of Option Markets

There are three distinct types of listed option markets in the United States. We shall briefly explain the primary differences between contracts:

OPTIONS ON INDIVIDUAL COMMON STOCKS—These are put and call options traded on the four securities exchanges in the United States. Options are written against specific securities, such as IBM, General Motors, etc. Options are priced against the market price of the underlying security. The contracts require the delivery of 100 shares per option upon exercise. However, they may be offset for cash settlement or left to expire. Currently, there are hundreds of securities on which options are available.

INDEX OPTIONS—These are put and call options traded on securities exchanges in the United States. Options are written against a (1) composite index or (2) industry index. Options are priced against the spot indexes. Cash settlement is required upon exercise or offset. No securities are deliverable against the contracts. Presently, there are only a small number of index options available, but the number of contracts will probably grow over the next five years.

FUTURES-OPTIONS—These are put and call options traded on futures exchanges in the United States. Options are written against index futures contracts. *Options are priced against the underlying index futures price, not the spot index price.* A futures contract is delivered upon exercise. However, contracts can be settled for cash upon offset.

The different types of option contracts have unique characteristics that affect the way they are priced in the marketplace. For example, options on individual stocks have greater perceived risk than index options because of the possibility of delivery of 100 shares of a security upon exercise. Similarly, futures-options are perceived to entail higher risk than index options because they can be exercised into underlying futures contracts. Consequently, higher-risk option contracts usually command greater premiums to compensate the writer for the additional risk.

Option premiums are a function of (1) volatility of the underlying index price, (2) time to expiration of the option contract, (3) strike price of the option, (4) prevailing risk-free rate (such as U.S. Treasury bills), and (5) the current index futures or spot price.

Option premiums will also vary among the different contract series. Some contract series are in greater demand than others. For example, a June 84 S&P 100 165 call might command a higher premium compared to a December 84 S&P 165 call because option buyers tend to exert a greater demand for the near-month maturity contract dates relative to more distant months, thus causing a relatively higher premium for the near-month maturity contracts.

1. Volatility of the Index Price

Volatility is the degree of price change over time. A commodity that fluctuated 30 percent over a 90-day period is 10 times more volatile than one that fluctuates 3 percent during the same period. A simple arithmetic expression can be used to give a crude estimate of volatility over a fixed period of time:

$$\frac{(\text{Highest price} - \text{Lowest price})}{\left(\dfrac{\text{Highest price} + \text{Lowest price}}{2}\right)} = \text{Volatility} = \frac{170 - 140}{155} = .19$$

For example, if June S&P 500 futures ranged from a high of 170.00 to a low of 140.00 during a 12-month period, an estimate of its annual volatility would be .19. A more accurate estimate of volatility can be computed by taking successively shorter intervals of volatility estimates, summing them, and then dividing by the total number of intervals:

$$\text{Volatility} = \frac{\sum_{1}^{n} (v1 + v2 + v3 \cdots vn)}{n}$$

where n = number of intervals.

Once traders have a calculated volatility index, they can rank and compare different indexes from lowest to highest volatility. The more volatile commodities command higher option premiums because they stimulate greater speculative buying. Less volatile indexes usually attract the more conservative option writers (sellers) because they want to reduce risks associated with holding an underlying futures contract. Less volatile indexes usually command smaller premiums because speculators are less interested in buying them.

2. Time to Expiration of the Option

Time to expiration is defined as the remaining time left (usually specified in days or weeks) between the purchase or writing of an option and its expiration date. An unsold or unexercised option expires worthless on its expiration date. Therefore, option buyers must take action prior to the expiration date if they are to redeem any value left in the option. The value of an option premium is related to its time value.

The value of a simple option is proportional to the square root of time. That is, a four-month option costs twice as much as a one-month option (the square root of four is two). In other words, the more time remaining in an option prior to expiration, the greater will be its premium. Naturally, a 120-day June NYFE 96 call offers a greater premium than a 30-day June NYFE 96 call. The relative value of an option premium drops at an accelerated rate as an option approaches its expiration date. Most speculators are not interested in buying options with only 10 or 20 days left to expiration. They would rather buy an option with greater time value.

3. Strike Price of the Option

The strike price designates the specific price at which an option writer incurs an obligation to an option holder. A call writer has a potential obligation to sell a futures contract, and a put writer has an obligation to buy a futures contract. The strike price of an option allows us to distinguish between *out-of-the-money* options versus *in-the-money* options. Also we can use the strike price to calculate the intrinsic value and true premium of an option.

Out-of-the-money call options are defined as those option series with a strike price above that of the current market value of the commodity. Out-of-the-money put options are those series with a strike price below that of the current market price. For example, if the current market price of June S&P 500 is 165.00, then all contract series with a strike price of 165 or higher would be out-of-the-money call options. All contract series with a strike price of 165 or lower would be out-of-the-money put options. The intrinsic value of an option is defined as the difference in dollar amount between the market price of the commodity and the strike price of the contract series. For example, if June S&P 500 futures were trading 167.00, and a June S&P 165 call had a premium of $2,500 (or 5.00 points, 1.00 point = $500), then the intrinsic value of an in-the-money-call option would be as follows:

$$\text{Current market price} - \text{Call option strike price} = 167.00 - 165.00 = 2.00 = \text{Intrinsic value}$$
$$\text{Call option premium} = 5.00 - 2.00 = 3.00 \text{ true option premium}$$

Intrinsic values and premiums for in-the-money puts are calculated as follows:

$$\text{Put option strike price} - \text{Current market price} = 170.00 - 167.00 = 3.00 \text{ Intrinsic value}$$
$$\text{Put option premium} = 7.00 - 3.00 = 4.00 \text{ true put option premium}$$

In-the-money call options are defined as those contract series in which the current market value of the commodity is above the strike price. In-the-money puts and calls have intrinsic value due to the favorable market price of the underlying futures contract.

Out-of-the-money options have no intrinsic value, only true premium, since it would be unfavorable for option holders to exercise their options and sell futures contracts at a profit. In-the-money options can be exercised and sold at their intrinsic value by the option holder.

Option buyers usually prefer to purchase out-of-the-money puts or calls because less money is required, whereas some option writers may prefer to sell at-the-market or in-the-money options against futures contracts to reduce risks associated with holding a futures position. The premium paid to the writer can also be applied toward margin requirements for the underlying futures contract.

4. Prevailing Risk-Free Rate

The prevailing risk-free rate affects the rate of return on any investment because interest rates are a measure of the cost of money. High interest rates indicate a shortage of money in circulation, whereas low interest rates indicate a relative surplus of money.

If all other variables in an option valuation formula except the short-term interest rates are held constant, an increase in the interest rate increases the premium of an option. To get an idea of why this is so, an increase in the interest rate reduces the present value of the exercise price of the option. Since the exercise price is a potential liability for the option writer, this increases the value of the option. An increase in the interest rate will have a greater effect on an option with a longer maturity than on an option with a shorter maturity. Thus, a change in interest rates will alter the relative values of near- and distant-month options. An increase in the interest rate has the same effect as a reduction in the exercise price of an option. A 1 percent decline in the price of a 90-day Treasury bill maturing at the same time as the option has the same effect as a 1 percent reduction in the exercise price. A change in the interest rate will not occur in isolation. During the same period there may be a change in the commodity price as well as a change in the volatility of the commodity. The change in option price will reflect the interaction of all these variables.

5. Current Spot Index or Index Futures Price

Stock index prices generally fluctuate over a wide range during a year in response to changes in investors' expectations of corporate earnings, economic news, and monetary events that affect the normal business cycle. Stock indexes often behave as leading economic indicators of business and monetary activities. Spot index prices represent the computed index value of the underlying securities comprising it. The changes in the spot price versus the futures price is called the *basis*. Basis fluctuations are important in the evaluation index futures prices. Index futures represent traders' expectations of what the spot index price should be. Index options are prices against the spot index price; whereas index futures-options are priced against a specific underlying futures price.

The Black and Scholes Model for Valuation of Option Premiums

The component variables that make up the "value" of a put or call option can be integrated into a mathematical formula to derive expected values for put and call premiums. The Black and Scholes (B&S) option pricing model was first developed in 1970, then revised in 1972. Fischer Black and Myron Scholes, professors at Massachusetts Institute of Technology, derived a mathematical option pricing model primarily for providing theoretical comparisons for over-the-counter (OTC) and listed securities options traded on the stock options exchange.

The B&S option pricing model has been used by securities investors to determine when any given stock option is overpriced or underpriced in relation to its expected value. The variables of time, strike price, current stock price, risk-free rate, and volatility can be fed into a computer to give a prospective option buyer or option writer an expected value that can be compared to the current market price. Once comparisons have been made, a determination can be made as to which options are the best buys and which ones are the best writes. This simply means to write (sell) those options that the B&S model says are overvalued, and buy those options that the model says are undervalued. Market analysts have developed modified versions of the B&S formula to account for the differences between index options, futures-options, and regular stock options. Modified versions of the B&S model are kept proprietary because brokerage and trading companies use them to market their research services and to trade for their own accounts.

The utility of the B&S model is that speculators and hedgers have available another tool for analysis of option pricing. Techniques of fundamental and technical analysis, applications of decision theory, and the B&S valuation formula can be utilized to enhance the profitability of an index options trading program to a considerable extent.

For example, when the model shows that the June S&P 100 165 call is undervalued because its expected value is $300 even though the market price is still at $250, the trader can assume that "in all probability" the actual price of the index could decline, but the model says that $300 is a fair price for the option. Therefore, if traders buy the June S&P 165 calls at $250 (which the model says should be offered for $300), they have bought a S&P call at a 20 percent discount from its theoretically valued price. Investors can utilize other analytic tools, such as technical and fundamental analysis of the underlying index, to prove or disprove what the B&S formula says the expected value of the call premium should be. No matter what the model says, if other information gleaned from fundamental and technical analysis does not confirm that a particular "undervalued option" (according to the model) is the one to buy, then it would be better to look for more attractive situations in which other tools of price analysis confirm the expected option value.

The main feature of the B&S model is that it attempts to create a rigorous formula to determine the expected value of a index option compared to what the current price is. The B&S model integrates five variables into a mathematical formula: (1) the price of the index futures, (2) time value until expiration of the option, (3) the risk-free rate, (4) volatility of the index futures price, and (5) the exercise price of the option. Thus, on an option with a fixed exercise price, an increase in one of the other variables will increase the value of the option.

Option Deltas and Hedge Ratios

Another feature of the B&S model is the *hedge ratio*. This ratio recognizes the fact that a 100-point move in the index futures price might not be matched by a 100-point move in the options price. A hedge ratio of .50 means that two options will make 100 points if the underlying futures price moves up 100 points. The *Delta* value is a number between .00 and 1.00 that measures the percentage movement of an option's price to the underlying index. For example, an at-the-market option has a delta of .50. A deep in-the-money option may have a delta of .90. See Table 5–3 for examples of S&P 500 option premiums and deltas.

On an option with a fixed exercise price, the hedge ratio increases with time to expiration and as the futures price increases. The hedge

Table 5–3
Option Premiums and Deltas Using the September S&P 500 Futures Contract

Strike Prices

Future Prices	Calls					Puts				
	160	165	170	175	180	160	165	170	175	180
165	14.0	11.65	9.6	7.8	6.3	9.25	11.65	14.35	17.35	20.6
	.57	.51	.45	.39	.34	.38	.44	.5	.56	.61
166	14.55	12.15	10.05	8.2	6.65	8.85	11.2	13.85	16.8	20.0
	.584	.52	.46	.4	.35	.366	.43	.49	.55	.6
167	15.15	12.7	10.5	8.65	7.0	8.5	10.8	13.35	16.25	19.4
	.596	.535	.47	.416	.36	.355	.416	.48	.535	.59
168	15.75	13.2	11.0	9.05	7.4	8.15	10.35	12.9	15.7	18.8
	.61	.55	.487	.43	.37	.34	.4	.465	.52	.58
169	16.35	13.8	11.5	9.5	7.75	7.8	9.95	12.45	15.2	18.25
	.62	.56	.5	.44	.38	.33	.39	.45	.51	.57
170	17.0	14.35	12.0	9.95	8.15	7.5	9.6	12.0	14.7	17.65
	.63	.57	.51	.45	.39	.32	.38	.44	.5	.556
171	17.65	14.9	12.5	10.4	8.55	7.15	9.2	11.55	14.2	17.1
	.64	.58	.52	.46	.407	.31	.37	.43	.49	.545
172	18.3	15.5	13.05	10.85	8.95	6.85	8.85	11.1	13.7	16.6
	.65	.59	.53	.476	.42	.3	.36	.42	.475	.53
173	18.95	16.1	13.55	11.35	9.4	6.55	8.5	10.7	13.25	16.05
	.66	.605	.546	.487	.43	.29	.346	.405	.46	.52
174	19.6	16.7	14.1	11.85	9.85	6.3	8.15	10.3	12.8	15.55
	.67	.616	.56	.5	.44	.28	.335	.39	.45	.51
175	20.3	17.35	14.7	12.35	10.3	6.0	7.8	9.95	12.35	15.05
	.68	.626	.57	.51	.45	.27	.325	.38	.44	.498

ratio can be used to maximize ratio writing returns. Ratio writing refers to writing (selling) two or more puts or calls options per futures contract held long or short. Ratio writing can be extremely risky because a large move in a brief period of time in the futures price can alter the hedge ratio significantly. Therefore, ratio writing should only be done by well-financed, sophisticated speculators. Portfolio managers who want to earn additional returns from portfolios could also use ratio writing as a viable hedging strategy.

The B&S formula can be a powerful trading tool when incorporated into an overall framework of technical analysis. Buying underpriced options or selling overpriced options will not generate profitable trades if the market trend runs contrary to the position. Whether the trader be a speculator or hedger, it is nevertheless important to develop procedures for evaluating the expected value of an option contract before buying or writing it.

6

Fundamental Factors for Forecasting Stock Index Prices

Common stocks are purchased by investors for the reason only to make a profitable and safe investment. An investor can have many reasons for the selection of stocks in his protfolio. The objective of fundamental analysis is to provide a rationale for making investment decisions based on value. The stock market competes for funds with other types of investments such as real estate, numismatic coins, government securities, and commodities. This chapter will describe and explain the fundamental factors that affect stock market prices and thus can be useful in forecasting the trend of stock index prices.

Even though technical analysis can be useful for timing the purchase and sale of index contracts, fundamental analysis is necessary for forecasting the extent and duration of a price trend. Fundamental analysis can provide the rationale for buying or selling stock index futures and options contracts.

Analysis of fundamental factors can be divided into three categories:

1. *General factors.* Events that affect the broad spectrum of common stocks. For example, rising interest rates tend to depress stock prices because investors will sell stocks to purchase high-yielding money market instruments.
2. *Industry group factors.* Events that affect certain industry groups more than others. Rising wages and benefit packages for miners will tend to depress prices for mining stock group. Rising labor costs can be detrimental to the earnings of the group.
3. *Firm specific factors.* Events that affect a specific company; for example, XYZ Corporation announces that it wants to buy all outstanding shares of ABC Corporation for 20 percent pre-

mium over current market price. The price of ABC will increase by 20 percent in expectation of XYZ's offer.

The impact of fundamental factors can be difficult to evaluate on the earnings of an industry group or company. This requires the skills of market analysts who specialize in methods of quantitative analysis. Most books describe methods for forecasting prices for individual stocks based upon prospects for sales, inventory, equity/debt ratios, etc. Since this book is concerned with a composite value of a portfolio of stocks listed as an index, the purpose of this chapter will be to outline fundamental factors that affect the overall stock market. The level of stock market prices reflect investors' expectations about the underlying growth and health of the national and global economies. Investors can receive numerous statistical information from government and private reporting services that paint a picture of the overall growth and health of world and U.S. economies.

Fundamental analysis of the stock market entails three distinct areas of research:

1. *The business cycle.* Study of the peaks and troughs in the general level of economic and business activity as measured by the gross national product (GNP) and other composite indicators. The business cycle represents the varying levels of the demand and supply of products and services produced by the economy, as well as total spending by consumers, businesses, federal, state, and local governments.

2. *The monetary cycle.* Study of the expansion and contaction of the availability and cost of money and credit as measured by the monetary aggregates; the value of the U.S. dollar compared to a basket of foreign currencies. The monetary cycle is superimposed on the business cycle in that they interact in a complex way to affect securities prices. Chapter 4 discusses the role of the Federal Reserve Board and its impact on the monetary cycle.

3. *Tax treatment of capital gains and dividends.* Study of the Internal Revenue Codes (IRC) as to how they affect the taxation of capital gains and losses. High tax rates on capital gains and dividends penalize the investor in securities, which discourages investment in the capital markets. Changes in the tax codes result from differences in beliefs, attitudes, and political pressures on members of Congress and the executive branch of government.

What Is a Business Cycle?

If we limited our discussion to the U.S. economy, a multitude of information and statistical data can be analyzed and interpreted within the context of the business cycle. Business forecasts are important news and receive broad coverage in the daily press. Because of the technical complexities and sophistication of the statistical devices used in predicting future events, forecasts are couched in terms that confuse readers, including professional investors. An understanding of the indicator approach to business cycles is essential to interpreting fundamental data for trading the stock index futures and options markets. Readers are referred to the *Business Conditions Digest (BCD)*, Superintendent of Documents, U.S. Government Printing Office. The *BCD* is published monthly and includes updated commentary with comprehensive graphs on economic indicators.

A business cycle is characterized by a series of peaks and troughs in economic activity. Economic activity is measured by various indicators compiled by the U.S. Department of Commerce, U.S. Treasury Department, Federal Reserve Board, National Bureau of Economic Research, Bureau of Labor Statistics. The National Bureau of Economic Research (NBER) developed the indicator approach to business cycle analysis. A business cycle consists of expansions occurring at about the same time in many economic activities, followed by similarly general recessions, contractions, and revivals that merge into the expansion of the next cycle. Thus, business cycles are alternating and recurring movements. They relate to aggregate economic activity, as distinguished from the cycle of an individual statistical series. The indicator approach to business cycle analysis uses expressions such as reference dates, peaks, troughs, turning points, composite indexes, and leading, coincident, and lagging indicators to provide a quantitative description of business cycles.

Business Cycle Indicators

Reference Dates

Reference dates are the turning dates, or peaks and troughs, of the business cycle. They have been dated from 1854 to 1975. These dates, termed *business cycle reference dates*, mark off 28 U.S. business cycles for that period. The cycles range in duration from 28 months to 117 months.

The expansion phase—the rise in business activity from the trough to the peak—has usually been of longer duration than the contraction phase—the decline from the peak to the trough. For the 28 complete cycles, the average expansion lasted 33 months, and the average contraction ran 33 months.

For seven post–World War II cycles, the disparity in length between the two-cycle phases is more evident—expansions averaged 48 months in contrast to an average contraction of 11 months. The longest expansion period in history was recorded from February 1961 to December 1969—a total of 106 months.

Coincident Indicators

Reference dates provide a framework for classifying individual economic series into three groups according to whether their turning points tend to lead, lag, or coincide with the turning points in general business. Individual series whose peaks and troughs roughly parallel those in general business are termed *coincident indicators*. Four major coincident indicators are:

1. Personal income, less transfers in 1972 dollars.
2. Index of industrial production.
3. Nonagricultural employment.
4. Manufacturing and trade sales in 1972 dollars.

The turning points of these individual series do not always coincide with the reference dates. Individual business cycle analysts sometimes prefer to designate peaks and troughs in general business on the basis of the behavior of a single indicator, particularly gross national product (GNP).

Lagging Indicators

The peaks and troughs of some economic series typically follow the turning points in general business. These series are called *lagging indicators*. They reflect business investment costs. Included in the group of six major lagging indicators are:

1. Commercial and industrial loans outstanding.
2. Average prime rate charged by banks.
3. Average duration of unemployment in weeks.
4. Ratio, constant dollar inventories to sales.
5. Index of labor cost per unit of output.
6. Ratio, consumer installment credit to personal income.

Leading Indicators

Turning points in some series typically precede the reference dates marking the peaks and troughs of general business. These series are accordingly termed *leading indicators* (see Figure 6–1). The 12 major series of indicators include such measures as:

1. Average workweek of production workers.
2. Average weekly initial claims for unemployment insurance.

Figure 6–1

Indices of Leading Economic Indicators

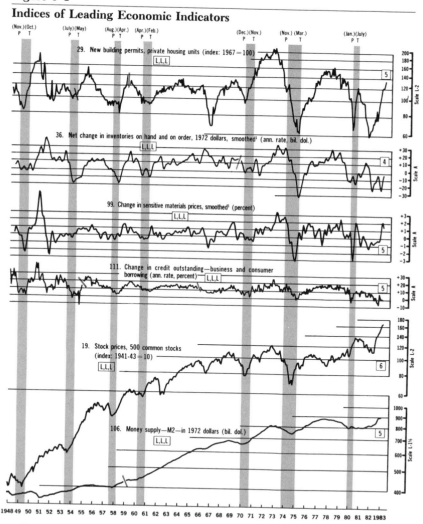

Source: *Business Conditions Digest,* June 1983.

3. Value of manufacturers' new orders for consumer goods and materials in 1972 dollars.
4. Index of business formation.
5. Index of stock prices, 500 common stocks.
6. Contracts and orders for plant and equipment in 1972 dollars.
7. Index of new private housing units.
8. Vendor performance, percent of companies receiving slower deliveries.
9. Net changes in inventories on hand and on order in 1972 dollars.
10. Change in sensitive materials prices.
11. Money supply—M2 in 1972 dollars.
12. Change in credit outstanding (business and consumer borrowing).

Composite Indexes

The number of months an individual series precedes or follows the turning points in general business varies from cycle to cycle. The average length of leads and the average length of lags at peaks differ from those at troughs. Thus, a summary measure can be more useful to the business cycle analyst than tracking an individual series. The Department of Commerce, Bureau of Economic Analysis, prepares the composite indexes and publishes its findings regularly.

There is one composite index for leading indicators, another for the coincident indicators, and a third for the lagging indicators (see Figure 6–2). Consistency of timing at both business cycle peaks and troughs was a major factor in determining which individual indicators were included in the composite indexes. Other criteria used to assess the individual series were economic significance, statistical adequacy, conformity to business expansions and contractions, smoothness, and prompt availability. The major series included in each composite index are discussed. Each series included is consistent in timing at both peaks and troughs.

Components of a Time Series and Seasonal Adjustment

An economic time series is an organization of data arranged in chronological sequence. Through seasonal adjustment, movements that recur year after year are removed from a series. These more or less repetitive movements within a year reflect primarily changes in business practices, weather conditions, and social customs. Seasonally adjusted series are used more and more in articles discussing

Figure 6–2

Comparison of Composite Indexes

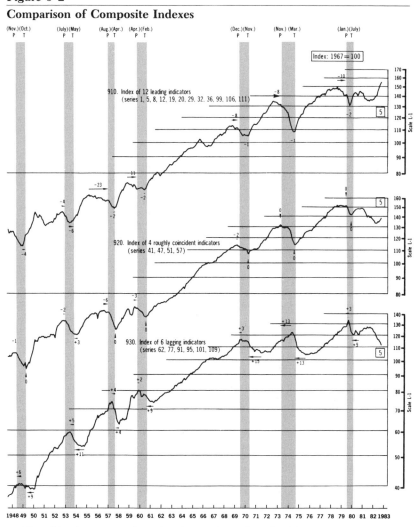

Note: Numbers entered on the chart indicate length of leads (−) and lags (+) in months from reference turning dates.

Source: *Business Conditions Digest*, June 1983.

the nation's economy since such series are easier to interpret for many purposes. For example, money supply figures tend to expand during the months of November and December to reflect increased consumer credit for purchases during the religious holidays. Thus, money supply figures are seasonally adjusted to reflect this expected expansion.

A statistical series as compiled—termed an Original series *(O)*— is represented as a product or sum of four components: *(a)* Trend *(T)*, *(b)* Cycle *(C)*, *(c)* Seasonal *(S)*, and *(d)* Irregular *(I)*. This statement translated into a formula is:

$$O = T \times C \times S \times I$$

To adjust for seasonal variation, the Original series *(O)* is usually divided by the seasonal factors *(S)*.

$$O/S = T \times C \times I$$

Seasonal patterns vary in amplitude from series to series. Also the seasonal pattern of a given series may change over time as social customs or business habits alter underlying conditions.

How to Use the Economic Indicators for Trading the Stock Indexes

The stock market itself acts as a leading indicator of turning points in the business cycle. This point confuses the uninformed investor who tends to buy stocks at the peak of the business cycle—when everything looks good—and sells stocks at the trough of the cycle— when business conditions look the worst. Why is this the case? One must remember that knowledgeable investors buy stocks on the expectation of higher corporate earnings and profits—which occurs near the trough of the business cycle. Similarly, these investors sell stocks on the anticipation of lower earnings and profits—which occurs near the peak of the business cycle. If we dissect the business cycle even further, it becomes clear why the expectation of higher earnings and profits occurs near the trough of the cycle and the expectation for lower earnings occurs near the peak of the cycle.

These events are generally negative to corporate earnings and profits. They occur near the peak of a business cycle and are therefore bearish to stock index prices.

1. High interest rates reflecting increased corporate borrowings to finance inventories, production, raw materials, and labor.
2. High labor and management costs reflecting shortages of qualified production and managerial personnel due to relatively high employment.
3. High producer prices reflecting shortages of raw materials and commodities.
4. High rate of inflation as measured by consumer prices reflecting excessive demand for finished goods and services.

5. High plant utilization reflecting the increased demand for manu-
factured products and finished goods. Management may decide
to borrow funds at high rates of interest to finance plant expansion beyond current capacity to accommodate the increased
demand for their products.

The events occur near the trough of a business cycle and are
generally positive to corporate earnings and profits. They are considered to be bullish to stock index prices.

1. Low plant utilization reflecting lack of demand for products
   and excessive capacity to expand production with little additional capital expenditures.
2. Low interest rates reflecting the reduced need to borrow funds
   to finance inventory accumulation, production, and labor costs.
3. High unemployment reflecting slack demand for labor and managerial personnel.
4. Low producer prices reflecting the slack demand for raw materials and commodities to produce finished goods.
5. Low rate of inflation as measured by lower consumer prices
   reflecting the decreased demand for finished goods and services.

Monetary and Financial Variables of the Monetary Cycle

Total spending by consumers, businesses, and governments affects
the general level of economic activity. In turn, decisions to spend
depend upon the availability and cost of money and credit. Thus,
there is a strong interrelationship between economic changes (the
business cycle) and financial changes (the monetary cycle). A fundamental analyst must understand the role of money and credit in a
free market economy.

The Federal Reserve System has the responsibility for regulating
the flow of money and credit to facilitate orderly economic growth
and a stable U.S. dollar. To perform this task, the Federal Reserve
collects and publishes statistical data on the country's banking and
monetary system. Chapter 4 describes in greater detail the role of
the Federal Reserve and its impact on business and the national
economy. Some of the key measures used in assessing the nation's
monetary and financial climate are:

MEMBER BANK RESERVES—In fostering orderly economic
growth, the Federal Reserve System (FRS) relies primarily on

its ability to increase or decrease the volume and cost of member bank reserves. The system requires that each member bank hold a fraction of its deposits as "reserves" at the Federal Reserve banks. The ability of the system to vary the fraction for "required reserves" is one tool of monetary policy. The difference between the total reserves and the required minimum is called *excess reserves*. When member bank borrowings from the FRS are deducted from excess reserves, the result is termed *free reserves* if the figure is positive and *net borrowed reserves* if negative.

MONEY SUPPLY—The Federal Reserve's objective in regulating the supply of member bank reserves is to exercise some control over the growth of total stocks of money and credit, since the availability of money and credit strongly influences the level of aggregate economic activity. Since money is not a precise concept, the FRS works with several forms of liquidity and definitions termed M1, M2, M3, etc. M1 is the narrowest definition of money; whereas M3 contains the broadest definition. M1 and M2 are measures of the money supply that are commented on most frequently by stock market and financial analysts. The FRS compiles and publishes data on these measures on a weekly and monthly basis.

COMMERCIAL BANK CREDIT—The current total bank credit series at all commercial banks provides data on U.S. Treasury securities, other securities, loans by type of lending, including lease financing receivables but excluding loans to commercial banks in the United States. The FRS collects from a sample of large commercial banks a detailed weekly statement of condition and from a subsample of these banks monthly information on commercial and industrial loans by type of borrower. These series are particularly sensitive to short-term deviations in the financial markets.

FEDERAL RESERVE CREDIT—The sum of three items—(1) total Reserve Bank credit, (2) monetary reserves (the gold stock and Special Drawing Rights certificates), and (3) Treasury currency—equals the sum of the following items: (1) currency in circulation; (2) Treasury cash holdings; (3) deposits (other than those of member banks) at the Reserve Banks, other Federal Reserve liabilities, and capital; and (4) member bank reserves. Increases in the first three items supply reserve funds, and decreases in them absorb reserves. In implementing monetary policy, the FRS takes into consideration the movements of each of these factors affecting reserves. The FRS supplies reserves to member banks primarily by purchasing securities in the open market. Conversely, open-market sales reduce bank reserves. Such open-market operations constitute a principal tool of monetary policy. If reserves are plentiful, member banks are able to expand their loans and investments—a bullish factor for the stock market. Also, pressure on interest rates is downward. If reserves are in short supply, the ability of the banking system to buy securities and make loans is restricted—a bearish factor for stock market prices. When the volume of reserves supplied through open-market operations is low, member banks may borrow temporarily from the Reserve Banks. A change in the interest rate charged—called the discount rate—is another policy tool to regulate the flow of money and credit in the banking system.

In summary, Federal Reserve System policies and open-market operations that expand the money supply and availability of credit in the banking system are considered to be bullish factors for securities and stock indexes. Whereas policies and operations that reduce money supply and credit are viewed as bearish factors to stock index prices. The important aspect of the analysis of monetary cycles is to monitor the trend in money supply and credit components to determine if they are expanding or contracting, and the corresponding effects they have on stock index prices.

A monetary cycle represents the peaks and troughs in the supply of money and credit. Some of the important indicators of the monetary cycle are:

1. The money supply—M2.
2. The value of the U.S. dollar compared to a basket of foreign currencies.
3. The discount rate as set by the Federal Reserve.
4. The federal funds rate.
5. Free reserves/net borrowed.
6. Long-term interest rates.

Figure 6–3 shows the relationship between the S&P Index, the federal funds rate, and the discount rate.

The Value of the U.S. Dollar

Special mention must be made regarding the valuation of the U.S. dollar compared to other foreign currencies, especially currencies of those countries with which the United States has trade

Figure 6–3

S&P Index, Federal Funds Rate, and Discount Rate

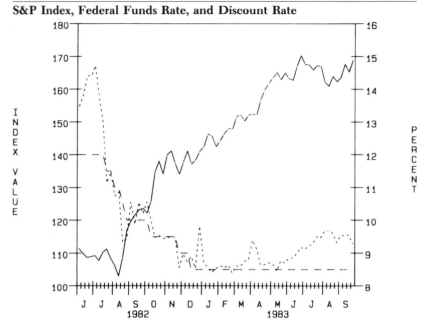

Source: *Heinold Marketwatch,* September 1983.

agreements. The buying power of the U.S. dollar can be measured
by the amount of other currencies that it can be exchanged for
on the foreign exchange markets. Many countries do not allow their
currencies to be traded on the foreign exchange markets for various
reasons. Because of the historic liquidity of the dollar and its wide-
spread use in international trade, it has been called the *reserve
currency* of the world. A strong dollar is symbolic of a strong America, vigorous economic and industrial activity, and the vitality of a
democratic form of government. Devaluation (reduction of buying
power) of the dollar is viewed as politically imprudent because of
its status as a reserve currency and all of its symbolic representations.

Dynamic economic activity and monetary strength encourage
active domestic and foreign capital investment in the United States.
Foreign investors must sell their respective currencies (e.g., Swiss
francs, Mexican pesos, Japanese yen) in order to buy U.S. dollars.
A strong dollar allows an importer to buy foreign-made products
and services at lower rate of currency exchange, while exporters
of American-produced goods and services become less competitive
on the foreign trade markets because buyers have to pay more dol-

lars relative to other currencies. A strong dollar is beneficial to those industry groups involved in importing foreign products and raw materials, whereas it is detrimental to the industry groups that must export American-made products and services. The U.S. balance of trade can experience large deficits if the country must import more goods and services than it can export. A long-term balance of trade deficit can affect the earnings and profits of American industries and service businesses—thus having a long-term negative impact on stock market and index prices.

Fundamental Analysis and Valuation of the Stock Indexes

A stock index is comprised of many different common stocks. Convertible securities, preferred stocks, rights, and warrants are not included in the composition of the stock indexes now traded on the commodities and options exchanges. Common stocks may be classified into approximately 92 distinct industry groups. Theoretically, there could be 92 separate stock indexes traded to match each industry group. Such a proliferation of stock index products would not prudent since it could dilute the capital formation process.

In performing fundamental analysis and valuation of a particular stock index, an analyst must first break down an index into its component parts. The component parts are:

1. The number of securities included in the index—are there 20, 100, 500, or 1700?
2. The major industry groups represented in the index—industrials, transportation, utilities, financial, computer, energy, etc.
3. The computation and weighting of the index—is the index price weighted or market weighted? Does each stock in the index have equal weighting with the others, or is the index weighted according to the number of shares outstanding for each security?
4. The specific securities that have the highest proportional value in the index. For example, IBM accounts for approximately 3.9 percent of the S&P 500 Index, while Foster Wheeler accounts for only .06 percent.

For simplicity sake, an index can be analyzed in much the same way as an individual security. For example, the securities in an index have the following components that can be averaged together to form a composite view of an index:

1. An average price of all the securities that represents the spot index price.

2. An average value of the corporate earnings.
3. An average dividend yield of the securities.
4. An average value for total return on the portfolio of securities, adjusted for stock splits and dividends.

Thus, we can derive certain ratios and statistics that have predictive value. They can be analyzed currently and historically. These numbers can be used to estimate future values for an index. They are:

1. The median of estimated price/earnings ratios.
2. The median of estimated yields.
3. The estimated median appreciation potential.

Table 6-1 compares the current and historical values for these statistics for the Value Line Index. The *Value Line Investment Survey* updates these values weekly in their publication.

Readers can make following observations from Table 6-1.

1. The top of bull index markets is characterized by *(a)* historically high price/earnings (P/E) ratios and *(b)* low dividend yields.
2. The bottom of bear markets is characterized by *(a)* historically low price/earnings (P/E) ratios and *(b)* high dividend yields.

Knowing the current P/E ratios and dividend yields in relation to market highs and lows for each index market can provide important clues as to when the top of a bull market, or the bottom of a bear market, is approaching.

How to Locate Information on the Industry Indexes

Industry indexes require specialized fundamental analysis with respect to the variables that affect the index and the prices of the

Table 6-1

Median of estimated price/earnings ratios	12.8%
Twenty-six weeks ago	10.0
Market low (12/23/74)	4.8
Market high (12/13/68)	19.0
Median of estimated yields	3.4
Twenty-six weeks ago	4.3
Market low (12/23/74)	7.8
Market high (12/13/68)	2.7
Estimated median appreciation potential	65.0
Twenty-six weeks ago	110.0
Market low (12/23/74)	234.0
Market high (12/13/68)	18.0

Source: *Value Line Investment Survey.*

underlying securities. The *Value Line Investment Survey*, Standard & Poor's *Stock Market Encyclopedia of the S&P 500*, and the *Dow Jones News/Retrieval Services* provide current information on industry groups.

Trade publications written for industry professionals, such as the *Oil and Gas Journal*, furnish important insights into the earnings and growth prospects for that industry—if one knows how to interpret the information and translate it into an investment strategy. As a warning, however, trade publications are usually overoptimistic, since their readers do not like to read bad news about their livelihood. In addition, there are investment advisory letters that specialize in industry-related securities. These advisory services provide buy and sell recommendations for specific issues in an industry group.

The AMEX Oil and Gas and Computer Technology Indexes can be affected by specific variables that may or may not affect other indexes. For example, the price of the Oil and Gas Index would be highly sensitive to news about OPEC pricing policies or deregulation of oil and gas production in the United States. The threat of a Mideast war—that would reduce oil supplies—could be bullish to the group of oil stocks.

The Computer Technology Index would be sensitive to foreign competition for cheaper and more innovative microprocessor technology. Price wars among the companies in this group are detrimental to their earnings and thus affect the individual securities prices as well as the industry index.

As more industry group indexes begin trading, a fundamental analyst/trader will become more specialized and concentrated on general and specific factors that affect a industry index. The chapters of the book that describe and explain the indexes, already listed for trading, will provide greater detail with regard to researching both fundamental and technical information on an index. Readers are referred to the primary trade journals and market advisory letters for each industry group as an important sources of information.

The Impact of Capital Gains Taxation on Stock Indexes

No discussion of fundamental analysis would be complete without describing the effects of the taxation of capital gains and dividends on trading the stock indexes. The taxation of dividends applies only to the underlying securities since index futures and options contracts do not receive dividend distributions. Chapter 15 presents the current interpretations of the Internal Revenue Code (IRC) rulings as they pertain to stock index futures and options for both speculative traders and stock portfolio managers (hedging applications).

The primary consideration is that changes in the IRC rulings must be evaluated with respect to having either positive or negative effects on the underlying securities comprising a stock index. Negative effects will be depressing to stock index prices. Positive effects will bolster index prices.

Capital formation through the purchase of common stocks requires equitable tax treatment for capital gains, losses, and dividends. Punitive taxation rulings discourage the purchase of securities and divert the flow of funds into alternate investment vehicles such as real estate, collectibles, and precious metals.

The primary areas of concern in interpreting IRC taxation rulings are:

1. The maximum and minimum tax rates for short-term capital gains and losses.
2. The maximum and minimum tax rates for long-term capital gains and losses.
3. The length of the holding period to qualify for long-term capital gains.
4. The amount of dividend exclusions allowable for corporations.
5. The requirements for tax-exempt status for various qualified pension/profit-sharing plans, e.g., IRAs, Keogh plans, corporate plans, etc.
6. The requirements for tax-exempt status for various investment-oriented institutions, e.g., trusts, nonprofit organizations, religious institutions, etc.
7. Special rulings such as "mark-to-market" rules for commodity futures and options transactions. Mark-to-market rules apply only to commodity and not to securities transactions.

In conclusion, IRC rulings change from time to time depending upon the political pressures placed on Congress and the executive branch by their constituencies, special interest groups, and lobbyists. Each change in the IRC rulings regarding securities and commodities transactions must be evaluated on its individual merits as to how it impacts the taxation of capital gains, losses, and dividends.

Other Fundamental Indicators Used to Analyze Stock Index and Option Prices

The following is a description of fundamental indicators that can be used to analyze stock index markets. They have limited value in forecasting stock index prices since the compiled data is made public after-the-fact. Investors in the stock index markets should be aware of them.

INSIDER TRANSACTIONS—These are purchases or sale of a large block of securities by executives, directors, or major shareholders of a corporation. These individuals are considered to be the most knowledgeable, and their activities in the market could signal either good or bad news for the market. Analysis of insider transactions is only relevant to the securities comprising a specific stock index, especially those securities that make up a large weighting in the index, e.g., IBM or the telephone company.

SPECIALIST SHORT SALES—A short sale is the sale of a security by an individual who does not own it—in expectation of a price decline. If the price of the stock declines as anticipated, the short seller can buy it back for a profit. These are made by professionals who have an intimate knowledge of the market and specific stocks. When specialists risk their own funds to sell short, they believe that the prices of certain stocks are going to decline. When their short sales are high (over 65 percent), it's a bearish indicator. When they reduce their short positions (under 35 percent), an improved stock market can be expected. These data are reported by several financial reporting services and publications.

BIG BLOCK ACTIVITY—The purchase or sale of large blocks of a specific stock or group of stocks can signal favorable or unfavorable developments on the horizon of the market. A large block is considered to be 25,000 shares or more. Usually investors who are buying or selling that quantity of stock are knowledgeable about events that are unknown to the general public and therefore buy or sell their holdings prior to the general announcement. The stock index trader should be cautioned that big block activity is only an indicator that should be confirmed by other data before making a trading decision.

7

The Value Line Composite Indexes

Introduction

Before going into a detailed overview of each stock index, let us review the similarities and differences between index futures and futures-options contracts. A futures contract is an *obligation* of a trader to perform in relation to a specific commodity at a specific point in the future. Let's say that a trader purchases an August gold futures contract on margin in February. By August, the trader must either take delivery (actual possession) of the gold and pay the balance of the futures price, or he must offset his long position by selling his contract before the delivery date. The margin he initially paid acts as a performance bond. It guarantees that he will purchase the gold if he is long or deliver the gold if he is short.

Index futures positions are *marked-to-the-market* daily. For example, if a trader buys a June Value Line futures contract at 190.00, he deposits $6,500 in *initial margins* with a broker. If the index price rises 1.00 to 191.00, the account equity has increased $500 for an *open trade equity* of $7,000. A customer may withdraw the $500 in profits from the broker (leaving a balance of $6,500 on deposit) if the index price does not close below 191.00.

If the Value Line futures price closes below 182.00 for an open trade equity loss of $4,000, a customer must make an additional deposit of $4,000 to the broker to maintain his position. This is called a *variation call* and is due the next day.

A futures-option is a right, not an obligation, to perform. Purchased options, unlike futures, must be paid in full and are not subject to marked-to-the-market rules. In contrast, written options are marked-to-the-market and margined according to the rules of the exchange. A customer who writes options is responsible for both initial and variation calls.

An option buyer, whether he purchases a put or a call, makes the decision to exercise his option. If he purchases a gold call, he can choose to exercise the option, thus taking a gold futures position at a predetermined price. If he purchases a put, he has the opportunity to sell a gold futures contract, again at a predetermined price, which is hopefully above the current market price of gold.

In either case, once an option contract is exercised, it becomes a futures contract. Normally, owning a futures contract means that the purchaser can take delivery of the physical commodity, be it gold, wheat, or hogs. It would be virtually impossible to deliver a portfolio of the numerous stocks that make up any of the stock indexes. Ultimate settlement for any index, whether traded on a commodity exchange or a securities exchange, is a cash *settlement.* For an explanation of how the cash settlement is computed on the various indexes, the reader is referred to Appendix B.

Comparison of Futures-Options versus Index Options

As stated above, an options purchaser has a choice of taking a position in the underlying futures. This allows him to take advantage of many different trading strategies without committing large amounts of capital. He is also able to take advantage of price movements in the underlying futures markets without assuming a position in that market. The option serves as an instrument for risk transference. Both futures-options and index options trading are conducted on regulated exchanges. The S&P 500 Index futures and futures-options are traded on the Index and Option Market (IOM) at the Chicago Mercantile Exchange (CME), the Value Line 1700 is at the Kansas City Board of Trade (KCBT), and the New York Stock Exchange Composite Index futures and futures-options is on the New York Futures Exchange (NYFE)—all are regulated by the Commodity Futures Trading Commission (CFTC).

The Securities and Exchange Commission regulates the Chicago Board Options Exchange where the S&P 100 Index option is traded, the American Stock Exchange where the Major Market and Market Value Indexes are traded, and the New York Stock Exchange, site of NYSE 1500 Composite Index options trading. The SEC also regulates the trading of the industry index options such as the AMEX's Oil and Gas Index and the Computer Technology Index. The S&P Integrated International Oil Index and Office and Business Equipment Index are traded on the CBOE.

All of the indexes that will be discussed are based on the underlying securities prices. One of the areas that must be touched is: What factors affect equity prices and, therefore, the prices of the indexes? Generally speaking, three kinds of risk affect equity prices: Market risk, industry risk, and firm specific risk. Market risk is the general risk that the price of a specific stock will rise or fall in relation to the market as a whole. Market risk is affected by expectations of changes in interest rates, national and international political and economic activities, inflationary expectations, and the credit cycle—those factors influenced by the activities and policies of the Federal Reserve Board.

Industry risk is composed of such items as labor disputes, consumer behavior, foreign competition, price/availability of raw materials, federal and/or state regulation, and obsolescence of a product—those things that influence an industry group.

Firm specific risk is the individual risk of doing business that a particular firm may have: company management, policies of the board of directors, corporate credit rating, and profits.

Industry and firm specific risk can be reduced through portfolio diversification. The management of market risk is more challenging. Until 1982, there was no truly effective hedging tool to reduce market risk. Then came the stock index futures and options contracts. Money managers now have a cost effective means of hedging stock portfolios. The primary advantages of using options are that they give the leverage of a futures contract while limiting a trader's risk. Now that we have reviewed the similarities and differences of these contracts, let's discuss them in detail. On February 14, 1982, the Value Line 1700 Index initiated stock index futures trading at the Kansas City Board of Trade (KCBT), Kansas City, Missouri. It was a history-making occasion for the commodity futures industry and the KCBT.

Specialist versus the Market-Maker System

On the principal stock exchanges (and certain options exchanges), *specialists* make the market for a particular index option. A specialist stands at the trading post and makes a market for an index option by announcing current bids and offers. When a broker approaches him and asks, "What's the market for the March 110 calls?" he'll receive an answer like: "5 bid, 5⅛ offered." Because the specialist is the only person obligated by exchange rules to make a market in that option, his bid and asked prices are the market. Simply, a specialist acts as the primary dealer in that option market. In addition, a specialist "keeps the book." The *book* is a listing of all outstanding orders that are not immediately fillable because they are too far from the current bid and asked prices. Index options traded on the NYSE and AMEX are specialist markets.

In contrast to the specialist system, certain exchanges such as the CBOE use the *market-maker* system for handling option orders. A number of floor traders who trade for their own accounts make a market in an index option. Market-makers are independent businessmen who act as principals; they are not brokers or agents for anyone else. Like specialists, market-makers have an affirmative obligation to make a market in the options they trade. At the CBOE, the *book* is kept not by a specialist but by an exchange employee called the Order Book Official. Orders on the book have priority over all other orders in the trading crowd at the same price. In this way, public traders get priority over professional traders.

Futures exchanges utilize a market-maker system for handling both index futures and futures-options contracts. Floor brokers gather in a trading pit surrounded by electronic displays of continuous price information. Floor brokers then engage in *open outcry* of bids and offers to other brokers to make a market.

Both the specialist and market-maker systems have advantages and disadvantages to them. Oftentimes, it is the customs and traditions of the exchange that determine which system will prevail in opening new contract markets.

History and a Brief Definition of the Value Line Composite Index

The Value Line Composite Index (VL) is an equally weighted geometric average of the approximately 1700 stocks included in the *Value Line Investment Survey*. The stocks included in the VL represent approximately 96 percent of the market value of all U.S. equities. Ninety percent of the stocks in VL are listed on the NYSE. However, in addition to the "blue-chip" stocks generally included in most indexes, VL includes the stocks of many "second-tier" companies. For this reason, VL is a much more volatile index than the S&P 500 or the NYSE Composite. The prices of "second-tier" stocks tend to be more volatile since their betas are usually higher—greater than 1.00—in relation to the more stable blue-chip stocks.

Over the long term, most indexes follow approximately similar trends. Where they differ is during the interim. The stock prices of small companies appear to turn down significantly before those of the more well-capitalized stocks. According to Lorie and Hamilton, in 1929 the equally weighted index reached its peak six months before the month-end peak of either the Dow Jones (DJ) or the S&P. It also reached its trough in 1932, one month before either of the other two indexes (Dow Jones Industrial Averages [DJIA] and S&P 500). During the bear market of 1973–74, the VL turned down fully 8 to 10 months prior to the DJ, S&P 500, and the NYSE Composite.[1] Lori and Hamilton have said, "[Equal weighted indexes] are more appropriate for indicating movements in the prices of typical or average stocks" and "are better indicators of the expected change in prices of stocks selected at random."[2]

Arnold Bernhard and Co. began publishing the Value Line Average (VLA) in 1961. Equally weighted geometric averages had been in use for 35 years prior to Bernhard and Co. deciding to use the equal weighting method. The original reason for developing the VL was not for general public use but to use as a tool for the evaluation of their own performance in stock selection and analysis. When a stock is included in the *Value Line Investment Survey,* the general feeling is that it has no more or less significance than any other. In the VL, Beatrice Foods has the same importance as General Motors or IBM.

Samuel Eisenstadt of Value Line feels that the VL is becoming better known and more popular with the general public for two reasons. With an increase in the number of stocks covered by the *Value Line Investment Survey,* the VL has gotten broader. There has also been a realization on the part of the investment public that the DJIA, the S&P 500, and the NYSE Composite do not reflect what's happening to the masses of stock prices. Historically there have been instances where the prices of the "blue-chip" stocks have been up and the prices of the majority of stocks have been down. The VL appears to be a better measure of the breadth of the market. In October 1982, Arnold Bernhard and Co. was reorganized under the name Value Line.

The company tries to be flexible in choosing the stocks to be covered by the *Value Line Investment Survey.* In order for a stock to be included in the survey, it must meet three basic criteria. It must have a reasonable market value (shares outstanding times market price). There must be a fairly strong trading volume that is an

---

[1] J. H. Lorie and M. J. Hamilton, *The Stock Market: Theories and Evidence* (Homewood, Ill.: Dow Jones-Irwin, 1982) p. 68.

[2] Ibid., p. 55.

indication of investor interest. And the degree of investor interest, as represented by the number of requests for information on a specific stock by their subscribers, is the final criteria. Stocks are rarely dropped from the survey. When a stock is dropped, it is removed because the company has gone bankrupt with little hope of revitalization and there is little investor interest, because of a merger, or because the company has gone private. Occasionally, a stock will be excluded because it has limited float, i.e., the majority of the shares outstanding are held by a specialized group such as a family that limits the trading volume. Parenthetically, Value Line itself went public in May 1983. It is not yet included in the *Value Line Investment Survey*. Four stock market indexes are computed for Value Line daily:

	Stocks
Value Line Composite Index	1700
Value Line Industrial Average	1500
Value Line Railroad Average	14
Value Line Utility Average	177

Computation of the indexes is performed by an outside firm. Since the Value Line Composite Index is the foundation for the KCBT Value Line futures contract, it is the index on which our attention will be focused.

How the Value Line Composite Index Is Calculated

When the VL was first published in 1961, it was calculated once a day. Now, because of the various products based on the spot index (symbol VLIC), it is calculated continuously throughout the trading day with a minute-by-minute dissemination via market information services. As stated previously, the VLA is an equally weighted geometric average. This means, unlike the S&P 500, the NYSE Composite, and the AMEX Market Value, which are market-weighted indexes, the stocks in the VL all have the same value. Each represents approximately 1/1700th of the index. One advantage of using an equally weighted geometric average is that it provides a distortion-free measure of the percentage change in stocks prices. Technically speaking, the VL is calculated as a geometric mean expressed an an index. The base value was set as of June 30, 1961. Base value = 100. Below is the procedure for calculating the daily closing value of the index. To arrive at a given intraday value, simply substitute the last price of a stock for the closing price. There are two terms with which the reader should be familiar before going into the actual calculation of the index.

Arithmetic average—the sum of n items (in this case n = stock price) divided by n.

$$(3 + 4 + 5) \div 3 = 12 \div 3 = 4$$

Geometric Average—$\sqrt[n]{\text{the product of all } n \text{ items}}$

$$\sqrt[3]{3 \times 4 \times 5} = \sqrt[3]{60} = 3.91$$

1. Divide each stock's closing price by the previous day's close (which should have been set at an index value of 100).
2. Geometrically average changes for all 1700 stocks.
3. The day's average change is then multiplied by the value of the average on the preceding day to get today's VL.

Adjustments in the VL are due to stock splits, listings, and delistings. To handle stock splits or dividends, the previous day's closing price is adjusted downward in the same ratio as the split or dividend, making the price equivalent to the post-split or post-dividend price for computing the percentage change. New listings are ignored on the first day of trading to establish an initial closing price on which a percentage change calculation can be based. For a more technical discussion of VLA calculation, the reader is referred to pages 10–17 of *The Future Is Here*, a brochure published by the KCBT. Correlation tables can be found in Appendix C.

Products Derived from the Value Line Composite Index

One reason the investing public has become more interested in the VLA is that it forms the basis for the Value Line futures contract traded at the KCBT. (Trading specifications are listed in Appendix B.) The KCBT, which is over 125 years old, has been known as an agricultural commodities exchange. However, in 1982–83, KCBT decided to broaden their market and expanded into the financial arena with the addition of a stock index futures contract. The KCBT pays a licensing fee to Value Line for the use of the index. On June 28, 1983, a record volume of 5,543 Value Line futures contracts were traded. Seats on the KCBT are currently being offered for around $62,000 for a class A membership and $22,000 for a class B membership. Class A members are allowed to trade any contract listed at the KCBT. Class B members may trade only the Value Line and the Mini-Value Line contracts. Using the Value Line futures contract can provide the hedger with price insurance for equity positions or a means by which to hedge stock options positions with a stock futures contract. A speculator might wish to trade Value Line futures to take advantage of broad market moves in the stock market. The Value Line futures can be used by quite a variety of traders:

1. New issue underwriters and syndicates wishing to hedge the value of stock inventories between purchase and sale.
2. Market makers, stock specialists, and institutional investors might chose to trade the Value Line futures contract to hedge a portfolio of stocks during periods of general market decline and weakness, to hedge large block positions, to reduce market risk when purchasing undervalued stocks in weak markets, to reduce the market risk of a short position in stocks, to improve timing of stock acquisition, or to protect uncovered positions in either puts or calls.
3. Executors of estates might find hedging the value of a stock portfolio advantageous during periods of market decline.

The Value Line futures contract has the highest price of all the index futures contracts. Contract value is determined by multiplying the current futures price by $500. For instance if the futures price is 200.00, the full contract value is $100,000. Because many traders are unwilling to put up the margin necessary on a contract of that size, on July 29, 1983, KCBT began trading futures on what is known as the Mini-Value Line futures contract. It is one fifth the size of the large Value Line futures contract. Contract value is $100 times the futures price. In the example used above, the contract value would be $20,000. This contract is more suitable for the small speculator and hedging smaller stock portfolios. Opening-day volume for the mini contract was 2,398 contracts. Complete contract specifications for both contracts can be found in Appendix B.

Until September 30, 1983, Value Line futures-options contracts were traded at the Chicago Board of Trade (CBOT). It was based on the KCBT's Value Line futures contract but was traded in Chicago due to a lack of space in Kansas City. Options trading began March 4, 1983. It was suspended with trading for liquidation only on May 23, 1983, due to a lack of investor interest. While the KCBT does not rule out trading Value Line futures-options, there are no plans at present to revive the contract.

Services Offered by Value Line

Value Line and its parent company, Arnold Bernhard and Co., have a distinguished history in the investment advisory and management industry. They provide numerous consumer services through their advisory publications and money management services and through computer applications for the investment and business communities. Publications include the *Value Line Investment and Advisory Survey*, the *Value Line Selection and Opinion*, the *Value Line OTC Special Situation Service*, and *Value Line Options and Convertibles*.

The money management services consist of various mutual funds managed by the company. A prospectus for each of the services is available upon request. Value Line's computer applications include the Value Line Data Base and CompuPower Corporation. Additional information is available by contacting:

Value Line
711 Third Ave.
New York, NY 10017

8

The Standard & Poor's Composite and Industry Indexes

The S&P 500 Index is a broad measure of the market value of 500 common stocks that reflects the general movement of the U.S. stock market. Because the S&P 500 represents stock market movement, it has become one of the U.S. Department of Commerce's Twelve Leading Economic Indicators. It is the yardstick against which all U.S. stock performance is compared. The S&P Index is used to compare the U.S. stock market to indexes on foreign stock exchanges. For example, the S&P 500 is compared against the *Financial Times Index* of the London Stock Exchange, or the *Commerzbank Index* of the Frankfurt Stock Exchange. The forerunner of the Standard & Poor's Corporation introduced an index that was a weekly measure of 200 stocks dispersed among 26 industry subgroups in 1917. It allowed the investor a quick tool with which to measure equity market movement and to spot market trends.

The roots of the Standard & Poor's Corporation go back to the Civil War era when Henry Varnum Poor published his *History of the Railroads and Canals of the United States.* This book, discussing the financial and operational details of the transportation industry, is considered to be the antecedent of investment publications in America. While doing research for the history, Mr. Poor discovered a dearth of information concerning the finances and operations of the country's railroads. Using his influence as editor of the *American Railroad Journal,* he was able to acquire the needed information from most companies. By 1888, Poor's son, Henry W. Poor, had published this country's first analysis of industrial securities, Poor's *Handbook of Investment Securities.* During this period, several other individuals were beginning to gather and disseminate corporate financial data to subscribers. In 1906, Luther Blake founded the Standard Statistics Bureau with that very purpose in mind. In 1941, Standard Statistics merged with Poor's to form the Standard & Poor's Corporation.

The S&P Index was expanded to include 500 stocks with 90 industry groups in 1957. It is currently composed of four major categories:

	Stocks
Industrials	400
Public utilities	40
Transportation	20
Financial institutions	40

The value of the stocks contained in the S&P 500 Index Portfolio is equal to approximately 80 percent of the market value of all the stocks listed on the New York Stock Exchange (NYSE). Originally, the stocks composing the S&P Index were only those listed on the NYSE. In the interests of maintaining a diversified portfolio and an accurate reflection of the securities market, Standard & Poor's began including some stocks listed on the American Stock Exchange (AMEX) and over-the-counter (OTC) stocks in 1976. The index also has added bank and insurance company stocks to further broaden its market coverage.

As the reader can see, the S&P 500 Index is a dynamic index, although the company tries to keep the changes to a minimum. It is the stability of the index that makes it a useful and accurate portfolio management tool. When additions and deletions are necessary, the decisions are made by the four Standard & Poor's executives who make up the S&P Index Administrative Committee. The committee consults with the S&P staff of industry and stock analysts prior to making any changes in the index. When a stock is removed from the S&P 500 Index, it is due to acquisition or merger of the company, to financial problems of the company, or to the fact that the particular subgroup is no longer representative of its industry. Additions of stocks to the index are needed to replace a dropped stock, preferably in the same industry group; to refine coverage of the index as is dictated by periodic review; or to establish a new industry group reflecting a broad, nontransitory interest in the group. Occasionally a whole industry group may be removed if it is no longer a viable part of the S&P 500 Index (sugar refiners), or a new index may be created (hardware and tools) to keep pace with an ever-changing economy. Stocks may also be transferred from one industry group to another. As an example of changes that are brought about in the index, let's take a look at what happened to the sugar refiners subgroup. By the fall of 1982, the sugar refiners subgroup was composed of three companies: Amalgamated Sugar, Holly Sugar, and Amstar. Amalgamated Sugar was dropped from the index when it was acquired by National City Lines. Holly Sugar was removed because it was a buy-out candidate and its market value was small. This left Amstar the lone company in the sugar refiners subgroup, distorting the effect Amstar had on the overall market value of the S&P 500 Index. Amstar was then transferred to the Foods subgroup restoring the balance of the S&P 500 Index.

How the S&P 500 Index Is Calculated

The S&P 500 is a market-weighted index. This means that each stock affects the index in direct proportion to its capitalization. Changes in the value of the index are proportionate to changes in the market value of the stock. In computing the S&P 500 Index, the first step is to figure the "weight" of each of the 500 stocks comprising the index. To do that, multiply the number of shares of stock outstanding by the market price per share.

Number of shares outstanding × Market price = Current market value

This determines the relative importance of a stock in the index. As of December 31, 1982, a stock like IBM (5.66 percent of the index) carried a greater "weight" in the index than a stock like Polaroid (.08 percent of the index). The second step is to determine the total current market value for the index as a whole. This is done by totaling the market values for all 500 stocks in the index. The last step is to compare the total dollar valuation to the base index value of 10, calculated from the base years 1941–43. An example from *Inside S&P 500 Stock Index Futures,* published by the Index and Option Market (IOM), a division of the Chicago Mercantile Exchange, will best illustrate these calculations.

Company	Number of Shares Outstanding		Price		Value
ABC	100	×	$50	=	$ 5,000
DEF	300	×	40	=	12,000
GHI	200	×	10	=	2,000
	Current market valuation				$19,000

If the 1941–43 value was $2,000, then $19,000 is to $2,000 as X is to 10.

$$\frac{\text{Current market valuation}}{\text{1941–43 market valuation}} \quad \frac{\$19,000}{\$\ 2,000} = \frac{X}{10}$$

Current index value $95 = X$

The S&P 500 Index is calculated periodically throughout the trading day and is available from the market information services.

There are several advantages in using the market-weighted index. It is a better measure of all stocks outstanding. It does not require the constant rebalancing that a geometrically weighted index does. The larger, more stable stocks have the greater influence on the index just as they do in the market. The market-weighted index has more flexibility to adjust for arbitrary prices changes in stocks such as issuance of rights, warrants, or stock splits. The base value is relatively constant. Correlation tables are in Appendix C.

Products Derived from the S&P 500 Index

Until 1982, the S&P 500 Index served as an instrument against which portfolio managers measured their effectiveness, but there was little that could be done with the S&P 500 Index itself as a stock portfolio hedging instrument. Portfolio managers were quite capable of limiting both industry and firm specific risk through portfolio diversification. But no matter how well diversified a portfolio was, its greatest exposure came from *market risk*. Market risk is responsible for the majority of stock price variance and effects nearly all stock prices to a varying degree.

S&P Index Futures and Futures-Options Traded on the Index and Option Market of the Chicago Mercantile Exchange

The Index and Option Market (IOM) of the Chicago Mercantile Exchange (CME) began trading the S&P 500 Index futures on April 21, 1983. Futures-options on the S&P 500 soon followed. The S&P Index futures were introduced in July 1983 after the IOM and the Chicago Board Options Exchange (CBOE) formed a joint agreement to trade corresponding indexes based on the S&P Composite and Industry Indexes. S&P 100 futures represent 40 percent of the value of the S&P 500 futures contracts. Both the IOM and the CBOE pay licensing fees to Standard & Poor's Corporation for the use of the S&P name and trademarks.

Until April 21, 1982, when the S&P 500 Index futures contract began trading, portfolio managers did not have an instrument that they could use to effectively manage the systematic risk in their portfolios. The arrival of the S&P 500 and 100 Index futures and S&P 500 futures-options contracts provides a cost-effective way of managing market risk. The 10 most heavily market-weighted stocks in the S&P 500 and 100 Indexes include:

American Telephone & Telegraph

IBM

Exxon Corp.

General Electric

General Motors

Eastman Kodak

Schlumberger

Standard Oil of Indiana

Mobil Corp.

Atlantic Richfield

Trading on the S&P 500 and 100 Index futures contracts has proved to be highly successful—with several thousand contracts being traded the first day. Appendix B lists the contract specifications for the S&P contracts.

S&P Index Options Traded on the Chicago Board Options Exchange

During the period when the IOM was expanding the S&P 500 Index to include futures-options, the CBOE developed the CBOE-100 Index which then began carrying its own options. Through mutual agreement on July 1, 1983, the CBOE-100 was officially renamed the S&P 100 Index. Trading on the S&P 100 futures at the IOM began July 14, 1983, where 20,000 contracts were traded the first week.

Since the spring of 1983, the number of index contracts has expanded. There are now four index option contracts trading on the CBOE: the S&P 100 (OEX) and 500 (SPX) index options, and two industry index options: the S&P Computer and Business Equipment Index (OBE) and the S&P Integrated International Oil Index (OIO). The industry indexes are much more industry specific and will aid the smaller investor in hedging his stock portfolio. The S&P industry indexes are less broadly based than either the Oil and Gas Index or the Computer Technology Index traded on the American Stock Exchange.

The most actively traded contract on the CBOE is the S&P 100 Index options; its futures are traded on the IOM of the Chicago Mercantile Exchange. They are two different aspects of the same entity. Both the options and the futures contracts of the S&P 100 Index consist of a broadly based market index of 100 stocks that have individual options listed on the CBOE. They also currently appear on the S&P 500 Index. This list includes most of the major blue-chip stocks. Like its big brother, the S&P 500 Index, the 100 Index tries to keep changes to a minimum. It is, however, periodically adjusted to reflect changes in capitalization that result from mergers, acquisitions, stock rights, etc. Again, like the S&P 500 Index, the 100 is a market-weighted index. The more shares of common stock outstanding, the greater the weight of the stock in the index.

The formula for the computation of the S&P 100 Index is the current market price of a given stock times the number of shares of common stock outstanding. This equals the current valuation for that particular stock. Then, the current values of all the stocks in the index are totaled to determine the aggregate market value of the index. The current value of the index is equal to the aggregate market value divided by the current market value times 100. By having the S&P 100 futures on one exchange (IOM) and the options on another (CBOE), the investor is given an opportunity to arbitrage the S&P indexes.

Composition of the S&P Integrated International Oil Index

As of August 31, 1983, the relative weightings of the six corporations composing the S&P Integrated International Oil Index (OIO) were:

Company	Weight as of August 31, 1983
Exxon Corp.	37.3
Gulf Oil	8.0
Mobil Corp.	15.1
Royal Dutch Petroleum	14.3
Standard Oil of California	14.4
Texaco, Inc.	10.9

Readers should notice that Exxon Corp. makes up over 37 percent of the proportional weight of this index.

Composition of the S&P Computer and Business Equipment Index

The 12 corporations used to construct the S&P Computer and Business Equipment Index (OBE) and their relative weighting as of August 31, 1983, are:

Company	Weight as of August 31, 1983
Burroughs Corp.	2.3
Control Data	2.1
Data General	.8
Datapoint	.5
Digital Equipment	5.8
IBM	73.0
NCR Corp.	3.3
Pitney-Bowes	.9
Sperry Corp.	2.3
Storage Technology	.7
Wang Labs.	4.2
Xerox Corp.	4.2

Readers should notice that IBM makes up 73 percent of the proportional weight of the index with the balance of the other 11 companies comprising only 27 percent of the index.

Services Provided by the Standard & Poor's Corporation

The Standard & Poor's Corporation offers many investment-oriented services to assist individual and institutional investors in planning and managing equities. Standard & Poor's publishes information regarding industry information relating to:

INDUSTRY INFORMATION: *Corporation Records, Financial Dynamics,* and *Industry Surveys.*

STOCK MARKET INFORMATION: *Earnings Forecaster, Stock Guide, Stock Reports, Stock Summary, The Outlook, Trendline Publications,* and *Watching Service.*

STATISTICAL INFORMATION: *Analysts Handbook, Daily Stock Price Record, Dividend Record, S&P Index Services,* and *Statistical Service.*

LEGAL INFORMATION: *Review of Securities Regulation.*

ELECTRONICALLY DISTRIBUTED INFORMATION: *Blue List Retrieval, Blue List Ticker, Bond Guide Retrieval System, Commercial Credit Information, COMPMARK, COMPUSTAT, Electronic Stock Reports, Fixed Income Management Systems, Municipal Fund Pricing, Stock Guide Retrieval System,* and *Stockpak.*

For additional information on Standard & Poor's services, write:

Standard & Poor's Corporation
25 Broadway
New York, NY 10004

The reader will find details of the S&P 500 Index futures contract, the S&P 500 futures and index options contract, the S&P 100 Index futures contract and the S&P 100 Index options contract in Appendix B. The uses of the S&P indexes as hedge instruments and/or speculative instruments are explained in Chapters 12 and 13.

9

Characteristics of the Major Market Index, Market Value Index, Oil and Gas Index, and Computer Technology Index

The American Stock Exchange (AMEX) originated 10 years after the Revolutionary War in 1793 as an out-of-doors marketplace. In 1911, trading rules for the New York Curb Market Association were established. During the bull markets of the early 1920s, trading was moved inside, and the name was changed to the New York Curb Exchange. In 1953, the New York Curb Exchange became the American Stock Exchange.

The exchange has a history of introducing innovative products. Equity options began trading on the AMEX in 1975. In keeping with its commitment to new product development, the AMEX has begun trading stock index options on four different indexes:

Market Value Index (XAM)

Major Market Index (XMI)

Oil and Gas Index (XOI)

Computer Technology Index (XCI)

There are many similarities among these indexes. Three of the indexes use the market-value weighting method of calculation of the index. The exception is the Major Market Index, which is an equally weighted price index. As discussed in Chapters 8 and 10, the market-value method gives greater weight to those stocks in the index that are more better capitalized than others. An equally weighted price index means that the percentage change in the price of any given stock will have the same affect on the index as the percentage change of any other stock. All of the indexes are updated

123

continuously and disseminated through market information services by the minute. All are traded like equity options.

As stated in Chapter 7, all of the AMEX indexes come under the jurisdiction of the Securities and Exchange Commission. Like the S&P indexes, there could be "crossover" regulation by the Commodity Futures Trading Commission (CFTC) if the Chicago Board of Trade implements its agreement with the American Stock Exchange to begin futures trading on two of the indexes. The Chicago Board of Trade will pay licensing fees to the AMEX for the use of the trademarked names *Major Market Index* and *Market Value Index*. As of this writing, the AMEX has only index options. No futures-options contracts are yet available on any of these indexes. Contract specifications for all four indexes appear in Appendix B.

The Market Value Index

The Market Value Index (XAM) consists of 800+ issues of common stock, warrants, and American Depository Receipts (ADRs) listed on the AMEX. It differs from other indexes in that it includes warrants and ADRs. These are midrange, growth-oriented companies. The initial base for the index was set at 100 in September 1973. In July 1983, the base was adjusted to one half of that and set at 50. All previous index closing values were also adjusted to reflect that change in the interest of historical consistency. Though the Market Value Index is a market-weighted index, it is not calculated exactly like the S&P indexes or the NYSE Composite Index. Because cash dividends are assumed to be reinvested, the Market Value Index is also known as a total return index. As of May 31, 1983, Wang Laboratories, Inc. Cl B, Imperial Oil Ltd. Cl. A, Gulf Canada Ltd., and Dome Petroleum Ltd. were the four largest component issues in the Market Value Index.

The Major Market Index

The Major Market Index (MMI) is a broad market index composed of 20 leading blue-chip industrial companies. It encompasses everything from communications to pharmaceuticals. It is the only one of the AMEX group that is an equally weighted price index. The stock prices used to compute the index are established on the stocks trading on the NYSE, not the AMEX. The stocks included in the Major Market Index are:

American Express	International Paper
AT&T	Johnson & Johnson
Coca-Cola	Merck & Co.
Dow Chemical	Minnesota Mining & Mfg.
Du Pont	Mobil
Eastman Kodak	Philip Morris
Exxon Corp.	Procter & Gamble
General Electric	Sears
General Motors	Standard Oil of California
IBM	U.S. Steel

The Oil and Gas Index

The Oil and Gas Index (XOI) is a market-weighted index of 30 leading U.S. corporations involved in oil and gas production. The base for this index was set at 100 on July 29, 1983. One of the primary advantages of both the Oil and Gas Index and the Computer Technology Index is that it will allow the small investor to hedge his stock portfolio. Many small investors do not have well-diversified portfolios. Rather, most have a large percentage of their investment capital tied up in one or two stocks, usually that of the company for whom they work. The small investor can then study the various industry indexes to see which is most representative of his portfolio and would be most appropriate for hedging. The five most heavily weighted stocks in the Oil and Gas Index are (in order of greatest percentage in the index as of September 1, 1983):

Exxon Corp.	17.0
Standard Oil of Indiana	7.9
Shell Oil	7.3
Standard Oil (Ohio)	7.3
Mobil Corp.	7.0

The Computer Technology Index

The Computer Technology Index (XCI) is a market-weighted index of 30 of the U.S. leading high technology stocks. On July 29, 1983, the base for the index was set at 100.00. Like the Oil and Gas Index, this index will allow the investor to hedge specific industry risk. The five most heavily weighted stocks in the index as of August 11, 1983 (in order of highest weighting), included:

IBM	53.92
Hewlett-Packard	7.92
Digital Equipment	4.16
Motorola	3.96
Tandy	3.33

Readers should notice that IBM makes up about 54 percent of the proportional value of the index.

10

The New York Stock Exchange Composite Index

The New York Stock Exchange Composite Index (NYSE Index) is a market-weighted index composed of all common stocks listed on the New York Stock Exchange (NYSE). The 1,505 stocks listed on the NYSE as of August 31, 1983, represent the lion's share of stock equity traded in the United States. Even though there are more companies listed over-the-counter (OTC), the stocks on the NYSE have a greater market value. The NYSE Index is highly representative of common shares traded on the NYSE. It does not contain OTC stock or stocks listed on other exchanges such as the Pacific Stock Exchange (PSE), the American Stock Exchange (AMEX), or the Philadelphia Stock Exchange (PHX). Companies listed on the NYSE tend to be better capitalized than those on other exchanges because the NYSE has the most stringent listing requirements of any of the U.S. securities exchanges. This index would be most useful to fund managers whose portfolios consist of NYSE-listed common stocks. It would be least beneficial for a manager with a portfolio of OTC stocks. It would not tend to be particularly volatile in relation to overall movements of the market. For this reason, it might not be the most appropriate contract for a speculator to trade. Five of the most heavily weighted companies listed on the NYSE are: IBM, AT&T, Exxon Corp., Schlumberger, and Standard Oil of Indiana. The expressed purpose of the NYSE Index is to reflect the increases and decreases in the value of common stocks. This is done in one of several ways: the first is the actual market value of the listed stocks as a total group (the NYSE Index as a whole); the second is a dollars-and-cents change in the current average price of all common stocks, known simply as "The Market"; and finally, the reader can get quotes on the various groups comprising the NYSE subindexes. The NYSE Index has two main parts: the NYSE Index itself and its four subindexes:

	Stocks
Industrials	1076
Transportation	51
Utilities	172
Financials	206

Before delving further into the NYSE Index and its related products, let's look at the evolution of the NYSE Index.

The History of the New York Stock Exchange

The NYSE is the oldest, most conservative, and best-known of the U.S. securities exchanges. The initial agreement between a group of stock traders meeting under a buttonwood tree created the beginning of what later became the NYSE. The approximate location of the early meeting place is believed to be 68 Wall Street in Manhattan. This first meeting occurred on May 17, 1792. The association of traders became known as the New York Stock & Exchange Board on March 8, 1817. The name was changed to the New York Stock Exchange in 1869.

The NYSE currently consists of 1,366 members with a seat of the exchange going for $420,000 as of October 7, 1983. In an effort to keep up to date, the NYSE has been installing new data processing equipment that should allow it to participate in electronic market making. The development of the NYSE Index is actually a by-product of the original computerization of the NYSE. To have manually computed a comprehensive stock index on a daily basis would have been prohibitive. When it was discovered that all of the data necessary for a comprehensive index was already being put into computers as a result of regular operations, the NYSE began working on designing their own stock index. On May 28, 1964, the exchange began daily computation of the composite stock index. At the close of trading on December 31, 1965, the exchange established the base against which its daily index calculations are computed. By July 14, 1966, the NYSE began publishing its composite index and the market change (dollars up or down) every half hour. The subindexes are computed hourly. The index is now computed minute by minute and is disseminated through the usual channels.

The NYSE Index evolved from the Securities and Exchange Commission Index which was also a market value-weighted index. The primary difference between the NYSE Index and the SEC Index was that the SEC Index was based on only 300 issues. The SEC Index was converted to the NYSE base on a weekly average basis for the period of time covering January 7, 1939, to May 28, 1964, so that the NYSE Index would have a historical data base.

The NYSE Index, like the S&P 500, is a market-valued index. This means that a stock with a broader capitalization base, such as IBM, contributes a greater percentage value to the index than a lesser capitalized stock such as Texas Commerce Bancshares. The calculation of the index is relatively simple if you follow the steps listed below.

1. Compute the market value of each of the 1,500+ stocks listed by multiplying the current market value by the number of shares outstanding of the stock listed on the NYSE.
2. Find the current *total* market value by adding all the sums in step 1.
3. Divide the current total market value by the *adjusted* base market value (more about how and why the base market value is adjusted in a moment).
4. Take the answer of step 3 and multiply it by 50 (the base market value set December 31, 1965) to get the current index value.

That's not so hard to do, is it? The reader must remember that it isn't done for one stock daily or even 10 stocks weekly. The calculations are based on over 1,500 stocks, and they are performed every half hour throughout the trading day. In numbers, the above calculations would look like this:

$$\frac{\text{Current total market value \$930 billion}}{\text{Adjusted base market value \$890 billion}} \times 50 = 52.25 \text{ index value}$$

The base was arbitrarily set at 50 because it was close to the actual average price per share on the NYSE at the close of trading on December 31, 1965. The base market value is adjusted to eliminate the effect that changes in capitalization, new listings, and delistings would have on the value of the index. This helps provide consistency in the value of the index. If a company adds new shares of stocks to its list, the new shares are expressed as a percentage of the current total market value of the stocks listed. That percentage is then added to the base, and the index is calculated as before.

The base must be adjusted for new listings and delistings in direct proportion to the change(s) in the aggregate market value of the list. When a company acquires an unlisted company, a change in the capitalization of the first company results, and the base market value must be adjusted. Rights offerings also involve adjustment of the base market value because they cause the capitalization of a stock to change. If no change in the capitalization of a stock occurs, no adjustment in the base value is necessary. For that reason, stock splits and stock dividends do not require an adjustment of the base; nor do mergers between two listed companies if there is no change in the total capitalization.

Unlike the Standard & Poor's Corporation and Value Line, the NYSE does not offer subscriber services or make investment recommendations. General information concerning the index and statistical data is available from the exchange. It has developed some new products which it is hoped will aid the investor in better managing his portfolio and optimizing his profit potential.

The New York Futures Exchange

On May 6, 1982, the New York Futures Exchange (NYFE), a wholly owned subsidiary of the NYSE, began trading NYSE Index futures. Over 6,000 contracts were traded the first day. The price of a seat on the NYFE rose from $4,000, before the introduction of the NYSE Index futures contract, to $6,000 in 1983. Presently, no other financial contracts are traded at the NYFE even though futures contracts on Treasury securities were once traded there. Although the NYFE is a subsidiary of the NYSE, they have separate physical locations. They are tied into each other via computer. On January 21, 1983, futures-options on the NYSE Index began trading at the NYFE. For both the NYSE Index futures and futures-options, the underlying value of the securities is equal to $500 times the index price. For example, if the index price is 100.00, the market value of the index is 100 × $500 = $50,000.

New York Stock Exchange Index Option

On September 23, 1983, trading began on the NYSE 1500 Index option at the NYSE—based on the NYSE Index. Although options are traded on many of the stocks listed on the NYSE, until the listing of the index options on the NYSE, no option contracts had ever been traded there. It is hoped that the NYSE and the SEC will reach an agreement so that other options can be listed on the NYSE. The value of the underlying securities in the index is equal to $100 times the index price. For example, if the index price is 100.00, the market value of the index is $100 \times \$100 = \$10,000$. Contract specifications for all three contracts are in Appendix B.

11

How to Trade Spreads, Straddles, and Combinations on the Index Futures and Options Contracts

This chapter describes how to trade stock index futures and option spreads to optimize gains while reducing risks associated with a simple long or short position. Previous chapters discussed fundamental and technical methods for analyzing and forecasting stock index price trends. These methods can be incorporated into an overall strategy for trading spreads. Expectations about future stock market prices and interest rate levels enter into formulating a spread strategy.

Trading stock index futures and option spreads can offer investors an opportunity for profit with less risk than an outright position. Another benefit in trading spreads is that exchanges and brokerage firms have reduced margin requirements and commissions for spread transactions. In spread trading, a trader relinquishes the opportunity to make substantial gains from outright positions (being net long or short) if he is correct in the analysis of the index market. A primary objective of a spread trader is to reduce the risk of carrying a sizable position in the market.

Many traders avoid trading spreads because they require additional thinking and research to make them work. However, the additional work can be well rewarded. Spreads can be an appropriate strategy for both novice and experienced traders depending upon their relative objectives, risk orientation, and level of sophistication.

Spread trading attempts to capitalize on the analysis of price differentials and price distortions. An efficient market greatly reduces the opportunities to make money. A spread trader looks for those opportunities where the market is inefficient—the price differentials become distorted due to technical factors or longer-term fundamental factors.

Before beginning to trade spreads, a trader must do substantial research to determine the following relationships and criteria:

1. What is the historical price range of the spread?
2. What has been the maximum price differential in the spread?
3. What has been the minimum price differential in the spread?
4. What fundamental and technical factors tend to distort the spread?
5. What is the estimated dollar risk and reward ratio if the spread is placed?
6. Where should I set a stop-loss order to close out the spread to reduce losses? Also, where should I take profits on the spread?
7. Can the spread be realistically executed at my price difference?
8. What is the best way to communicate my spread order to a broker so that he can place it correctly?

Types of Index Futures Spreads

A spread is a position that consists of both a long and short futures or options position in the same stock index or between two price-related index contracts. Spread transactions may be put on between the primary composite stock indexes and the corresponding subindex contracts. Transactions between index contracts traded on securities exchanges and the commodity exchanges are not recognized as spreads for margin purposes since a customer would be required to post margin on both the long and the short side of the transaction.

The best way to understand spreads is to illustrate with examples. There are several categories of spreads and many types of strategies investors can use to reduce risks. The primary types of stock index spreads are described as follows:

INTRA-MARKET SPREAD—A long and short position between two different months of the same index contract, for example, long one March S&P 100/short one June S&P 100 Index.

INTER-MARKET SPREAD—A long and short position between two price-related index contracts; the months may be identical or different, for example, long one March S&P 500/short one March Value Line.

BULL SPREAD—Being long an index contract in a nearby month and short a deferred contract; for example, long one March

S&P 100/short one December S&P 100. Bull spreads usually make money in a rising stock market, when the nearby month is at a deep discount to the deferred.

BEAR SPREAD—Being short an index contract in a nearby month and long a deferred contract; for example, short one March New York Composite/long one December New York Composite. Bear spreads usually make money in a declining stock market, when the nearby month is at a premium to the deferred.

What Is the Carrying Charge?

Before proceeding further, the concept of *carrying charge* should be explained. Carrying charge is the cost of holding a position in the market as reflected by the price differences between the consecutive months. Call option premiums of the index options should reflect these carrying charges as well. Carrying charges also reflect the future dividend distributions that would occur if one owned the underlying securities of an index. Companies comprising an index pay out quarterly dividends to the shareholders. The value of an index temporarily drops when these companies go ex-dividend by an amount of the dividend distribution. The same event occurs when a single security, such as General Motors, goes ex-dividend. Dividend distributions will have a greater impact on the smaller indexes, such as the CBOE's S&P International Oil Index (6 major oil companies) or the AMEX Major Market Index (20 blue-chip stocks), which are composed of a small number of issues compared to the NYSE 1500 Composite.

All exchanges require that customers have certain margin balances in their accounts in order to place on and maintain spread positions. Margin funds represent a cost to the customer since he could be earning interest on them if they were held as a fixed income security. Table 11–1, using the VL, illustrates carrying charge relationships.

The price differences between the months partially reflect the cost of holding an index contract in the market. Since the stock index contracts specify cash settlement upon expiration, carrying charges in these markets represent the cost of borrowed capital to finance contract margins at the prime rate or higher. Carrying charge costs will vary with the amount of margin funds required by the exchanges—the more margin required, the higher the carrying cost differential between months. In addition, the price

Table 11-1

S&P 500 Spot and Futures Closing Prices (September 16, 1983)—500 Times Index Price

Month	Price	Difference	Carrying Charge
Spot index	166.25	—	—
December 83	168.95	2.70	$1,350.00
March 84	170.35	1.40	700.00
June	171.35	1.00	500.00
September	172.35	1.00	500.00
December 84	173.35	1.00	500.00

differences reflect the bullish or bearish expectations of the overall stock market. As a general rule, carrying charges increase when interest rates are rising and fall when rates are declining. The cash settlement aspect of these contracts simplifies the computation of carrying charges since the costs of delivery, warehousing, and insurance are eliminated. In addition, carrying charges vary directly with the expectations of dividend payouts from the underlying securities. Carrying charges would be significantly higher if actual stock certificates were delivered at expiration of the contract.

What Is the Basis?

Another important concept to understand in trading spreads is the relationship between the spot index price and the futures contract price. This is called the *basis*. Basis is defined as the spot index price minus the futures index price.

$$Basis = Spot\ index\ price - Futures\ index\ price$$
$$0 = 155.00\ (S\&P\ 500) - 155.00\ (March\ S\&P)$$
$$+1.00 = 153.00\ (S\&P\ 500) - 152.00\ (March\ S\&P)$$
$$-1.00 = 154.00\ (S\&P\ 500) - 155.00\ (March\ S\&P)$$

A trader cannot put on a spread between the spot index and a index futures because there is no contract market for a spot index contract. Analysis of historical basis relationships, however, can provide indicators when the actively traded index contracts become overbought (too bullish) or oversold (too bearish). The basis is at a premium when the spot index price is greater than the nearby futures price (positive basis). The basis is at a discount when the spot price is less than the nearby futures price (minus basis). Basis relationships tend to become distorted during a trading day due to technical

Figure 11-1

Basis Spread Chart: Value Line Futures versus Spot Index (January 3–
April 29, 1983)

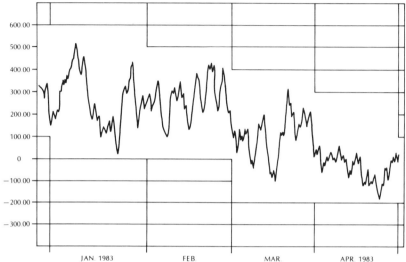

Source: Kansas City Board of Trade.

factors and inefficiencies of the market. An astute trader can take
advantage of these distortions if he has done his homework.

If the nearby futures price is at a deep discount to the spot price
(positive basis), this suggests a bull spread because traders will tend
to buy futures to bring the basis in line. The futures price is undervalued in relation to the spot price. One should remember that
the spot and nearby futures prices will converge near the expiration
date of the futures contract.

If the nearby futures price is at a large premium to the spot
price (minus basis), this suggests an opportunity for a bear spread
since traders will tend to sell the nearby futures to realign the basis.
The futures price is temporarily overvalued in relation to the spot
price.

Examples of Intra-Market and
Inter-Market Spreads

The following examples will exhibit various types of spreads using
price charts to show the fluctuations in the spread and basis relationships.

Example 1

Long one December Value Line/short one December S&P 500 at Value Line 18.00 over S&P. Margin requirement for spread is $6,500.

	December Value Line	December S&P 500
April 25	188.00	160.00
June 25	210.00	172.00
Results	+22.00	−12.00
	$11,000 profit	$6,000 loss

Net result: 22.00 − 12.00 = 10.00 × 500 = $5,000 net profit

$$\text{Return on margin} \frac{\$5,000}{\$3,500} \times 100 = 143 \text{ percent}$$

Example 2

Long one June Value Line/short one December Value Line at 1.00 December over June. Margin requirement for spread is $500.

	June Value Line	December Value Line
May 23	195.00	196.00
May 30	205.00	204.00
Results	+10.00	−8.00
	$5,000 profit	$4,000 loss

Net result: 10.00 − 8.00 = 2.00 × 500 = $1,000 net profit

$$\text{Return on margin} \frac{\$1,000}{\$400} \times 100 = 250 \text{ percent}$$

How to Trade Index Option Spreads

Option spreads may appeal to investors who do not want to trade index futures contracts. Put and call options on the various stock indexes are traded on both securities and commodities exchanges. Option spreads require a different risk-orientation and analysis than trading index futures contracts. Many futures traders do not like to trade options because of the high-cost premiums they command. The cost of premiums reduces the leverage of their position—thus reducing the opportunities for profit. Also, many traders do not have the tools available for evaluating the put and call premiums to determine which option premiums are overpriced and underpriced. Pricing of options requires sophisticated models that are available through brokerage firms that specialize in options research and analysis. The Black and Scholes (B&S) model has been modified to evaluate index option premiums by several research firms. The B&S Model is useful in determining which options are undervalued and which ones are overvalued. A spread trader wants to buy an undervalued option and correspondingly sell an overvalued option. The use of the B&S model does not guarantee a profitable trade; however, it does give an option spread trader an edge in the placing on and closing out position at favorable prices. Correct analysis of the market trend is the key factor in determining the outcome of a position.

Option spreads offer an alternative approach to buying puts and calls outright since the net premium cost can be reduced. Two basic types of option spreads are discussed: those where two options have different exercise prices (known as a vertical spread) and those where two options have different expiration dates (known as a horizontal spread). Since the purchase of an option requires a payment (termed a *debit*) from the customer and the sale of an option results in a payment (termed a *credit*) to the customer, an account will either have a credit or debit at the initiation of a spread. If a customer pays more than he receives, he has bought the spread, or put the spread on at a debit. If a customer receives more than he paid, he has sold the spread, or put the spread on at a credit. In both cases, the profit or loss in a spread results from the price difference between the two options increasing or decreasing as the price of the underlying index changes and as the expiration date approaches. The primary advantage of credit spreads over debit spreads is that the additional premium credits can be kept on deposit in Treasury bills with the brokerage firm. Since Treasury bills earn interest, this reduces the cost of holding a spread.

VERTICAL OPTION SPREAD—A long and short position between two strike prices of the same option class and expiration date; for example, long one June S&P 150 call/short one June S&P 155 call. This type of spread may also be called a *price spread.*

HORIZONTAL OPTION SPREAD—A long and short position between two different months with the same or different strike prices; for example, long one June S&P 150 call/short one September S&P 150 call. Another name for this type of spread is a *calendar spread* because different expiration months are involved.

BUTTERFLY OPTION SPREAD—A combination of two long options and two short options at three different strike prices of the same option class and expiration date; for example, long one New York Index at 92/ short two New York Indexes at 90/and long one New York Index at 88. This type of spread has its maximum profit potential if the spot price settles at the middle strike price (90). The maximum premium requirement and risk is limited to the debit to put on the spread. The butterfly spread can have a very high reward/risk ratio compared to other spreads for a small debit—sometimes as much as 6 to 1.

CREDIT SPREADS—A credit spread results when one sells an option for a greater premium than one buys another one for on an opening transaction. The objective of a credit spread is to receive premium credit with a limited risk. Credit spreads usually require additional margin deposits depending upon its structure. Risk is limited to the difference between the strike prices minus the net premium credit received. Credit spreads may be bullish or bearish depending upon the composition. An example would be: long a January AMEX Major Market Index (MMI) 125 call/short a January Major Market Index 120 call for a credit of 2½ points.

DEBIT SPREADS—A debit spread results when a trader sells an option for lesser premium than he buys another one for on an opening transaction. The objective of a debit spread is to reduce the cost of holding a long put or long call position. The risk is usually limited to the debit (but not necessarily so). Debit spreads usually offer a higher reward to risk ratio than credit spreads. Debit spreads may be bullish or bearish depending upon the composition. An example would be: long an October Major Market Index (MMI) 120 call/short an October Major Market Index 125 call for a debit of 1¾ points

STRADDLE—A combination of a put and call option with the same exercise price and expiration dates; for example, long one March Value Line 180 call/long one March Value Line 180 put. Straddles are different from spreads as later examples will illustrate. Buying straddles can be a profitable strategy in highly volatile, indecisive markets.

STRANGLE—A combination of a put and call option with the same expiration date but different strike prices; for example, long one October Major Market Index 120 call/long one October Major Market Index 115 put. Strangles are similar to straddles in that they can be profitable in highly volatile, indecisive markets.

Examples of Spreads

The basic mathematics of a spread may seem confusing at first to a new trader. We have provided the examples of different types of spreads to clarify them. Let us assume the following prices for the June S&P 500 call options:

Vertical Call/Debit Spread

Option Series	Price	Premium	Futures Price
June 160 call	2.00	$1,000	154.50
June 155 call	4.00	2,000	154.50

Let us further assume that you put on a spread by buying the S&P June 155 call at 4.00 and simultaneously selling the June 160 call at 2.00. Since the customer paid more than he received, he has put on this spread with a debit of 2.00, or $1,000.

Now let us assume that time has passed, the June S&P index has risen in price, and the two options now look like this:

Option Series	Price	Premium	Futures Price
June 160 call	3.00	$1,500	158.00
June 155 call	8.00	4,000	158.00

Note that the difference in price between the two options has changed from 2.00 to 5.00. If the customer closed out his spread at this point by selling the option previously bought and repurchasing the option previously sold, the net result would be as follows:

June S&P 155 Call	June S&P 160 Call
Bought at 4.00	Sold at 2.00
Sold at 8.00	Bought at 3.00
Gain = 4.00	(Loss = 1.00)

Net Gain = 3.00 = $1,500 profit

In the preceding example, an investor would have made a greater gain by simply being long the June 155 call instead of putting on a spread. This is hindsight, since the spread reduced his risk by $1,000.

Let us now consider a horizontal, or calendar, spread to determine how it works. Horizontal spreads require that an investor be short an option in the nearby expiration month and long an option in a deferred month. Let us look at the following calendar spread: short one March S&P 150 call/long one June S&P 150 call. The objective of a calendar spread is to capture time value as the short option in the nearby month approaches expiration. Time value deteriorates rapidly as the expiration date approaches. Time value can be applied toward reducing the cost of the long option in the deferred month. The premium credit from the short option finances the premium debit of the long option. The primary risk in this strategy is premature exercise of the short option. There are procedures for handling this kind of risk when it occurs.

Horizontal Call/Debit Spread

March S&P 150 Call	*June S&P 150 Call*
Sold at 3.00	Bought at 7.00
Expired at 0	Sold at 6.00
Gain = 3.00	(Loss = 1.00)

Net gain = 2.00 = $1,000 profit

In this example, an investor could have stayed long a June S&P call with a cost basis of only 4.00 instead of selling his position at 6.00, if he thought the June index price was going to move significantly higher. Nevertheless, the trader achieved his objective of capturing the 3.00 ($1,500) time value held in the March contract when he initiated the spread. This strategy can be very profitable if an investor is neutral to bearish on the stock market for the near term but bullish longer term.

The following examples illustrate credit spreads using the AMEX Major Market Index (MMI). Value of index equals 100 times index price. A spread trader usually has to post additional margin with his broker to put on credit spreads.

Vertical Call/Credit Spread

January MMI 120 Call	*January MMI 125 Call*	*Spot Index*
Sold at 4.00	Bought at 1.50	124.50
Expired at 0	Expired at 0	119.50
Gain = 4.00	(Loss = 1.50)	

Net gain = 2.50 = $250 profit

A vertical call/credit spread makes money if the index price declines and conversely loses money if the index rises. Therefore, it is a bearish spread. The risk is limited to the price difference between the strike minus the net credit received. In the example above, the risk was limited to: $125 - 120 = 5.00 - 2.50 = 2.50 \times 100 = \$250$.

Vertical Put/Credit Spread

October MMI 115 Put	October MMI 110 Put	Spot Index
Sold at 4.00	Bought at 1.00	112.50
Expired at 0	Expired at 0	117.50
Gain = 4.00	(Loss = 1.00)	

Net gain = 3.00 = $300 profit

Figure 11-2

Value Line versus S&P 500 Spread Chart

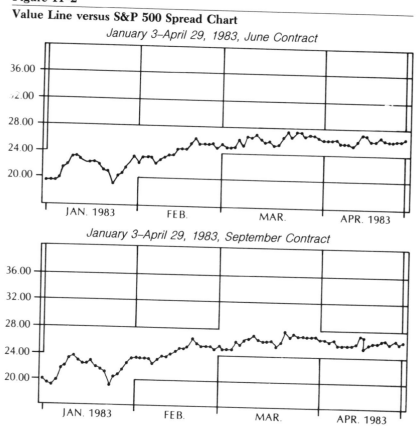

January 3–April 29, 1983, June Contract

January 3–April 29, 1983, September Contract

Source: Kansas City Board of Trade.

Figure 11–3
Value Line versus NYSE Composite Spread Chart

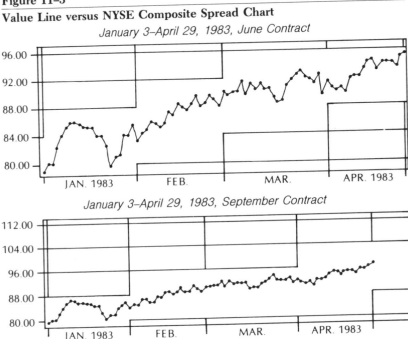

January 3–April 29, 1983, June Contract

January 3–April 29, 1983, September Contract

Source: Kansas City Board of Trade.

A vertical put credit spread makes money if the index price rises and conversely loses money if the price falls. Thus, it is a bullish spread. The risk is limited to the difference between the strike prices minus the net credit. In the example above, the risk is limited to $115 - 110 = 5.00 - 3.00 = 2.00 \times 100 = \$200$.

How to Trade Option Straddles and Strangles

The term *straddle* is often used interchangeably for *spread*. In options, spreads, straddles, and strangles represent different positions in the market. Buying straddles and strangles can be a profitable strategy in highly volatile, indecisive markets.

Straddle. A straddle is a combination of a put and call option with the same exercise price and expiration dates; for example, long one June New York 84 call/long one June New York 84 put.

Let us use the New York Composite Index futures options (NYSE) as an example of a straddle:

June NYSE 84 Call	*June NYSE 84 Put*	*Futures*
Bought at 2.00	Bought at 2.10	83.80
Sold at 7.00	Sold at 0.10	89.25
Gain = 5.00	(Loss = 2.00)	+ 5.45
	Net gain = 3.00 = $1,500 profit	

Strangle. A strangle is a combination of a put and call option with the same expiration date but different strike prices; for example, 'ong one June NYSE 88 call/long one June NYSE 84 put.

Let us use the New York Composite Index options (NYSE) as an example of a strangle:

June NYSE 88 Call	*June NYSE 84 Put*	*Futures*
Bought at 2.00	Bought at 2.20	85.80
Sold at 6.50	Expired at 0	94.50
Gain = 4.50	(Loss = 2.20)	+8.70
	Net gain = 2.30 = $1,150 profit	

An investor should purchase a straddle or strangle only when the volatility of the index price is greater than the combined volatilities of the put and call options.

Volatility of the Indexes and Inter-Market Spreading

Each stock index has a different volatility factor associated with it. This volatility factor is called an *index beta* coefficient. By convention, the S&P 500 Index has a beta of 1.00. The S&P 500 Index is the statistic used by the U.S. Department of Commerce to compare U.S. securities markets to foreign stock markets. Other stock indexes, such as the Dow Jones averages (DJA), NYSE 1500, VL 1700, and AMEX Market Value Index, are compared against the S&P 500 with respect to volatility. An index beta is a product of a combination of (1) the proportional average of the betas of the underlying securities in the index and (2) the method of computing the index.

A comparison of index betas can be useful in developing inter-market spreading opportunities. It follows that certain indexes have higher, or lower, betas than the S&P 500. For example, the cash beta for the Value Line Average (VLA) has a beta of 1.21. This means that the VLA rises approximately 21 percent more than the S&P 500 Index in a bull market. Similarly, it declines 21 percent more in a bear market. The VL leads the market both going up and coming down. This suggests the following guidelines for inter-market spreading:

1. *In a rising market.* Buy the high beta index futures or options contract and sell the low beta index in anticipation of the spread widening in favor of the high beta index.
2. *In a declining market.* Buy the low beta index futures or options contract and sell the high beta index in anticipation of the spread narrowing in favor of the low beta index.

See Figures 11–2 and 11–3 for examples of spread charts of the Value Line Index futures versus the S&P 500 and the NYSE Index futures.

Arbitrage Trading

Arbitrage trading is a special form of inter-market spreading. An arbitrageur buys index contracts in one market and sells an equivalent value in another market. For example, an arbitrageur may buy seven NYSE index futures and sell four S&P 500s. He buys the undervalued index and sells the overvalued index against it. He takes profits when the price relationships "become normal again." Arbitrage traders monitor the spread relationships between the spot and futures indexes to determine their relative values. Arbitrage trading is relatively low risk if done properly. Consequently, arbitrageurs place large orders (several hundred or thousand contracts) to achieve their profit objectives.

Arbitrageurs play an essential role in keeping the index markets in line with others. Arbitrage interests can generate a significant portion of the open interest and trading volume in the index markets. However, arbitrage trading is usually done by floor traders who pay low exchange clearing fees. In addition, they must monitor markets constantly and maintain instantaneous communications between markets to place orders. In conclusion, arbitrage trading performs a crucial role in maintaining efficient index and options markets by contributing to open interest, volume, and correcting price distortions. Arbitrage is a sophisticated form of trading of the indexes and not suitable for most speculators or investors.

Summary and Conclusions

The authors offer the following guidelines for trading spreads, straddles, and combinations.

1. Analyze the major and intermediate trends of the market to determine your fundamental orientation toward the market and the type of position you want to place. Technical analysis is an important tool for determining trends (refer to Chapter 5).
2. Analyze the respective betas (volatility factors) for each index contract traded. High beta indexes rise faster in bullish markets and decline faster in bearish markets.
3. Look for technical aberrations in the market to put on position in order to obtain maximum profit opportunity with defined risk.
4. Determine stop-loss points and profit-taking objectives before initiating position.
5. With options spreads, look to buy undervalued options and sell the overvalued options as determined by a fair-pricing evaluation, such as the Black and Scholes Model.
6. Analyze basis relationships to look for deep discount or premium situations.
7. A spread trader should use strict money management rules even though he has reduced risks by trading spreads. Preservation of capital should be the primary goal of the trader.

12

Trading Strategies for Index Futures and Options

With the basics behind us, we can now proceed with the interesting subject of trading strategies. The format of this chapter provides readers with a situation, an opinion on the market, and alternative strategies to profit from that situation. We have simulated the reasoning process used by successful traders to analyze a situation, formulate an opinion about the market, and then develop an appropriate trading strategy for profiting from that opinion. Successful traders use a combination of fundamental and technical analysis along with strict rules for managing equity. They look for opportunities in the market where the potential profits are at least three to four times that of the estimated risk.

This chapter describes speculative trading strategies and guidelines for management of risk capital. Examples of speculative trading situations are presented to assist readers in understanding these strategies. A *speculator* attempts to anticipate price changes and to profit through buying and/or selling index futures contracts. He assumes price risk to make capital gains—without owning common stocks or equivalent securities. In a legal sense, any commodity futures trader who is not defined as a bona fide hedger by the Commodity Futures Trading Commission (CFTC) is a speculator.

A *hedger* is an investor who desires to reduce price risk of a portfolio of securities. Speculators assume the risk of index price movement that hedgers want to reduce in managing their portfolios. Index and options contracts function as efficient risk transfer instruments between speculators and hedgers. Hedging strategies are designed to offset losses in a portfolio of securities with profits in the index futures or options markets. Hedging strategies are described with examples in Chapter 13.

Oftentimes investors turn bullish, bearish, or neutral on the market, and they are not aware of the alternative strategies available to profit from their opinions. We will present the time-tested strategies. However, readers may modify them in a way to fit their trading objectives. Before proceeding further, we will present some guidelines for trading the index and options markets.

Guidelines for Speculative Trading

Most speculators who trade futures and options contracts lose money. This statement is true regardless if one trades pork bellies or the S&P 100 Index contracts. These markets provide only an opportunity to make money—the market guarantees nothing. The financial rewards for the successful trader can be enormous. Few investment vehicles allow an investor with limited capital to parlay it into a fortune within a short period of time. Enormous profits can result from leverage, since futures and options contracts control market value 8 to 10 times greater than the funds required.

However, there are questions that speculators should ask that can serve as useful guidelines for trading. These guidelines can help traders increase their odds of winning:

1. What is the major trend of the market? What assumptions and tools of analysis did I use in arriving at this conclusion?
2. What is my profit objective on this trade?
3. What is amount of risk on this trade? What percentage of my total equity am I risking on this trade?
4. Where should I set a stop-loss order on this position?
5. At what price level should I enter the market?
6. At what price levels should I add to a profitable position?
7. What are my rules for money management?

This chapter provides a guide to developing a speculative trading strategy once a trader has formulated an opinion about the stock market and in particular the direction of a specific stock index contract. Advantages and disadvantages of each strategy are presented to give readers an idea of when and when not to use a particular strategy. This opinion may be derived from a fundamental or technical approach, or a combination of these methods. There are five primary opinions one can have regarding the stock market:

1. *Bullish opinion.*   The belief that the price of the stock index will rise higher in the near future.

2. *Bearish opinion.* The belief that the price of the stock index will decline in the near future.
3. *Neutral opinion.* The belief that the price will remain in a narrow, sideways trading range with small volatility.
4. *Major move expected, direction uncertain.* The belief that the stock market will make a major move, but the direction of that move is uncertain.
5. *Stay-out-of-market opinion.* The investor has no opinion and does not take positions in the market until a price trend or pattern develops.

We will describe strategies under categories 1, 2, 3, and 4 that an investor may consider before he takes a position.

Guidelines for Managing Risk Capital

The authors will present some useful guidelines for managing risk capital and account equity. Our experience over the years shows that money management is as important as being "right about the market." A speculator may have a correct opinion regarding where the market is headed but lose money because he does not apply good money management. High leverage in the futures markets can work in your favor. However, it usually works against the inexperienced trader because there is a strong tendency for him to stay with a losing position too long—hoping that it will turn around in his favor—which is rarely the case. The guidelines we recommend are:

1. Maintain twice the required margins in a brokerage account for each futures contract traded. For example, if the initial margins for an S&P 500 Index futures contract is $6,500, then maintain at least $13,000 in the account to trade one contract.
2. Do not risk more than 3 to 5 percent of your account equity on each trade. For example, in a $20,000 account, risk no more than $600 to $1,000 per trade. If the volatility of the market is greater than the estimated dollar risk, reject the trade. This rule helps a trader cut losses quickly and preserves equity until another opportunity comes along.
3. If an account is sufficiently capitalized to take multiple positions, average into a position, rather than take on two or three contracts at one price. For example, a trader could buy three S&P 100 futures at 167.00, 166.50, and 167.80—instead of buying all three contracts at one price.

4. Set profit objectives based upon estimated reward to risk ratios, or an estimated price objective derived from technical or fundamental analysis. Speculators must make large profits on a few winning trades to offset the many small losses they have to take in "testing the market."
5. If the risk of the futures market is too great to assume, consider trading index options and option spreads that offer limited risk opportunities.

Before proceeding, we should define some terms that will be used in describing trading strategies:

An *opening transaction* occurs when a customer initiates a new position in the market.

A *closing transaction* occurs when a customer liquidates his positions in the market.

A *stop-loss point* is the price where a customer closes out his position.

A *profit objective* is the price where a customer desires to take profits after initiating a position.

A *synthetic option* is a combination of a futures position and an protective option position. For example, (1) a long futures with a long put option or (2) a short futures with a long call option.

A *synthetic future* is a combination of a (1) long call and short put or (2) long put and short call. The credit from the short option partially offsets the debit of the long option.

Writing an option occurs when a customer sells either a put or call option on an opening transaction. The customer receives a premium credit when he writes an option.

An *uncovered written option* is a put or call option sold as an opening transaction without an offsetting position in the cash or futures markets. This is a high-risk position for a speculator.

Ratio writing describes a strategy of selling multiple options against an underying futures or option position. For example, sell two June S&P 500 calls at 165 versus a long S&P futures contract or sell one long S&P 500 call at 160.

Delta is a measurement of relative movement of the index price versus the change in option price. For example, if the spot Major Market Index (MMI) rises 2 points, the call option may only rise 1 point. The delta is said to be .50.

A *credit* occurs when a customer writes an option in his account.

A *debit* occurs when a customer purchases an option for his account.

Position and Exercise Limits and Reportable Requirements for Speculative Traders

Futures and securities exchanges, in cooperation with governmental agencies, monitor the activities of large speculators and their positions. Daily surveillance of reportable speculative positions is done in the interest of the public to prevent price manipulation of index futures and options markets to the disadvantage of smaller traders and hedgers. The cash settlement feature of these markets prevents a "market squeeze" situation, which can occur in other futures markets (e.g., silver market) if there is a shortage of deliverable supply upon expiration of the contract.

The Commodity Futures Trading Commission (CFTC) regulates index futures and futures-options markets. The Securities and Exchanges Commission (SEC) regulates index options markets.

Each of these agencies has a market surveillance unit for monitoring the volume of trading and type of activity (speculative or hedging) on each exchange. In addition, the exchanges, in cooperation with the governmental agencies, impose position and exercise limits for each contract market as well as reporting requirements. These position and exercise limits and reporting requirements are different for each contract market and may change upon notification by the exchange.

A *position* and *exercise limit* is the maximum number of contracts net long or net short in all contract months combined that a speculator can take on.

A *reportable position* is the number of contracts on one side of the market that must be reported to the exchange and regulatory agency on a daily basis regardless of whether the customer is a bona fide hedger or speculator.

We have provided some examples of position and exercise limits and reportable positions *for speculator traders* as of this writing (see Table 12–1). *Customers should consult with their brokers or the exchanges to receive updated information on these limits and reporting requirements to avoid violation of exchange and governmental regulations.*

We will present the following situations with fundamental and technical information from which bullish, bearish, and neutral opin-

Table 12–1

Contract Market	Exchange	Position and Exercise	Reportable Positions
S&P 500 futures	IOM	5,000 contracts	100 contracts
S&P 100 futures	IOM	10,000	25
S&P 500 options	IOM		25
NYSE futures	NYFE		100
NYSE options	NYFE		25
Value Line	KCBOT		25
Major Market Index	AMEX	15,000	200
Market Value Index	AMEX	10,000	200
Oil and Gas Index	AMEX	8,000	200
Computer Technology	AMEX	4,000	200
S&P 100 options	CBOE	15,000	200
S&P 500 options	CBOE	15,000	200
S&P International Oil	CBOE	4,000	200
S&P Computer and Business	CBOE	4,000	200
NYSE 1500 Composite	NYSE	25,000	200

ions about the stock market can be inferred. Our objective is to assist traders in developing knowledge-based opinions about the index markets and then translate them into sensible trading strategies. The following situations are derived from a combination of fundamental and technical information presented in Chapters 5 and 6. Given this information, a trader can formulate an opinion and then devise an appropriate strategy within the desired risk/reward parameters. *The following situations and examples are presented for illustration purposes only—not actual trade recommendations.*

Situation for Bullish Opinions

Fundamentals. Minutes from the Federal Reserve Open Market Committee (FOMC) indicate that the Fed will add reserves to the banking system, ease up on credit, and lower the Federal funds rate in the months ahead. It is expected that the Federal Reserve will soon lower the discount rate 1.0 percentage point because the annual rate of inflation is at 4 percent. The Fed has added reserves to the banking system by performing system repurchase agreements (REPOS). The Index of Leading Indicators released by the Department of Commerce showed a 2 percent gain after being down for three consecutive quarters. Economists are talking about this being the trough of the recession. Housing starts showed an impressive 12 percent gain. Auto sales posted a 10 percent gain. Several major New York banks lowered their broker loan rate 1.5 percentage points. M2, a broad measure of U.S. money supply, has been growing at moderate rates for three months. Corporate earnings for the Dow Jones Industrial companies are expected to be up sharply for the current quarter. Congress is considering legislation to lower capital gains taxation by 20 percent and increase the dividend exclusions. Specialists on the New York Stock Exchange are accumulating "blue-chip" issues on 10-point declines in the Dow Jones Averages (DJA). Big block activity has picked up in recent weeks. Insider reports have shown a large increase in executives buying stock of their corporations. A strong U.S. dollar has encouraged foreign investment in the stock and bond markets.

Technicals.   The S&P 500 Index appears to have a formed a head and shoulder bottom at the 150–152 level on the weekly bar chart. The S&P 500 Index is nearing a 20-week cycle low on the charts. Volume and open interest in the S&P 500 Index futures market have declined substantially over the past 10 days. Volume of shares traded on the NYSE and the AMEX has declined during recent sessions. Bullish consensus figures have fallen to 20 percent. Relative strength indicators are at the 25 percent level. Momentum oscillators appear to be oversold. The Dow Jones Transportation and Utility Indexes failed to confirm a new low in the Industrial Index. The put to call ratio on the S&P 100 options have shown a dramatic increase in buying puts by the public. The weekly charts of DJA indicate good buying support at the 1070 to 1080 level. The 3-week moving average for the Value Line Index is about to cross over the 10-week average to the upside—signaling a trend change to upward market.

Situation for Bearish Opinion

Fundamentals.   The Board of Governors of the Federal Reserve (FRB) has hinted that it would tighten up on credit to reduce corporate and consumer credit. FRB officials have voiced concern about the return of double-digit inflation. They are talking about setting strict target objectives for M1 and M2—to reduce the excessive growth in the money supply. The Fed has been draining reserves from the banking system by performing matched sales. Several major New York banks have raised their prime rates and the broker loan rates 2.0 percentage points in three weeks. The Index of Leading Economic Indicators showed a 3 percent decline after rising for six consecutive quarters. Housing starts and auto sales also showed substantial declines during the current quarter. Unemployment figures for the current quarter were reported to be 4 percent. Corporate earnings are expected to be flat or down for many companies comprising the Dow Jones Industrials. Economists are saying that business and economic activity are nearing a peak. Large block activity on the NYSE has shown a distribution pattern of blue-chip stocks on rallies. Congress is considering legislation to raise taxes on corporate profits, capital gains, and dividends to reduce large federal budget deficits.

Technicals. The S&P 500 Index has formed a triple top pattern at the 170–172 level on the weekly bar charts. The S&P 500 Index is nearing a 20-week cycle high on the charts. Volume and open interest has been declining on rallies and increasing on declines in the index. The Transportation Index of the Dow failed to make a new high as the Industrial Index did. The Dow Jones Industrials appear to meet overhead resistance at the 1270–1275 level. Bullish consensus figures have stayed at 85 percent for two weeks. The put/call ratio on the S&P 100 indicates unusually active call buying by the public. The 3-week moving average for the Value Line Index crossed over the 10-week moving average to the downside—signaling a downward trend.

Situation for a Neutral Opinion

Fundamentals The fundamentals for a neutral opinion involve little change in current Federal Reserve System policies. The Board of Governors are reasonably content with the rate of economic activity, money supply growth, and availability of credit to corporations and consumers. Economic and business activity proceeds at a slow pace. No dramatic changes in congressional or administrative policies are anticipated. The world situation is relatively stable—no major wars or military conflicts. The rate of inflation is staying below 4 percent. The indexes of leading, coincident, and lagging indicators are staying relatively unchanged.

Technicals. The S&P 500 Index has been fluctuating between 150 and 154 for 12 weeks. The daily volatility for S&P 500 Index ranges from 15 to 30 points. Bullish consensus figures have ranged from 47 to 53 over a 12-week period. The volume and open interest have stayed low but remained constant during this period due to the dull market activity.

Situation for a Major Move— Direction Uncertain

Fundamentals. The fundamentals involve a major change of events about to occur—either expected or unexpected—that market analysts cannot accurately assess without more information. These events could pertain to an unexpected war, political assasinations, trade embargoes, dramatic but uncertain changes in the tax laws. The market is anticipating important news that investors and analysts cannot properly assess without more information. The impact of these events can have a short-term but dramatic effect on the market—causing a major rise or fall in index prices depending upon their content. Usually, the stock market does not respond favorably to shocking news. Investors liquidate holdings until the relevance of the news events can be assessed with respect to their investments.

Technicals. The S&P 500 Index has been trading in a wide congestion area from 150 to 160. Volume and open interest statistics have surged dramatically over the past week. The daily volatility ranges from 200 to 300 points. A close above 160 level on high volume suggests an upside breakout (bullish situation). A close below 150 on high volume indicates a breakout to the downside (bearish situation).

Stay-Out-of-the-Market Opinion

There are times when a speculator should liquidate his positions and take a vacation from the market. Even though active traders may find this hard to do, it is essential to preserving one's trading capital. The stock market enters periods during which the fundamental and technical patterns are confusing. If a trader cannot form a knowledge-based opinion on the market within a framework of reasonable assumptions and data, he should stand aside and wait for an opportunity to re-enter the market. Please refer to Chapters 5 and 6, which can assist traders to decide when to stay out of the market.

Examples of Bullish Strategies

Example 1

OPINION: Strongly Bullish.
STRATEGY: Buy Index Futures.

RISK: Unlimited—traders should use stop-loss orders.

POTENTIAL PROFIT: Unlimited.

MARGIN REQUIREMENT: Varies with the index contract and the brokerage firm.

EXAMPLE OF STRATEGY: Buy December S&P 500 futures at 155.00.

COMMENT: The problem with buying futures contracts is the capability of meeting margin calls should the position go against you. Traders should use stop-loss orders to prevent excessive losses in a position.

Example 2

OPINION: Strongly Bullish.

STRATEGY: Buy index futures/buy put options (synthetic call).

RISK: Limited by the premium paid for the put option.

POTENTIAL PROFIT: Unlimited.

MARGIN REQUIREMENT: Varies with the index futures and the brokerage firm.

EXAMPLE OF STRATEGY: Buy December S&P 500 futures at 155.00. Buy December S&P 500/155 put option for premium of 4.

COMMENT: This strategy provides a good hedge against adverse price movement in the futures position. It allows traders to hold on to their position for some time.

Example 3

OPINION: Strongly Bullish.

STRATEGY: Buy call options.

RISK: Limited to the premium paid for the option.

POTENTIAL PROFIT: Unlimited—intrinsic value of the options at expiration less initial premium paid.

MARGIN REQUIREMENT: No margin requirement—options are fully paid for purchase.

EXAMPLE OF STRATEGY: Buy December NYSE 90 call at 2.00.

COMMENT: Buying call options is suitable for traders who do not want to meet margin calls and are willing to pay a high premium for doing so.

Example 4

OPINION: Mildly Bullish to Neutral.

STRATEGY: Buy index futures and sell call options.

RISK: Unlimited—traders should use stop-loss orders on both positions.

POTENTIAL PROFIT: Limited to the time value of the option plus the amount, if any, that the option is out-of-the-money.

MARGIN REQUIREMENT: Varies with the index contract and the brokerage firm.

EXAMPLE OF STRATEGY: Buy December NYSE futures at 90 and sell a December NYSE 90 call option.

COMMENT: The written call provides some protection against the long futures position. Stop-loss orders should be used to prevent excessive losses in the futures.

Example 5

OPINION: Mildly Bullish to Neutral.

STRATEGY: Sell put options.

RISK: Unlimited—traders should use stop-loss orders.

POTENTIAL PROFIT: Limited to premium received.

MARGIN REQUIREMENT: Varies with the index contract and the brokerage firm.

EXAMPLE OF STRATEGY: Sell June S&P 100/150 put option for a premium of 3.

COMMENT: Selling put options is a good method for earning premium income or acquiring an underlying position in the futures at a lower-cost basis.

Example 6

OPINION: Strongly Bullish.

STRATEGY: Synthetic long futures—buy calls and sell puts.

RISK: Unlimited—traders should use stop-loss orders.

POTENTIAL PROFIT: Unlimited.

MARGIN REQUIREMENT: Varies with the index contract and the brokerage firm.

EXAMPLE OF STRATEGY: Buy June S&P 100/150 calls and sell June S&P 100/150 puts.

COMMENT: A synthetic long futures position is equivalent to being long in the futures market with all of the inherent risks. Traders should use stop-loss orders to prevent excessive losses in a position.

Examples of Bearish Strategies

Example 1

OPINION: Strongly Bearish

STRATEGY: Sell index futures.

RISK: Unlimited—traders should use stop-loss orders.

POTENTIAL PROFIT: Unlimited.

MARGIN REQUIREMENT: Varies with the index contract and the brokerage firm.

EXAMPLE OF STRATEGY: Sell June S&P 500 futures at 165.00.

COMMENT: The main problem with selling futures contracts is the capability of meeting margin calls should the position go against you. Traders should use stop-loss orders to prevent excessive losses in a position.

Example 2

OPINION: Strongly Bearish.

STRATEGY: Sell index futures and buy call options (synthetic put).

RISK: Limited to time value of the option plus the amount, if any, that the option is out-of-the-money.

POTENTIAL PROFIT: Unlimited—futures profit less option less option premium paid.

MARGIN REQUIREMENT: Varies with the index contract and the brokerage firm.

EXAMPLE OF STRATEGY: Sell June S&P 500 futures at 155.00 and buy June S&P 500 155 calls.

COMMENT: This strategy provides a good method of hedging a short futures position to limit losses. The call option is a form of insurance against excessive losses and margin calls.

Example 3

OPINION: Strongly Bearish.

STRATEGY: Buy put options.

RISK: Limited to the premium paid for the option.

POTENTIAL PROFIT: Unlimited—Intrinsic value of the options at expiration less initial premium paid.

MARGIN REQUIREMENT: No margin requirement since options are fully paid for at time of purchase.

EXAMPLE OF STRATEGY: Buy June S&P 100/165 puts for a premium of 3.

COMMENT: Buying put options is suitable for traders who are bearish the market but do not want to meet margin calls should the position go against them. They are willing to pay a premium for this right.

Example 4

OPINION: Mildly Bearish to Neutral.

STRATEGY: Sell index futures and sell put options.

RISK: Unlimited—traders should use stop-loss orders on both positions to limit risk.

POTENTIAL PROFIT: Limited to time value of option plus the amount, if any, that the option is out-of-the-money.

MARGIN REQUIREMENT: Varies with the index contract and the brokerage firm.

EXAMPLE OF STRATEGY: Sell June S&P 500 futures at 165.00 and sell a June S&P 500 put at 165 for a premium of 3.

COMMENT: This strategy provides a good method for protecting a short futures position. Traders should use stop-loss orders on both positions.

Example 5

OPINION: Mildly Bearish to Neutral.

STRATEGY: Sell call options.

RISK: Unlimited—traders should use stop-loss orders.

POTENTIAL PROFIT: Limited to the premium received.

MARGIN REQUIREMENT: Varies with the index contract and the brokerage firm.

EXAMPLE OF STRATEGY: Sell June NYSE 98 calls for a premium of 3.00.

COMMENT: This is a high-risk strategy since the profit potential is limited to the premium received, whereas the risk is unlimited. Traders should use stop-loss orders to prevent excessive losses.

Example 6

OPINION: Strongly Bearish.

STRATEGY: Synthetic short futures—buy puts and sell calls.

Risk: Unlimited—traders should use stop-loss orders.

POTENTIAL PROFIT: Unlimited.

MARGIN REQUIREMENT: Varies with the Index contract and the brokerage firm.

EXAMPLE OF STRATEGY: Buy June S&P 100/155 puts and sell June S&P 100/155 calls.

COMMENT: A synthetic short futures positions is equivalent to being short in the futures market with all of the inherent risks of a futures position. Traders should use stop-loss orders to prevent excessive losses.

Examples of Neutral Strategies

Example 1

OPINION: Neutral.

STRATEGY: Sell a straddle.

RISK: Unlimited—traders should use stop-loss orders.

POTENTIAL PROFIT: Limited to the premiums received.

MARGINS REQUIREMENT: Varies with the index contract and the brokerage firm.

EXAMPLE OF STRATEGY: Sell June S&P 100/155 call and sell June S&P 100/155 put options.

COMMENT: This strategy works well in a sideways market where the market lacks a trend. The straddle writer can collect substantial premiums using this strategy. Traders are advised to use stop-loss orders in case the market develops a decisive trend.

Example 2

OPINION: Neutral.

STRATEGY: Sell a strangle—combination of a put and call.

RISK: Unlimited—traders should use stop-loss orders.

POTENTIAL PROFIT: Limited to the premiums received.

MARGIN REQUIREMENT: Varies with the index contract and the brokerage firm.

EXAMPLE OF STRATEGY: Sell June S&P 100/155 call and sell June S&P 100/150 put options.

COMMENT: Writing a strangle is a good method for collecting premiums in a sideways market. This strategy is somewhat safer than writing straddles because of the difference in strike prices.

Examples of Major Move Expected— Direction Uncertain

Example 1

OPINION: Major move expected—direction uncertain.

STRATEGY: Buy a straddle—combination of a put and call.

RISK: Limited to the premiums paid for the put and call.

POTENTIAL PROFIT: Unlimited—instrinsic value of the options at expiration less initial premium paid.

MARGIN REQUIREMENT: No margin requirement—options fully paid for at purchase.

EXAMPLE OF STRATEGY: Buy June S&P 100/155 call and buy June S&P 100/155 put options.

COMMENT: Buying straddles is good method for profiting from major moves in the market. A trader pays a large premium for this right which reduces the profit potential of this strategy.

Example 2

OPINION: Major move expected—direction uncertain.

STRATEGY: Buy a strangle—combination of a put and call.

RISK: Limited to the premiums paid for the options.

POTENTIAL PROFIT: Unlimited—instrinsic value of the options at expiration less initial premium paid.

MARGIN REQUIREMENT: No margin requirement—premiums fully paid for at purchase.

EXAMPLE OF STRATEGY: Buy June S&P 100/155 call and buy June S&P 100/150 put options.

COMMENT: Buying strangles is basically the same strategy as buying straddles. A trader pays less premium for buying a strangle than a straddle.

13

Hedging Strategies for Portfolio Managers, Individual and Institutional Investors

This chapter is written for individual investors as well as financial executives and fiduciaries who are responsible for managing sizable securities portfolios. The material is particularly relevant to registered investment advisors, bank trust officers, pension fund managers, corporate treasurers, underwriters, risk arbitrageurs, and institutional fund managers.

Application of the stock index futures and options to portfolio management could increase a manager's performance if integrated into the overall structure of a portfolio. Because of the newness of these markets, most textbooks on portfolio management and theory do not include chapters on the utility of index futures and options contracts as hedging tools. This chapter will only serve to introduce the subject in a manner that may encourage further scholarly works in this area.

The economic justifications for the index futures and options markets were that they would be used as risk transfer instruments to hedge systematic and unsystematic risks associated with managing a portfolio of common stocks. A portfolio manager is called a hedger—one who lays off a portion of his risks to a speculator by the process of buying and selling index futures and options contracts. The speculator assumes the risks that the hedger wants to lay off in expectation of making a trading profit.

This section describes the many approaches to developing hedging strategies for reducing price risks associated with holding common stocks and equivalent securities. In the opinion of the authors, there are some strategies that are not appropriate for hedging purposes. Other professionals may disagree with us, but we shall explain the reasons for our opinion.

What is a Hedging Strategy?

Hedging is defined as the initiation of a position in a futures or options market that is intended as a temporary substitute for the sale or purchase of the spot index, e.g., the S&P 500. The objectives of using the index futures and options markets for hedging are:

1. To reduce the price risk associated with the purchase or owner-ship of the underlying securities of an index.
2. To generate additional credits to an investment account—thus offsetting the risk of ownership.
3. To engage in an active management program of *dividend capture.* A corporate investment manager can use a combination of index futures and options contracts to enhance the dividend yields on his portfolio by timing sales and repurchases with ex-dividend dates of the underlying securities in the index. This can be an appropriate strategy to use on indexes composed of a relatively small number of stocks, such as the CBOE S&P International Oil Index. Of the six major oil companies in the index, Exxon Corporation makes up approximately 37 percent of the proportional value.

A hedging strategy assumes that there is a close correspondence in price fluctuation between the underlying portfolio of securities and the hedging instrument. In reality, a perfect relationship rarely exists unless the composition of securities in the portfolio duplicates those of the spot index exactly. Imperfect correspondence between the spot index and a specific portfolio is called *basis risk.* For example, during a specific period, the value of the New York Stock Exchange Index (NYSE) may appreciate 15 percent, whereas the value of a specific portfolio may only appreciate 10 percent. The difference of 5 percent represents the basis risk. In mathematical terms, we can say that the *correlation* between the value of the NYSE Index and the portfolio was less than 1.00. To minimize this type of risk, a money manager should determine the degree of corre-lation between the value of his portfolio and a particular index. A *correlation coefficient* of .95 indicates a strong relationship between the price movement of an index and the securities of a portfolio. A correlation coefficient can never exceed 1.00. If it is less than .70, the degree of variance (basis risk) between the price movements of an index and the portfolio may be too great to use an index contract as a reliable hedging instrument.

Hedging strategies, while reducing risks, also can limit potential profits in an underlying securities position. Professional investors have to evaluate the trade-off between reduced risks versus lower profits. *The purpose of hedging with index futures and options contracts is to bring about an adjustment in the expected risk versus the expected return on a securities portfolio that is cost effective and within the parameters determined by the portfolio manager or investor.*

The Structure of a Securities Portfolio

A typical portfolio may include common stocks, convertible securities, fixed income securities, money market instruments, and cash equivalents. Cash equivalents are considered to be Treasury bills, commercial paper, or repurchase agreements (REPOS).

Portfolio managers will restructure their portfolios with changing expectations about the marketplace. Also, they tend to favor certain industry groups over others at any given time and concentrate their holdings in those groups. At particular times in the business cycle, certain industry groups have a greater relative strength than others. In addition, special situations may make certain groups stronger or weaker in relationship to the overall market. For example, precious metals stocks experienced a meteoric rise when the price of gold bullion rose from $400 to $800 an ounce in 1979. The precious metals group then fell out of favor with investors as gold bullion prices fell to under $300 per ounce in 1982.

Portfolio managers ferret out undervalued companies within an industry group and accumulate shares in those companies. They will then sell shares in that industry group considered to be overvalued when their profit objectives have been reached. For example, when the prices of oil and gas exploration companies rose during the 1970s due to the booming demand for oil and gas supplies and OPEC's cartel pricing policies, money managers purchased these companies at highly inflated price/earnings multiples. Their portfolios outperformed the general market until the worldwide recession (1980–82) caused agonizing surpluses of crude oil and refined products. Prices of these companies plummeted as investors sold their holdings on expectations of lower profits. Portfolios with concentrated holdings of energy companies showed a dismal performance during this period.

Another example occurred with financial lending institutions during the period of ultra-high interest rates in 1980–82. The earnings of the savings and loan group were severely impacted during this period. Stock prices plummeted as many savings and loan companies declared bankruptcy or reported sharply lower profits for several quarters. As interest rates came down and the profit margins increased, this group rebounded quickly as was reflected in the price of their shares.

The Analysis of Betas in a Portfolio

Beta is a measure of the sensitivity to change of a stock's price in relation to overall fluctuations in the S&P 500 Index. A beta of 1.50 indicates a stock tends to rise (or fall) 50 percent more than the S&P 500. Beta is used to measure the stock market risk inherent in any diversified portfolio of 17 or more stocks. To calculate the beta of a portfolio, take a proportional average of the betas of the stocks comprising the portfolio. A beta of 1.00 means that a particular stock fluctuates exactly with the S&P 500, while a beta of .80 indicates that a stock fluctuates less than the overall stock market.

A *beta coefficient* for a stock is derived from a least-squares regression analysis between weekly percentage changes in the price of stock and weekly percentage changes in the S&P 500 over a five-year period. Betas are periodically adjusted for their long-term tendency to regress toward 1.00.

In rising (bullish) markets, high beta stocks (betas greater than 1.00) tend to outperform the overall market. Likewise, in declining (bearish) markets, low beta stocks (betas less than 1.00) decline less than the general market. Stated another way, high beta stocks tend to make more money in bullish markets, while low beta stocks tend to lose less money in bearish markets.

Index futures and options contracts can be a cost-effective way of adjusting the average beta of a portfolio of securities without buying or selling additional securities—thus saving commission costs. Please refer to the sample portfolio given in Table 13–1.

The *Value Line Investment Survey* publishes weekly information on a stock's price, estimated price/earning ratio, estimated yield, and beta. In addition, the *Value Line Investment Survey* ranks individual stocks with regard to timeliness of purchase, technical performance, and safety on a scale from 1 to 5. It also ranks industry groups with respect to relative strength and future performance. Value Line, however, covers approximately 1,700 stocks.

Table 13-1

Sample Portfolio

Security	Price	Number of Shares	Dollar Value	Beta
AMF Inc.	16	1,000	$16,000	1.20
Abbot Labs	48	1,000	48,000	1.05
Blue Bell	36	1,000	36,000	.80
Tandy Corp.	42	1,000	42,000	1.45
Totals		4,000	$142,000	4.50

Source: *Value Line Investment Survey*, August 19, 1983.

To properly use the beta concept in hedging market risks, one must determine (1) the betas for each stock in the portfolio, (2) the average beta of the portfolio, and (3) the correlation between it and the specific index to be used as a hedging instrument, i.e., the S&P 500.

Methods of Hedging Portfolio Risks

There are many methods to hedge price risks in a securities portfolio. With these new hedging instruments available, a portfolio has a choice of reducing price risks associated with (1) a specific company, (2) a specific industry, or (3) market fluctuations. Here are a few examples:

1. Writing covered call options against specific securities. For example, sell an IBM July 120 call against 100 shares of IBM.
2. Buy put options for specific stocks to offset risk of decline. For example, buy a General Motors (GM) October 60 put against 100 shares of GM.
3. Selling securities short against the box.
4. Diversify holdings among unrelated industry groups.
5. Diversify holdings of companies within an industry group with the strongest relative strength.
6. Purchase convertible securities (bonds or preferred) instead of the underlying common. Convertibles tend to rise with the common in rising markets but are resistant to declines in falling markets because of their higher yield.
7. Sell an index futures contract against a diversified portfolio of stocks. For example, sell a June S&P 500 futures contract to protect against market risk.

8. Buy index futures as a substitute purchase for actual securities at a later date. For example, buy a December S&P 100 Index futures as a substitute purchase for blue-chip issues.
9. Buy a put option on an industry index. For example, buy a December AMEX Oil and Gas 105 put to protect against a decline in value of oil and gas stocks.
10. Sell a call option on an industry index. For example, sell an AMEX Computer Technology March 105 call to receive premium credits on a portfolio of computer stocks.
11. Sell put options against cash reserves to increase yields. For example, sell an S&P 100 December 160 put for a premium credit of 4.
12. Credit call option spreads to generate additional credits while limiting risks of a written option. For example, sell a January AMEX Major Market Index (MMI) 125 call/buy a January Major Market Index 130 call for a credit of 2½ points.

Options on Individual Options versus Index Options

If protection on a specific stock is required, one should consider puts and calls on an individual stock. However, if broader-based coverage is desirable, then one should consider the advantages of index options. Index options are traded on market averages—such as the NYSE Index, or on industry groups—such as the AMEX Oil and Gas Index and Computer Technology Index. Options on the indexes offer several advantages over put and calls on individual stocks:

1. Written calls on individual stocks *can limit profits* on a stock if a dramatic rise occurs. For example, if a fund manager sold October IBM 80 calls for a premium of 4 and IBM rises to 100 per share, the calls will be exercised at 80. The fund manager experiences an opportunity loss of $16 per share on his position. The alternative strategy would be to sell calls on the AMEX Computer Technology Index. The fund manager retains the IBM and earns additional premium income from the written calls since index contracts require cash settlement and not the delivery of specific stocks.

2. Written calls on individual stocks can be exercised prior to their ex-dividend date. A fund manager holds a sizable position in *Exxon, Mobil,* and *Texaco,* on which he has written calls. Prior to the ex-dividend dates, the calls are exercised on him. He must deliver the stocks and thus *forfeit substantial dividend income.* An alterna-

tive strategy would be to write calls on the S&P International Oil Index. He can still retain his stocks and earn the dividend income along with the premium credits from the index calls.

3. Index options offer broad-based coverage for a portfolio for *less commission costs* since actual delivery of stocks is not required as they might be if one traded options on individual stocks. Index options can be traded without having to disturb the underlying portfolio. For example, if a fund manager holds 20 blue-chip stocks that comprise the AMEX Major Market Index (MMI) and he believes that a 20 percent decline in the index could occur over the next 60 days, he has a choice of (1) selling all his stocks with hope of repurchasing them at lower prices, (2) buying puts on each stock for protection, or (3) buying puts on the Major Market Index for broad-based protection. The third example provides reasonable protection against a 20 percent market decline for economical commission costs.

Strategies Not Recommended for Hedging

There are numerous strategies not recommended for hedging portfolio risks. The authors are expressing an opinion here that other professionals may disagree with. The determination of what is or is not an appropriate hedging strategy is a matter of judgment and degree of sophistication of the investor. The strategies we do not recommend are:

1. Buying call options. Call options are wasting assets that expire worthless 70–80 percent of time to the benefit of the writer. This means that option buyers make money only 20–30 percent of time. Buying call options is a speculative strategy because it increases market risks, not reduces them. On the other hand, writing call options is a conservative strategy since it generates premium credits—thus reducing either firm, industry, or market risks.

2. Debit call spreads. The same argument applies for debit call spreads as for buying call options. However, option spreads improve the odds of making money by reducing the premium cost of the long option. Please refer to Chapter 11 for explanation of option spreads.

3. Debit put spreads. Buying put options provides a certain amount of "insurance" against the downside risk of a market decline, while not limiting the upside potential for profits. No one can estimate the downside risk of the stock market. For example, the NYSE Index might decline only 5 percent, or it might decline 25 percent.

Debit put spreads limit the protection that might be needed in a major downside correction in the market.

Measurement of Portfolio Manager's Performance

The primary task of a portfolio manager is to increase the value of his portfolio. In order to do this, he must select quality securities from diverse industry groups to structure his portfolio. The active manager must establish criteria for selection based upon guidelines for acceptable risks and expected return on capital. He must also decide which yardstick to use for measuring performance. He must balance the component assets of the portfolio to enable him to meet current and future liabilities, such as administrative, legal, accounting, and reporting expenses. If he is managing a pension fund, he must be concerned about liabilities resulting from retirement, disability, and early withdrawals. Opportunities in the stock market, however, do not wait until he has investment funds available. Proper application of the index and options markets can allow him to improve timing for the purchase and sale of securities as well as generate premium credits.

Money managers are usually paid incentive fees based upon their performance in the appreciation of their portfolios compared to a standard index of measurement such as the S&P 500 Index. For example, let us assume that the S&P 500 Index rose from 125 to 135 during a six-month period—a gain of 8 percent. Table 13–2 shows a comparison of three different money managers who select securities from the S&P 500 group and thus use the S&P 500 Index as a performance measure.

Manager A's performance would be rated high with a +8 percent gain compared to managers B and C. Managers B and C would be rated mediocre since their performance was on par with or below average to the S&P 500 Index.

Before describing the various strategies that investors and portfolio managers can employ for hedging these risks, a few basic concepts

Table 13–2

Manager	Portfolio Gain	S&P 500	Difference	Performance Rating
A	16%	8%	8%	High
B	8	8	0	Average
C	2	8	−6	Below average

Figure 13–1

S&P 500 Basis Chart—60 Days

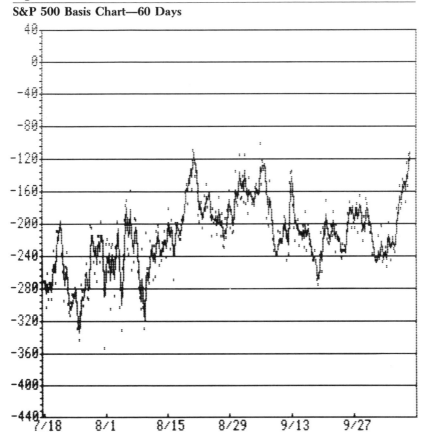

Source: *ADP Comtrend,* October 1983.

must be introduced and explained. The concept of *basis* is very important to the hedging process. *Basis* is defined as difference between the spot index price and the futures price. Refer to Figure 13–1 of a basis graph plotted over a 60-day period.

Position and Exercise Limits and Reportable Requirements

The activity of the index futures and options markets is regulated by the exchanges and several governmental agencies. The Commodity Futures Trading Commission (CFTC) regulates index futures and futures-options markets. The Securities and Exchanges Commission (SEC) regulates index options markets.

Each of these agencies has a market surveillance unit for monitoring the volume of trading and type of activity (speculative or hedging) on each exchange. In addition, the exchanges, in cooperation with the governmental agencies, impose position and exercise limits for each contract market as well as reporting requirements. These position and exercise limits and reporting requirements are different for each contract market and can change upon notification by the exchange.

A *position and exercise limit* is the maximum number of contracts net long or net short in all contract months combined that a bona fide hedger can take on.

A *reportable position* is the number of contracts on one side of the market that must be reported to the exchange and regulatory agency on a daily basis regardless if the customer is a bona fide hedger or speculator.

We have provided some examples of position and exercise limits and reportable positions for *bona fide hedgers* as of this writing (see Table 13–3). *Customers should consult with their brokers or the exchanges to receive updated information on these limits and reporting requirements to avoid violation of exchange and governmental regulations.*

Table 13–3

Position and Exercise Limits and Reportable Positions

Contract Market	Exchange	Position and Exercise Limits	Reportable Positions
S&P 500 futures	IOM	None contracts	100 contracts
S&P 100 futures	IOM	None	25
S&P 500 options	IOM	None	25
NYSE futures	NYFE	None	100
NYSE options	NYFE	None	25
Value Line	KCBOT	None	25
Major Market Index	AMEX	15,000	200
Market Value Index	AMEX	10,000	200
Oil and Gas Index	AMEX	8,000	200
Computer Technology	AMEX	4,000	200
S&P 100 options	CBOE	15,000	200
S&P 500 options	CBOE	15,000	200
S&P International Oil	CBOE	4,000	200
S&P Computer and Business	CBOE	4,000	200
NYSE 1500 Composite	NYSE	25,000	200

Examples of Hedging Strategies Using Index Futures

The authors present the following hedging strategies that an investor can employ using index futures. Each strategy is presented as a situation with an objective. The results are then analyzed on a one-contract basis demonstrating best-case and worst-case-scenarios.

Example 1

Situation. An institutional portfolio contains two-year Treasury notes scheduled to mature in three months. Upon maturity, the money will be allocated for buying $1 million worth of blue-chip securities. The fund manager believes that the S&P 500 Index is prime for an immediate 15-point rise (from 150 to 165) because his research indicates that interest rates will drop 200 basis points and second-quarter corporate earnings reports will be sharply up. The fund retains cash reserves of $100,000 that can be used for short-term commitments.

Objective. To achieve a substitute purchase of $1 million worth of securities prior to the actual purchase of the securities in anticipation of a major rise in the market averages.

Strategy. To buy 13 December S&P 500 Index futures at 150. He deposits $3,500 per contract, or $45,500 in hedge margins, with a broker. The commodity exchange does not require a customer to pay interest on debit balances. His positions are marked-to-market daily for maintenance calls.

Example 2

Situation. An institutional portfolio contains 35 percent stocks listed on the New York Stock Exchange, 35 percent stocks listed on the American Stock Exchange, and the remaining 30 percent traded on the over-the-counter (OTC) market. The fund manager believes that the market is ripe for a 10 percent downside correction during the next 30 days, but he is unsure because his market indicators have given mixed signals. His research shows that the value of his portfolio correlates highly with the Value Line Index. The average beta of the stocks in the portfolio is 1.25, which suggests it is vulnerable if the market correction comes as forecast.

Objective. To achieve a substitute sale of $2 million worth of securities in anticipation of a downside correction in the market. The fund manager wants to adjust the average beta of his portfolio from 1.25 to 1.00 by the sale of Value Line Index futures.

Strategy. To sell 21 December Value Line Index futures at 190.00. He must deposit hedge margins of $3,500 per contract, or total margins of $73,500. For protection, he places a stop-loss at 192.00 to close out his futures positions for a loss of $1,000 per contract, or $21,000 for all contracts.

Examples of Hedging Strategies Using Index Options

The following examples illustrate hedging applications using index options. Each example is presented as a situation with an objective. The results are then analyzed on a one-contract basis demonstrating best-case and worst-case scenarios.

Example 1

Situation. A bank trust officer manages a sizable portfolio comprised of 20 major oil and gas companies for the bank's customers. The average dividend yield on the portfolio is 4.5 percent. Money market instruments are currently yielding 12 percent. In addition, the value of the portfolio has declined during recent years as oil and gas prices fell due to a global recession. However, he believes that the oil and gas industry group will recover as the U.S. economy improves. The bank's customers have complained that they want a higher return on their holdings. They ask him what he recommends to increase their return without having to sell their stocks. The AMEX Oil and Gas Index closed at 105.40.

Objective. To achieve a higher return on current holdings without having to actively trade the stocks.

Strategy. To develop a program for writing calls on the AMEX Oil and Gas Index to earn premium income for the bank's trust accounts. To sell 100 December 110 calls on the AMEX Oil and

Gas Index for a premium of 3½. Upon the sale of call options, the broker credits the bank's account with $35,000 in premiums. The bank must deposit $3,300 per contract or total margins of $330,000 in cash or equivalent securities for initial margins.

Example 2

Situation. An investment manager for a company that manufactures peripheral devices for leading computer companies has been accumulating shares of these companies. He believes that their prospects for long-term growth and price appreciation are excellent. Recently, he heard rumors that the second-quarter earnings reports could be sharply lower due to cutthroat competition and price-cutting in this industry group. He wants protection against a dramatic decline in prices for his holdings if these rumors prove true.

Objective. To achieve protection against a dramatic price decline in a portfolio of computer technology stocks without selling them.

Strategy. To buy 100 September 95 puts on the AMEX Computer Technology Index for a premium of 2. The index closed at 97.50. He must deposit $200.00 per contract, or $20,000, in cash with the brokerage firm to cover the purchase.

Example 3

Situation. An aggressive institutional investor holds substantial cash reserves in 90-day Treasury bills. He wants to commit a portion of these funds to the stock market when the Treasury bills mature. He prefers to buy stocks selected from the S&P 100 Index. In the meantime, he wants to enhance the yield on the Treasury bills— currently yielding 8 percent. Also, he believes that the stock market will present some excellent buying opportunities within 90 days. The S&P 100 Index closed at 156.30.

Objective. To achieve a higher return on cash reserves prior to making a commitment in the market.

Strategy. To write (sell) 50 September 155 puts on the S&P 100 Index for a premium of 3. The brokerage firm will allow him to deposit Treasury bills in lieu of initial margins for writing put options. He must deposit $4,650 per contract, or total margins of $232,500.

Example 4

Situation. An individual investor with a large holding of 10 blue-chip stocks is dissatisfied with the total return on his investments. He is approaching retirement age and does not want to take risks. The value of his portfolio has risen only slightly in eight months. Further analysis of his portfolio reveals that it correlates highly with the AMEX Major Market Index (MMI). He wants to increase his current return without forfeiting an opportunity for unusual profits should his stocks rise dramatically. He seeks the advise of a broker who recommends writing credit call spreads. The AMEX Major Market Index closed at 119.

Objective. To increase the return on a conservative portfolio of securities while participating in a dramatic rise in the stock market.

Strategy. To sell 50 AMEX January Major Market Index 120 calls at 5 and buy 50 January 130 Major Market Index calls at 1 for a credit of 4. The investor must deposit $600 per contract, or total margins of $30,000. The brokerage firm will allow Treasury bills to be used in lieu of cash.

Example 1—Substitute Purchase of Stocks Using S&P 500 Index Futures

On March 1, the portfolio manager valued the securities that he was planning to purchase at $975,000. One million dollars worth of U.S. Treasury notes matured on June 1. The June S&P 500 futures were 150.00. Thirteen futures contracts of S&P 500s purchased at 150.00 represent $975,000 market value of securities. S&P 500 futures positions will be closed out when the actual securities are purchased.

Transaction Summary—10 Percent Market Decline

Purchase 13 June S&P 500 on March 1 at 150.00	$975,000
Stock market declines by 10% by June 1 (S&P 500 = 135.00)	877,500
Net loss on futures	(97.500)
Purchase stocks June 1 for	877,500
Gain on portfolio	97,500
Loss on futures	(97,500)
Loss on stocks by hedging	$ –0–

Had the market rallied rather than declined, the following would have resulted:

Transaction Summary—10 Percent Increase in Stock Market

Purchase 13 June S&P 500 on March 1 at 150.00	$ 975,000
Stock market rises by 10% by June 1 (S&P 500 = 165.00)	1,072,500
Net gain on futures	97,500
Purchase stocks on June 1 for	1,072,500
Loss on portfolio	(97,500)
Gain on futures	97,500
Loss on stocks by hedging	$ –0–

Example 2—Substitute Sale of Stocks Using Value Line Index Futures

On May 2, the portfolio manager valued his securities that he is planning to hedge using the sale of 21 December Value Line contracts at 190.00 at $1,995,000. Twenty-one Value Line futures contracts represent $1,995,000 worth of securities. He sets a stop-loss order at 192.00 on his futures position to prevent further losses should the market rally.

Transaction Summary—10 Percent Market Decline

Sell 21 December Value Line on May 2 at 190.00	$1,995,000
Stock market declines by 10% by December 1 (Value Line = 171.00)	1,795,500
Net gain on futures	199,500
Loss on portfolio	(199,500)
Gain on futures	199,500
Loss on stocks by hedging	$ –0–

Had the market rallied rather than declined, the following would have resulted:

Transaction Summary—10 Percent Increase in Stock Market

Sell 21 Value Line Futures on May 2 at 190.00	$1,995,000
Stock market rises but position stopped out at 192.00 for loss	2,016,000
Net loss on futures	(21,000)
Value of portfolio if stock market rises by 10% by December 1 (Value Line = 209.00)	2,194,500
Gain on portfolio	199,500
Loss on futures	(21,000)
Gain on stocks by hedging	$ 178,500

Example 1—Sale of AMEX Oil and Gas Index Calls against Portfolio of Stocks

The bank trust officer valued his portfolio of oil and gas securities on October 2 at $1,050,000. He intends to sell 100 December 110 AMEX Oil and Gas calls for a premium of 3½ ($350), which will be credited to his account. He believes that call writing will reduce the risk of owning his stocks should the market decline and add premium income to it should the market rise or stay unchanged. The call writer receives the full credit upon expiration if the index price is less than the exercise price. The AMEX index closed at 105.00.

Transaction Summary—10 Percent Market Decline

Sell 100 December AMEX Oil and Gas 100 calls for premium of 3½ ($350) credit	$ 35,000
Stock market declines by 10% by December 1 (AMEX Oil and Gas Index = 94.50)	(105,000)
Net loss on portfolio	(70,000)
Value of portfolio by December 1 (AMEX Index = 94.50)	945,000
Loss on portfolio	(105,000)
Gain by writing calls	35,000
Net loss on portfolio	(70,000)

Had the market rallied rather than declined, the following would have resulted:

Transaction Summary—10 Percent Increase in Stock Market

Sell 100 December AMEX Oil and Gas 110 calls for premium of 3½ ($350) credit	$ 35,000
Stock market rises by 10% by December 1 (AMEX Index = 115.50)	105,000
Gross gain on portfolio	140,000
Value of portfolio if stock market rises by 10% by December 1 (AMEX Index = 115.50)	1,155,000
AMEX options repurchased at 115.50 for loss of 2 ($200)	(20,000)
Gain on portfolio	140,000
Net loss on options	(20,000)
Gain on stocks by writing calls	$ 120,000

Example 2—Purchase of AMEX Computer Technology September 95 Puts against Portfolio of Stocks

The investment manager valued his portfolio of computer technology securities on July 5 at $975,000. He intends to purchase 100

September AMEX 95 puts for a premium of 2 ($200) which will be debited to his account. He believes that the computer stocks may decline. The AMEX Computer Technology Index closed at 97.50.

Transaction Summary—10 Percent Market Decline

Buy 100 December AMEX Computer Technology 95 puts for premium of 2 ($200) debit	$ (20,000)
Stock market declines by 10% by September 16 (AMEX Computer Technology Index = 87.75)	(97,500)
Gross loss on portfolio	(117,000)
Value of portfolio by September 16 (AMEX Index = 87.75)	877,500
Loss on portfolio	(117,000)
Value of AMEX puts—made gain of 7.25 = 95 − 87.75	72,500
Net loss on portfolio	$ (44,500)

Had the market rallied rather than declined, the following would have resulted:

Transaction Summary—10 Percent Increase in Stock Market

Buy 100 September AMEX Computer Technology 95 puts for premium of 2 ($200) debit	$ (20,000)
Stock market rises by 10% by September 16 (AMEX Index = 107.25)	97,500
Gross gain on portfolio	77,000
Value of portfolio if stock market rises by 10% by September 16 (AMEX Index = 107.25)	1,072,500
AMEX options expired worthless for loss of 2 ($200)	(20,000)
Gain on portfolio	77,000
Value of puts	–0–
Net gain on portfolio	$ 77,000

Example 3—Sale of September S&P 100/155 Puts for Premium of 3 ($300)

The investment manager wants to earn additional income on his cash reserves. He writes S&P 100/155 puts for a 3 ($300) credit. In addition, he wants to purchase certain blue-chip stocks if the S&P 100 Index declines below 143; otherwise he will not add to his existing portfolio. The securities he wants to purchase are currently valued at $780,000. The S&P 100 Index closed at 156.00.

Transaction Summary—10 Percent Market Decline

Sell 50 September S&P 100/155 puts for premium of 3 ($300) credit	$ 15,000
Stock market declines by 10% by September 16 (S&P 100 Index = 140.40)	78,000
Gross gain on holdings	93,000
Value of portfolio by September 16 (S&P 100 Index = 140.40)	702,000
Gross gain received in purchasing stocks	78,000
Net loss on value of S&P 100 puts	(58,000)
Net gain by writing puts	$ 20,000

Note: The investment manager purchased additional securities since the S&P 100 Index declined below 143 which was his entry level. The gain received from writing puts was applied against the acquisition cost of the stocks. Writing puts incurred a net loss of $58,000 (the difference between 155 and 140.40 plus the premium credit of 3).

Had the market rallied rather than declined, the following would have resulted:

Transaction Summary—10 Percent Increase in Stock Market

Sell 50 September S&P 100/155 puts for premium of 3 ($300) credit	$ 15,000
Stock market rises by 10% by September 16 (S&P 100 Index = 171.60)	78,000
Gross gain on portfolio	93,000
Value of portfolio if stock market rises by 10% by September 16 (S&P 100 Index = 171.60)	858,000
S&P 100 options expired worthless for gain of 3 ($300)	15,000
Gain on portfolio	93,000
Value of puts	–0–
Net gain on portfolio	$ 93,000

Note: The investment manager did not purchase additional stock because the S&P 100 did not decline to his entry level. The gain generated by writing puts accrued to the overall value of his portfolio.

Example 4—Sale of January AMEX Major Market Index 120 Calls/Buy January AMEX Major Market 130 Calls for Premium of 4 ($400) Credit

The investor wants to earn additional income on his stock portfolio. He places on a credit spread using the AMEX Major Market Index (MMI) calls. The Major Market Index closed at 119.

Transaction Summary—10 Percent Market Decline

Sell 50 January MMI 120 calls for premium of 5 ($500) credit	$ 25,000
Buy 50 January MMI 130 calls for premium of 1 ($100) debit	(5,000)
Stock market declines by 10% by January 20 (AMEX MMI Index = 107.10)	(59,500)
Net loss on value of portfolio	(39,500)
Value of portfolio by January 20 (AMEX MMI Index = 107.10)	535,500
Net gain by writing credit spread	20,000
Loss on portfolio value	(59,500)
Net loss on portfolio value	$(39,500)

Had the market rallied rather than declined, the following would have resulted:

Transaction Summary—10 Percent Increase in Stock Market

Sell 50 AMEX MMI 120 calls for premium of 5 ($500) credit	$ 25,000
Buy 50 AMEX MMI 130 calls for premium of 1 ($100) debit	(5,000)
Stock market rises by 10% by January 20 (AMEX MMI = 130.90)	59,500
Gross gain on portfolio	79,500
Value of portfolio if stock market rises by 10% by January 20 (AMEX MMI Index = 130.90)	654,500
Gain on portfolio	59,500
Net loss on credit call spread	(34,500)
Net gain on portfolio	$ 25,000

14

How to Use Personal Computers for Financial and Investment Analysis

The arrival of low-cost personal computers has expanded investors' access to financial information that was difficult to obtain several years ago. The development of solid-state microprocessors and memory storage devices allows executives and investors to search for, retrieve, and store financial data for review and analysis. The authors believe that personal computers will become an essential tool for information retrieval and analysis within the coming decade. Investors and financial executives who are not aware of the applications of personal computers will be at a disadvantage to those who understand and regularly use this new technology. The use of a computer in no way guarantees that an investor will make profitable trading decisions. It is a tool for organizing, storing, and retrieving information to make efficient use of one's time. The authors strongly recommend to all readers that they learn about this new information technology and the impact it will have on our society as a whole.

The new microcomputers can perform the following functions:

1. Data processing and computational functions.
2. Graphics display of statistical data.
3. Word processing and report generation applications.
4. Development of user-written programs.
5. Electronic filing system for data storage and retrieval.
5. Access to remote data bases via telecommunication networks.
7. Data base management and filing system.
8. Spread sheet applications for doing "what if" projections.
9. Electronic mail delivery.

Microcomputers are electronic devices that store and manipulate symbolic and numeric data in a binary format. A bit is the smallest unit of binary organization. Groups of eight bits form bytes, which represent numbers, letters, and special symbols that are stored in the computer memory and instruct the microprocessor to perform computational and manipulative functions. A kilobyte is a standard unit of computer memory capacity. Kilobyte (abbreviated as K) is 1,024 bytes, which represents about 205 five-letter words of text. For example, a microcomputer with a 16-K memory contains 16,384 bytes of memory, or 3,277 five-letter words of text.

Computer hardware usually consists of a video display, keyboard, microprocessor, and a permanent memory storage device. Printers are required to obtain a hard-copy printout of results. A microprocessor is the heart of the computer and is called a *computer on a chip* because of its small size. A microprocessor controls all of the input/output (I/O) functions of a computer through a system of solid-state, integrated circuits. Until recently, the eight-bit microprocessor was the only type available for personal computers. A new generation of 16- and 32-bit microprocessors is now becoming commercially available. The new microprocessors have from four to eight times the speed and random-access-memory (RAM) capacity than the eight-bit microprocessor has. In addition, they allow more direct memory access (DMA) since their random-access-memory capacity is substantially greater. The technological developments of microprocessor, floppy disk, hard-disk drives, and bubble memory allow low-cost storage of large amounts of information in a tiny space. A word of caution about buying the 16- or 32-bit computers: software has not been fully developed or tested for them. A prospective buyer should evaluate his application needs within the framework of software availability before buying. A faster computer is useless to an owner if the programs are not available to run it. Many of the popular investment and financial analysis programs will be converted from the 8-bit to the 16- and 32-bit computers when commercially feasible.

A computer program describes the set of instructions that are converted from a programming language (such as *BASIC* or *FORTRAN*) into binary codes that a microprocessor can act upon. The generic term for a computer program is *software* to distinguish it from *hardware*. Many computer vendors are marketing packaged programs that perform specialized accounting and financial applications. A computer program is considered to be "user-friendly" if it comes with an easy-to-read documentation manual and with program prompts that guide the user through it with a minimum of error. Writing a user-friendly computer program is a painstaking job and may require several years of work before it can be released for sale to the public. In general, the quality of computer software is rising while prices are falling because of the availability of a mass market of personal computer owners. Programs that perform word processing, data file management, and general accounting applications are available from most computer vendors at reasonable prices. Refer to Appendix D for a partial listing of packaged computer programs that are available for commodity and stock market analysis.

Many of the newly designed microcomputers use an integrated approach to program control. A user can load several different programs into memory. For example, he can split the video screen into several work areas. He can display a price chart of a stock in one area; write a report on the stock in another area; and perform computations with respect to the stock's price, earnings, and dividends in yet another area. The user can shift data from one area into another by using standard commands. These features will allow a user to work on several projects at one time and move information back and forth through the use of integrated program commands.

Videotex is an umbrella term used to cover both broadcast teletext and telephone transmission viewdata systems. The use of personal computers in telecommunications is a recent phenomenon. An individual can dial a telephone number and access a subscriber data base that contains voluminous amounts of information presented in a menu format. A data base is an organization of information by files that can be accessed and updated for regular use. Some vendors are marketing portable computers that come equipped with built-in phone connections to access on-line information services, such as the *Dow Jones News/Retrieval Service, Compuserve,* and *The Source.*

For example, an investor can access the *Dow Jones News/Retrieval Service* to receive stock quotes and financial information regarding individual companies or industry groups or general information on securities markets. Other data bases, such as *Compuserve* and *The Source,* allow a subscriber to read financial sections of major newspapers and specialized investment services that offer advice on securities and commodities markets. This information is offered in a *menu* format that permits readers to select their areas of interest. See Figure 14–1 for example.

There are many types of microcomputers on the market now. A potential buyer of a personal computer should determine his needs, availability of packaged programs (software), price range, and list of available options—such as printers, expandable memory, and programming languages. The development of computer programs for microcomputers is still in its infancy. Many computer

Figure 14–1

Menu Format for *Dow Jones*
News/Retrieval Service

//MENU

Master Menu
Copyright (C) 1983
Dow Jones & Company, Inc.

Type   For

A   Dow Jones Business
       and Economic News
B   Dow Jones Quotes
C   Financial and Investment
       Services
D   General News and
       Information Services

owners prefer to write programs that instruct the computer to perform specialized applications. A programmer will develop an algorithm, which is a prescribed set of rules for solving a specific problem. For example, if a user wants to compute a 10-day moving average for tracking the S&P 500 Index, he can write a program to sum the daily prices of the index and then divide by the total number of days.

Advanced Programming Applications

Computers were originally designed to perform operations that were too tedious and time-consuming for humans to perform. The operations of a computer are limited by its memory capacity and the program that instructs it. The computer can be programmed to perform the following useful applications, among others:

1. Develop quantitative models for the analysis of a portfolio of securities with respect to composition of securities, changes in valuation, dividend payouts, price/earnings ratios, length of holding period, convertibility.
2. Develop price forecasting models based on projected earnings and historical price/earnings ratios.
3. Develop valuation models for put and call option pricing to determine "fair values."
4. Develop technical trading models for stock index futures to optimize profits.

Future Applications of Microcomputers

A new generation of computer microprocessors and software currently being designed will be capable of simulating artifical intelligence (AI). AI is defined as the capability of a computer system to perform functions normally concerned with human intelligence, such as learning, adapting, reasoning, self-correction, and automatic improvement.

LISP is a interpretative language compatible with the development of procedures for simulating artifical intelligence. LISP is an acronym for LISt Processing. This language was developed for the manipulation of symbolic strings and recursive data.

The combination of advanced microprocessors and high-level languages like LISP could add a dimension to the development of heuristic models of stock market behavior.

Information Services

Information services containing price data, news reports, and fundamental and technical information are now available for only a few dollars per hour of user time. With most services, you pay an initial subscription charge and user fees for the amount of time your computer is connected to a host system. The user fees vary according to the types of services used and the time of day. There are only a half a dozen major consumer-oriented data banks, though new ones are being added each year, and the services of existing data banks are being expanded. Generally, these services offer stock and/or commodity price data, news articles, and statistical data regrading companies and specific markets. The following is a brief list of the major consumer-oriented data bases; many new ones are being added each year. Chapter 16 describes how to find out more details about these services.

> DOW JONES NEWS/RETRIEVAL SERVICE
> COMPUSERVE INFORMATION SERVICE
> THE SOURCE
> NEW YORK TIMES INFORMATION SERVICE

How to Access an Information Service

A personal computer owner may have to purchase additional equipment before he can access information services. A computer must have a modem and an RS-232 communications board installed before it can communicate with the host computer of an information service via the telephone. Many new models of personal computers come already equipped with these devices.

A modem is the abbreviated word for modulator-demodulator, which is a thin, box-like electronic device that allows computers to talk with each other via the telephone lines. There are two types of modems: acoustic coupler and direct-connect. A RS-232 communications board is required to effect communications between the computer and a host system. The RS-232 board is purchased from the vendor and lies within the computer itself.

Modems transmit information at different speeds, known as the baud rate, between a personal computer and a host information service. Generally, special software is needed to make a personal computer emulate a terminal. Before a modem can communicate with a host system, certain settings must be made to make them compatible. They are as follows:

> DUPLEX: Full or HALF
> ORIGINATE or ANSWER mode
> BAUD RATE: 300 or 1200
> PARITY: ODD or EVEN

After a subscriber has dialed a telephone network line, he must *log on* the host system. The subscriber dials up the host system via a network communcations system. In many cases, a local call is made instead of a long-distance call. This can save subscribers a lot of money over many hours of usage. *Log on* procedures include the typing in of an identification number and a password, which the host system checks out before allowing the user to gain access to the system's data banks. The following is a sample *Log on* procedure for the *Dow Jones News/Retrieval Service:*

> PLEASE TYPE YOUR TERMINAL IDENTIFIER: A
> PLEASE LOG IN: DOW1;;
> WHAT SERVICE PLEASE????? DJNS
> ENTER PASSWORD: 110034SECRET

After a subscriber has finished accessing the host system, he logs off the system, which terminates the connection between the host system and the personal compputer.

The Basics of Programming

A program is a list of instructions that enable a computer to perform a specific task—for example, to compute the 20-day moving average of a stock price. Without a program, a computer is as lifeless as a phonograph without a record. The program, or set of instructions, can be written in one of many programming languages—BASIC, FORTRAN, PASCAL, COBOL. BASIC is a popular language to learn and use because of its reference to English words such as *print, read, data, input, remark, run, save, load,* which have an intuitive meaning to a user.

Writing programs for personal use that perform reliably can take many days of work. Even experienced programmers take hours to successfully "debug" a program before entrusting its use to a business or financial application. Test data are usually run through the newly written program to ensure the accuracy of results. It is easy to make simple programming mistakes that output totally ridiculous results.

The difficulty in writing reliable programs has given birth to a new multimillion-dollar industry—that of software development for personal computers. There are now many "packaged" programs available that can perform powerful business and financial applications. As software engineering and design become more adaptable to the novice user, it will become unnecessary for a person to learn programming since he can set up his own parameters and functions within the framework of an existing program.

VisiCalc[1] is an electronic spread sheet program that has a wide range of uses in financial planning and forecasting. Other programs are available for performing portfolio management, technical analysis, and fundamental analysis. Users of VisiCalc can set up their own parameters and applications and execute the program without having to learn a programming language.

The authors believe that portable microcomputers will be as common as attache cases are for executives and professional persons in the near future. The development of miniaturized mass storage devices will enable executives to store and retrieve information quickly as well as access data banks for making sales, marketing, or financial decisions.

Guidelines for Evaluating Application Software

The authors have developed a set of guidelines for evaluating software packages for personal computers. A "software package" is a set of computer programs developed and marketed by a vendor to perform specific applications—whether they be investment analy-

---

[1] VisiCalc is a trademark of VisiCorp. Inc., 2895 Zanker Road, San Jose, CA 95134.

sis, record-keeping, or portfolio evaluation. An application is a specific function of a program, such as (1) computing moving averages; (2) displaying bar graphs; or (3) updating files of stock prices, earnings, and dividend data.

These guidelines are the result of 10 years of experience in buying and using software products. Refer to Appendix D for a description and evaluation of software packages for investment analysis.

1. A prospective buyer should make a list of specific applications and functions he wants from a package at a stated price.
2. A package should be compatible with the computer you own or intend to purchase.
4. A package should be marketed by a reputable vendor who will warrant and properly service the products.
5. A prospective buyer should avoid purchasing version number 1.0 or 1.1. The version number indicates how long the software package has been on the market. Look to buy version 2.0 or 3.0, if available.
6. A package should be "menu driven," i.e., the user can select functions of the program by menu number.
7. A package should come with a detailed and readable documentation manual with ample illustrations and examples for users.
8. A prospective buyer should contact at least two or three persons who have used the package for several months. He should ask them specific questions about the utilities of the package and if they are satisfied with it.
9. A prospective buyer should request a demonstration of the software package from an experienced salesperson. The salesperson should be aware of the package's benefits as well as its limitations in performing the desired applications.

In conclusion, the availability of personal computers will allow investors and traders to access timely fundamental information and technical data that should prove useful in trading the stock index futures and options market.

15

Tax Treatment of Profits and Losses

This chapter will discuss the current rules and regulations regarding taxation of stock index futures, futures-options, and index option contracts for (1) speculative traders, (2) investors in common stocks, (3) securities broker/dealers, and (4) tax-exempt investments.

Readers are forewarned that tax rulings may change after publication of this book, and readers should therefore seek assistance from a qualified tax attorney or certified public accountant for individual tax situations. Material presented in this chapter will serve only as guidelines to the current interpretations of the Internal Revenue Codes (IRC).

The Economic Recovery Tax Act of 1981

Prior to 1981, commodity futures were taxed according to length of holding period. If positions were held longer than six months, the resultant capital gain or loss was treated as long term. All positions held six months or less were treated as short-term capital gains or losses.

The Economic Recovery Tax Act of 1981 (ERTA) changed tax rulings regarding commodities and securities transactions. All speculative futures transactions became subject to *Mark-to-Market* rules, whereas securities transactions were not. Mark-to-market rulings were implemented to eliminate the abusive use of "commodity tax straddles." Tax straddles were used to defer income and short-term capital gains from one tax year into the next and, under certain conditions, convert short-term gains to long term. ERTA also defined a regulated futures contract (RFC) as:

1. Requiring delivery of personal property for an interest in such property.
2. Subject to year-end, "mark-to-market" system.
3. Traded or subject to the rules of a domestic board of trade designated as a contract market by the Commodity Futures Trading Commission or Secretary of the Treasury.

The Technical Corrections Act of 1982 (TCA) amended the ERTA definition of an RFC to include cash settlement contracts, such as the stock index futures. TCA deleted the provision under ERTA that a contract must require the delivery of personal property to qualify as an RFC. This change now allows stock index futures contracts to be considered as RFCs and thus qualify for the 60/40 long-term/short-term split.

Explanation of the Mark-to-Market Concept

Commodity futures exchanges in the United States utilize a unique system of margining and accounting for every futures contract's gain or loss on a daily basis. A trader may receive any gain on his position in cash as a matter of right after the market close. If a futures position has increased in value at the close of the market, the net increase in the position is computed and transferred to the trader's account before the beginning of the next trading session. A trader has the right to withdraw the full amount of his gains immediately every trading day. If a trader's position decreases in value at the close of the market, he may have to post additional margin funds with the broker to maintain his position. Money paid on position losses is paid into the exchange clearing corporation that transfers such amounts to accounts that gained in value at the close of the market. The daily accounting that includes the determination of contract settlement prices and margin adjustments to reflect gains and losses is called *marking-to-market.*

The mark-to-market system applies to futures and *written* futures-options contracts. *Long* futures-options positions are not marked-to-market because long options are fully paid for at time of purchase and thus are nonmarginable contracts.

ERTA has adopted a mark-to-market system for the taxation of regulated futures contracts. Because a taxpayer who trades index futures contracts receives profits as a matter of right or must pay losses in cash daily, Congress believed it appropriate to measure the taxpayer's futures income on the same basis for tax purposes. The IRS applied the doctrine of constructive receipt to gains in a futures trading account at year-end.

Types of Index Futures and Options Contracts

The reader must distinguish among the four categories of contracts traded and realize that the tax treatment of each category may be different.

1. Stock index futures contracts.
2. Index futures-options contracts.
3. Index options (classified as securities).
4. Equity options (classified as securities).

Index futures-options are "options on RFCs" since they can be exercised into underlying futures contracts. Index options and equity options are considered to be "options on physicals." Index options represent cash settlement contracts on an underlying composite index of stocks. Equity options represent contracts that can be exercised for delivery of 100 shares of an underlying stock, e.g., put and call options on General Motors.

Tax rulings as applied to futures and options can be classified as either *speculative* or *hedging* transactions. Furthermore the resultant gains or losses from these transactions can be divided into four general categories depending upon the nature of the transaction and its outcome. The categories are:

1. Short-term capital gains and losses.
2. Long-term capital gains and losses.
3. Ordinary income.
4. Ordinary losses.
5. 60/40 long-term/short-term capital gains split.

Stock index futures are classifed as regulated futures contracts (RFCs), which are taxed at a 60/40 long-term/short-term capital gains split. Stock index futures-options (i.e., commodity options) may be taxed the same as RFCs or may be taxed similarly to options on stocks (equity options). Proposed legislation leans toward the taxation of index futures-options on a 60/40 basis.

Speculative positions in the stock index futures and options transactions are taxed as either long- or short-term capital gains or losses. Investor positions, in which index futures or options are traded against a position of common stocks, are considered to be capital asset transactions, and the resultant gains and losses are taxed accordingly.

Taxation of Index Options

As of this publication, *the IRS has made no specific rulings regarding the tax treatment of index options,* which include options on the market indexes and industry indexes. Since these instruments are closely akin to equity options and are traded on securities exchanges, the general opinion is that their tax treatment will be similar to equity options.

Equity options are considered to be capital assets for nondealers. Long options must be held for a period longer than one year to qualify for long-term capital gain. However, listed equity options are only available for a period of nine months or less. Premiums received from written options are treated as short-term capital assets regardless of the holding period. Thus, all option premiums, profits, and losses are short term.

Index options may have a distinct advantage over equity options once IRC rulings are specified. Buying or writing index options against a portfolio of stocks should not affect the holding period established by an investor. In contrast, the IRS has specified certain situations where the purchase or sale of an equity option would alter the holding period of the underlying security to the disadvantage of the investor. For example, if a put is bought on a specific stock, such as Exxon Corporation, the holding period for the stock would begin the day the put was purchased instead of the date when the stock was purchased. Obviously, this regulation discourages investors from buying puts on specific stocks to protect their position unless the put is purchased the same day as the stock.

Bona Fide Hedging Transactions

The Internal Revenue Code (IRC) explains *hedging* as any transaction in the index futures or options markets entered into by a taxpayer in the normal course of his trade or business primarily to:

1. Reduce price risk of holding a portfolio of common stocks that closely tracks the price changes of a general market index or

specific industry index. The index contract used becomes designated as the hedging instrument.

2. Reduce risk of interest rate changes regarding borrowings made or to be made, or obligations incurred or to be incurred, by the taxpayer.

The taxpayer is expected to clearly identify the transaction as a hedging transaction before the close of the markets on the day the transaction was entered. If an investor in a portfolio of common stocks is using the index futures and options markets for bona fide hedging purposes, he may be exempt from the year-end marked-to-market, short-sale, and wash-sale rulings. Profits and losses for bona fide hedge accounts are treated as ordinary income or loss.

Trading Activities of Broker/Dealers and Market-Makers

A broker/dealer may be a sole proprietor, partnership, or corporation in the business of buying securities and reselling them to customers for a markup or commission. The trading activities of securities broker/dealers and market-makers are considered to be business-related income if the transactions are not identified as investments for their own account. Profits and losses from their trading activities qualify as ordinary income or loss since they are in the business of buying securities for resale as dealers. If certain trading activities are identified as investments for the dealer's account, then they may qualify for capital gains treatment.

Tax Treatment of Hedging Transactions on a Portfolio of Securities

For investment accounts, all profits and losses generated from the purchase or sale of the index futures or options contracts are taxed as ordinary income or loss within the restraints of the overall tax liability of the securities portfolio being hedged. Brokerage commissions must be used to adjust the gain or loss for transactions.

For investors who wish to speculate in the stock index and options markets as well as use them as hedging vehicles, brokerage firms can designate separate accounts. One type of account can be approved for speculation and another for hedging transactions. Brokers usually designate these different accounts by a number series that identifies the account as either speculative or hedge. Profits and losses generated from the purchase or sale of futures and options are subject to the same tax as a regular speculator.

Tax-Exempt Investments

If a securities portfolio is exempt from taxation, e.g., a qualified pension fund, trust, or retirement plan, bona fide hedging transactions should not produce any taxable consequences as unrelated business income. We recommend that fiduciaries who manage tax-exempt investments receive an opinion from the appropriate tax authorities before using these instruments.

Tax Treatment of Speculative Transactions

Tax Treatment of Long and Short Futures Transactions

A holder of a long or short futures position is subject to the 60/40 ruling with regard to short- and long-term capital gains regardless of the length of the holding period of the contracts. The 60/40 ruling was a radical departure from traditional taxation policies. In addition, all open long and short futures positions are marked-to-market at the end of the tax year. For example, if a trader is short a S&P futures contract on December 31 with a profit of $1,000, he must report a $1,000 profit as a capital gain even though the contract has not been closed out. Similarly, if the position has incurred a ($1,000) loss, he must report it as a capital loss for that year.

The 60/40 ruling allows the trader to do the following:

1. Forty percent of the net profits (or losses) are taxed as short-term capital assets regardless of the length of the holding period.
2. Sixty percent of the net profits (or losses) are taxed as long-term capital assets regardless of the length of the holding period.
3. The maximum tax rate under the 60/40 rule is 32 percent.

Tax Treatment of Futures-Options Purchases

A futures-option is a capital asset to its holder. A trader must distinguish between long and written (short) options with respect to the IRS tax rulings. A long option is a purchased put or call in which the holder pays the premium in full. An option holder can let his option expire, exercise it into a futures contract, or offset it by selling it. An option holder incurs no tax consequences until an option (1) expires, (2) is exercised, or (3) is sold to offset position. The IRC rulings make no distinction between puts or calls with regard to taxation. Long and short futures-options will probably receive the same tax treatment under proposed legislation.

Tax Treatment of Written Put and Call Futures-Options

A written (short) call option is a potential obligation by the writer to receive a short index futures contract from the call holder. A written put option is a potential obligation by the writer to receive a long index futures contract from the put holder. Premiums paid by the put and call holders are deferred until termination of the transaction (obligation). If a put or call expires unexercised, the capital gain will be equal to the net premium received in the opening writing transaction. For a closing purchase transaction (option writer buys back option prior to expiration), the capital gain (or loss) will be the difference between the premium originally received and the price paid in the closing purchase transaction.

If an option is exercised, then the entire transaction is treated as a purchase or sale of an underlying futures contract. The premium is considered to be a part of the purchase or sale price of the futures contract. Call option premiums received by the writer increase the sale price of the futures contract to the buyer. Put option premiums received by the writer reduce the purchase price of the futures contract.

Written options are subject to the mark-to-market rules (the same as RFCs) at the end of the tax year. Net profits (and losses) are then subject to the 60/40 rules (same as RFCs). In summary, written futures-options are taxed the same as futures contracts with respect to the length of the holding period and the 60/40 rules.

Spreads and Straddles

Spreads

Spreading is the simultaneous purchase and sale of futures-options of the same class (puts or calls) on the same underlying index futures, differing only in maturity date, strike price, or both. Spreading futures contracts or futures-options are not subject to any special tax rules. Each component of the spread is treated as an individual transaction and generally taxed according to the rules discussed previously.

Straddles

Straddles pertain only to option contracts. A straddle is the simultaneous purchase or sale of an equal number of puts or calls on the same underlying index futures with identical maturity dates and striking prices. Each component of a straddle is treated as an individual transaction and generally taxed according to the rules previously discussed. All premium income (or loss) to straddle writers from a closing transaction or lapse of an option is taxed the same as futures contracts. There is no special significance to the straddle itself. It is taxed according to its separate components.

Long-Term versus Short-Term Capital Gains Treatment

As most investors are aware, long-term capital gains receive favored tax treatment under the Internal Revenue Code. Under the current law, long term applies to capital assets held over 12 months, and short term pertains to capital assets sold within one year of purchase. The main exception to these rules involves regulated futures contracts (RFCs) that are marked-to-market at year-end and taxed on a 60/40 split basis as explained earlier.

1. Short-term gains are subject to the full income tax rate.
2. Short-term losses can only offset $3,000 of ordinary income, includes short-term capital gains.
3. With long-term capital gains, only 60 percent of the profits are taxed. Thus, the maximum tax rate for those in the highest tax bracket (50 percent) is 20 percent, 40 percent or 50 percent.
4. Long-term losses are always deductible against ordinary income on a two-for-one basis (i.e., every $2 loss offsets $1 of income to an annual limit of $3,000, and excess losses can be carried forward). In addition, long-term losses are deductible against long-term gains on a dollar-for-dollar basis.

A taxpayer should always separate the results into short-term and long-term categories and then offset them for the best tax benefits.

Deductions Relating to Trading Activities

Certain expenses incurred in trading activities may be deducted in computing taxable income. Other expenses may be used to adjust the gain or loss on a transaction. This distinction depends upon the appropriate tax law. Securities broker/dealers take their deductions as business expenses. Investors take their expenses as itemized deductions. For nonprofessional traders or investors, commissions must be used to adjust the gain or loss; they may not be taken as a deduction. For broker/dealers, commissions may be deducted as a business expense. Market-makers and specialists can deduct expenses as business deductions.

Conclusions

This concludes the chapter on the tax treatment of stock index futures and options transactions. Investors are strongly urged to obtain the assistance of a qualified tax consultant if in doubt about the tax status of any index futures or securities transactions. Tax rulings in this area are often complex and subject to periodic revision. Tax considerations should be integrated into an overall speculative or investment program in order to derive maximum benefits available under current tax laws. Ignorance of the tax consequences of these transactions can lessen the profitability of an otherwise viable trading program.

References

Chicago Commodites and Securities Tax Update, Vol. 1, nos. 2 and 9, ed. Dennis J. Santoni. Chicago: Coopers & Lybrand, 1983.

Faircloth, T. A., and R. F. Sennholz. *Tax Treatment of Commodity Futures.* Cedar Falls, Iowa: Center for Futures Education, 1983.

Tax Consequences of Futures Option Trading. Publication by the Chicago Board of Trade, Coffee, Sugar & Cocoa Exchange, and the Commodity Exchange. New York, 1983.

Tax Considerations in Using CBOE Options. Chicago: The Chicago Board Options Exchange, 1976.

16

Sources of Information and Computer Data Bases

There are numerous sources of written information, charting services, stock market advisory services, and computer data bases available at reasonable prices for individual and institutional investors. We have selected some of these sources as representative of the industry in order to highlight the specialty services they provide.

The Wall Street Journal, 200 Burnett Rd., Chicopee, MA 01021—A daily publication that covers current news, feature articles, and price data on credit, stock, options, and commodity markets. Important columns are: Abreast of the Market, Heard on the Street, Credit Markets, and Commodities.

The Journal of Commerce, 110 Wall St., New York, NY 10005—A daily publication with current business and economic data and commentary regarding major industries, such as oil and gas, computer technology, banking, and finance.

USA Today Money Section—A daily publication that cover news and price data on securities and options markets. Updates stock indexes graphically. Important columns are Moneyline and Daily Analyst.

The New York Times, 229 West 43d St., New York, NY 10036—A daily publication that covers news and price data on commodities, options, and securities markets. The business section has excellent articles on current events and their effects on the financial markets.

Barron's, 200 Burnett Rd., Chicopee, MA 01021—A weekly publication that covers current news, feature articles, and price data on credit, securities, options, and commodities markets. Serves as a weekly review of market activity with in-depth interpretation of major events that affect the financial markets. Important columns

203

are Up and Down Wall Street, The Striking Price, Current Yield, The Trader, and the Statistical Section.

Financial Times, 75 Rockefeller Plaza, New York, NY 10019— A publication commenting on the European perspective of American and foreign business and economic activities. The publication analyzes and interprets the effects of American political and economic events on European financial markets.

Consensus, 30 West Pershing Rd., Kansas City, MO 64108—A weekly publication containing excerpts of commentaries and research reports disseminated by major brokerage firms to their customers.

Futures Magazine, 219 Parkade, Cedar Falls, IA 50613—A monthly magazine devoted to in-depth articles on commodity markets. Periodic coverage is given to the stock index futures and options markets. The articles are nontechnical and highly educational to a new trader.

Dow Theory Forecasts, 7412 Calumet Ave., Hammond, IN 46324-2692—A weekly newsletter with stock market commentary and reports, articles, and specific recommendations regarding securities. The service focuses on the tenets of the Dow Theory for making its recommendations.

The Elliott Wave Theorist, P.O. Box 1618, Gainesville, GA 30503—An advisory letter written by Robert Prechter that covers securities and commodities markets. The letter emphasizes the application of Elliott Wave Theory to forecast major peaks and troughs in stock market and commodity prices.

The Professional Tape Reader, P.O. Box 2407, Hollywood, FL 33022—An advisory letter published by Stan Weinstein that offers investors information and recommendations on selections of securities. The service focuses primarily upon charting, cyclical analysis, and other technical methods for its recommendations.

The Zweig Forecast, 747 Third Avenue, New York, NY 10017— An advisory letter written by Dr. Martin Zweig, a highly regarded authority on securities markets. His service provides a combination of technical and fundamental approaches to stock selection and risk management.

Money Market Services, Inc., 490 El Camino Real, Belmont, CA 94002—A multinational corporation that advises institutional investors on Federal Reserve policies, credit, and foreign currencies markets. *MMS* has a staff of economists and credit market analysts who provide detailed technical and fundamental analysis to their clients. *MMS* does not provide specific reports on the stock market or recommendations regarding securities. *MMS* provides weekly and monthly reports of U.S. and international credit markets. Important information services are FEDWATCH, FEDWIR, and Weekly Economic Survey. Services are available via several videotex computer data bases, such as *Dow Jones News/Retrieval Services,* Compuserve, and Telerate.

Value Line Investment Survey, 711 Third Avenue, New York, NY 10017—A weekly publication that provides comprehensive analysis of securities that comprise the Value Line 1700 Index. Value Line lists and ranks securities with respect to industry group, timeliness of purchase, safety, dividend yields, and betas. Each stock in the index is given a detailed write-up with regard to its prospects for growth and income potential. Value Line is written for both both individual and institutional investors. Value Line has a computer data base available to subscribers via several videotex services.

Standard & Poor's Corporation, 25 Broadway, New York, NY 10004—Standard & Poor's provides a large variety of services for private and institutional investors. It provides detailed information on listed, over-the-counter stocks as well as bonds and commercial paper markets. Detailed information on stocks in the S&P index can be found in the *Stock Market Encyclopedia of the S&P 500.* The company has available two computerized data bases: COMPMARK and COMPUSTAT. The 500 Index is one of the leading economic indicators used by the Department of Commerce to measure the level of business activity.

Business Conditions Digest, Superintendent of Documents, U.S. Government Printing Office, Washington, DC 20402—The BCD provides monthly statistics on the leading, lagging, and coincident indicators of the economy. The publication uses comprehensive graphs, indexes, and historical charts to show the interrelations among these indicators.

Survey of Current Business, Department of Commerce, Superintendent of Documents, U.S. Government Printing Office, Washington, DC 20402—A monthly publication that is a primary source for economic statistics. Includes some articles.

Federal Reserve Publications, Board of Governors of the Federal Reserve System, Washington, DC 20551—The following is a brief selection of publications offered by the FRS. Some are free, while others have a subscription charge. *Federal Reserve Bulletin, Federal Reserve Chart Book, U.S. Financial Data Research Department, Statistical Releases G.7 and H.6.*

Commitments of Traders in Commodity Futures with Market Concentration Ratios, Commodity Futures Trading Commission, 2033 K Street, N.W., Washington, DC 20581—A monthly government report on the market positions of large and small speculative and commercial traders. Not a useful report for trading, but recommended reading for educational purposes only.

Computer Data Bases

Dow Jones News/Retrieval Services, P.O. Box 300, Princeton, NJ 08540—The *Dow Jones News/Retrieval Service* provides a computer data base of reports and prices available for a large number of stocks. The service can be accessed by a personal computer for a low monthly cost depending upon the time used. The service provides current and historical price quotes, corporate earnings estimator, Disclosure, Media General Financial services, Weekly Economic Survey and Updates, Wall Street Journal Highlights, Wall Street Week Online, and a directory of symbols for stocks, bonds, mutual funds, and options. A Free Text Search is available that saves costs in locating information in the data base. This is an excellent and affordable service for investors who own a personal computer. *Dowline* Magazine keeps subscribers informed as to changes in the data base.

CompuServe Information Service, 5000 Arlington Centre Blvd., Columbus, OH 43220—CompuServe is a computer data base, which has a wide variety of information providers who contribute information and statistical data for stocks and commodities. The MicroQuote and QuickQuote programs allow a subscriber access to information on approximately 40,000 stocks, bonds, and mutual funds. A subscriber can obtain detailed information on a company with respect to its balance sheet, projected earnings, and other relevant financial information. CompuServe is not an advisory service. It makes available information and data, which the subscriber can then use. *Today* Magazine keeps subscribers updated with respect to changes in the data base. CompuServe is a low-cost service available to personal computer owners in the United States and Canada.

The Source, P.O. Box 1305, McLean, VA 22101—A popular data base for personal computer owners that contains regularly updated business news, stock and bond prices, commodity news and prices, investment advice and analytical tools, and financial modeling and accounting programs.

The Value Line Data Base—II, Value Line, Inc., 711 Third Avenue, New York, NY 10017—The data base contains historic annual and quarterly financial records for over 1,600 industrial, transportation, utility, retail, bank, insurance, and finance companies; savings and loan associations; and securities brokers. The annual data begin in 1955, quarterly figures in 1963.

Commodity Information Service Company, 327 South LaSalle St., Chicago, IL 60604—CISCO provides a computer data base of prices and programs for technical analysis for the commodities markets. CISCO does not contain a data base of securities or bond prices. It does maintain a data base of stock index futures and options prices. It does not provide any fundamental information or news reports on either commodities or securities. CISCO has numerous computerized trading systems that can be accessed via personal computer. This service might be useful for experienced computer users who trade commodity contracts using a technical systems approach.

National Computer Network of Chicago, 1929 N. Harlem Avenue, Chicago, IL 60635—An extensive data base of bond, securities, options, and index futures prices. NCN has a library of programs for investment and financial analysis. Data can be downloaded into microcomputers in the evening.

Chronometrics, 327 S. LaSalle St., Chicago, IL 60604—The company provides a real-time computer service called COMPACT, which can be used for evaluating put and call options on stock indexes, gold, and Treasury bonds. The COMPACT menu offers traders extensive routines accessed via a remote database for pricing options evaluating portfolio positions and trading strategies. COMPACT offers 28 opportunity scans of different spread types and simple positions.

Monchik-Weber, 11 Broadway, New York, NY 10004—On-line, real-time options and futures quotes, analysis capabilities, theoretical values, strategy evaluation, and simulation features. All futures, indexes, equities, and their options.

On-Line Response Inc., 327 S. LaSalle St., Chicago, IL 60604—Developed the PC QUOTE System, which is an on-line, real-time information service for securities, options, index futures, and index options markets. Information on 60 stocks can be formatted by the user. The system allows users to monitor quotes and evaluate real-time values and profit and loss for stock portfolios. This system allows investors to keep accurate records of buys, sells, dividends, interest income, and expense and cash entries.

Software Options Inc., 19 Rector St., New York, NY 10006—Option support services, including quotations, strategies, training programs, trading and back office systems. Developers of software packages for micros, including the COTS/Fair Value system.

The Options Group, 50 Broadway, New York, NY 10004—A consulting group that specializes in stock, debt, and foreign currency options. Offers TOG, an on-line, interactive system for evaluating futures and options on stock indexes. The service provides pricing and strategy analysis to meet needs of brokers, traders, arbitrageurs, and investment managers.

Charting Services

The following is a list of charting services that track stock index and stock market prices. Before subscribing to a charting service, we recommend that you receive a sample copy for review to determine that it fulfills your requirements.

Commodity Perspective, 327 S. LaSalle St., Chicago, IL 60604— A weekly service that provides large-scale, daily charts for stock index futures contracts with volume, open interest, 4-, 9-, and 18-day moving averages, and a TREND-A-LIZER for each commodity.

Commodity Chart Service, 75 Montgomery St., Jersey City, NJ 07302—A weekly service that provides daily, weekly, and monthly bar charts and technical comments for stock index futures contracts. A Computer Trend Analyzer section and spread charts are provided.

Financial Futures Charting Service, Data Lab Corporation, 200 W. Monroe St., Chicago, IL 60606—A weekly service that provides bar charts for cash and futures markets for financial instruments.

Commodity Price Charts, 219 Parkade, Cedar Falls, IA 50613— A weekly charting service developed by the publishers of *Futures Magazine.* The service provides 4-, 9-, and 18-day moving averages, Relative Strength Indexes, basis graphs, trend line analysis, chart formations, and point and figure charts.

List of Commodity and Securities Exchanges

The following is a list of exchanges that provide information and data on the stock index and options markets. They will mail information upon request to the Public Relations Departments.

American Stock Exchange, 86 Trinity Place, New York, NY 10006.
Chicago Board Options Exchange, 141 W. Jackson Blvd., Chicago, IL 60604.
Chicago Board of Trade, 141 W. Jackson Blvd., Chicago, IL 60604.
Chicago Mercantile Exchange, 444 W. Jackson, Chicago, IL 60606.

Kansas City Board of Trade, 4800 Main, Kansas City, MO 64112.

New York Futures Exchange, 20 Broad St., New York, NY 10005.

New York Stock Exchange, 11 Wall St, New York, NY 10005.

Philadelphia Stock Exchange, 1900 Market St., Philadelphia, PA 19103.

17

Proposed New Listings of Index Futures and Options Markets

The following contract markets have been approved but were not trading prior to the completion of this book. They could begin trading in January, 1984.

Pacific Stock Exchange Technology Index

The Pacific Stock Exchange's (PSE) Technology Index is an index option on 100 stocks that are listed on the New York Stock Exchange, (NYSE) American Stock Exchange, (AMEX) and NASDAQ (over-the-counter). About 22 issues are dually traded on the Pacific Stock Exchange (PSE) and other exchanges. The index option will trade on the January cycle with the expiration dates corresponding to regular equity options. The option contract specifies cash settlement. The value of the index will be 100 times the spot index, e.g., 125.00 × $100 = $12,500.

The PSE Technology Index is composed of 100 underlying securities representing a broad spectrum of companies principally engaged in manufacturing or service-related products within the advanced technology field. The advanced technology field includes bio-genetic engineering, computer, medical technology, microprocessor devices, satellite and telecommunication stocks. The index contains the following breakdown of companies with respect to the exchange listing:

	Companies
New York Stock Exchange	49
American Stock Exchange	6
Nasdaq (OTC)	45
Total	100

The PSE Index has a beta of 1.60 compared to the S&P 500 Index over a five-year period, which indicates that it has a higher volatility than most market indexes. The PSE Index is price weighted with the following securities having the highest relative weighting as of August 26, 1983:

	Symbol	Price
Motorola, Inc.	(MOT)	133¼
International Business Machines	(IBM)	121⅝
NCR Corporation	(NCR)	115⅛

Approval for trading this index was delayed because of a definitional problem it raised with the Securities and Exchange Commission (SEC). The SEC has tried to distinguish between *narrow-based* and *broad-based* indexes. A broad-based index is an index on the market, such as the S&P 500, whereas a narrow-based index is one on a specific industry group, such as the S&P International Oil Index. The PSE Index falls somewhere between these two categories. The differences between a narrow-based and broad-based index are important for an exchange. In the opinion of the SEC, a broad-based index should qualify for higher position and exercise limits and lower margin requirements than a narrow-based index. A narrow-based index would be margined similar to equity options (30 percent of index value plus in-the-money or minus out-of-the money). Broad-based indexes are margined at 10 percent of index value plus in-the-money or minus out-of-the money. A broad-based index is considered to entail less risk due its diversified composition of securities. In addition, only broad-based indexes could qualify to have a corresponding index futures contract available. Therefore, if the PSE Index is considered to be a narrow-based index, it would not qualify for the lower margining requirements or the availability of a futures contract. As of this writing, the SEC has not provided an operational definition to distinguish between narrow-based or broad-based indexes. See Figure 17–1 for a five-year price chart of the PSE Technology Index.

New Industry Index Listings of the Philadelphia Stock Exchange

The Philadelphia Stock Exchange (PHLX) applied for approval for trading options on two industry indexes to begin December 1983. These indexes are called (1) Gold/Silver Index and the (2)

Figure 17-1

Comparison of Indexes (indexes adjusted 12/31/82 = 100)

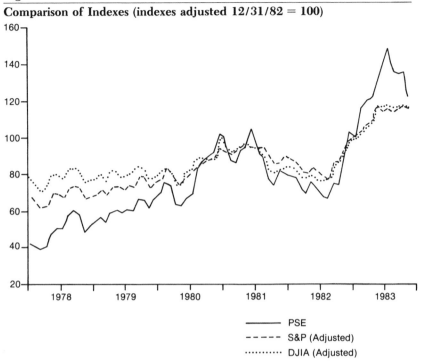

- ——— PSE
- – – – – S&P (Adjusted)
- ·········· DJIA (Adjusted)

Gaming/Hotel Index. They are classified as a narrow-based and thus subject to higher margin requirements and lower position and exercise limits. Both indexes are capitalization-weighted and require cash settlement. The expiration cycles of the options are monthly and/or quarterly. The market value of each index is 100 times the spot index price, e.g., $100 × 110.00 = $11,000.

Several years ago, the Philadelphia Stock Exchange pioneered trading in listed options on foreign currencies, such as the British pound, Canadian dollar, German mark, Swiss franc, and Japanese yen. In addition, the exchange has numerous equity-based options listed for trading.

Specifications for the Gold/Silver Index

The Gold/Silver Index is composed of the following underlying issues as of December 2, 1983:

	Symbol	*Percent of Market Value*
ASA Ltd.	(ASA)	11.42%
Callahan Mining Corp	(CMN)	2.95
Campbell Red Lake	(CRK)	26.08
Dome Mines Ltd.	(DM)	21.79
Hecla Mining Co.	(HL)	7.82
Homestake Mining Co.	(HM)	23.31
Sunshine Mining Co.	(SSC)	6.63

Figure 17–2

Gold/Silver Index

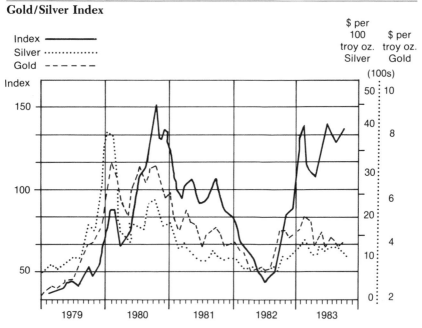

The symbol for the Gold/Silver Index is XAU. Note that Campbell Red Lake, Dome Mines, and Homestake Mining comprise over 70 percent of the market value of the index. Initially, position limits are 6,000 contracts on the same side of the market. See Figure 17–2 for a four-year price chart of the Gold/Silver Index.

Specifications on the Gaming/Hotel Index

The gaming/Hotel Index is composed of the following underlying issues as of December 2, 1983:

	Symbol	Percent of Market Value
Bally Mfg. Co.	(BLY)	9.55%
Caesars World, Inc.	(CAW)	5.54
Golden Nugget, Inc.	(GNG)	8.75
Holiday Inns, Inc.	(HIA)	31.52
Hilton Hotel Corp.	(HLT)	25.53
MGM Grand Hotels	(GRH)	4.80
Ramada Inns, Inc.	(RAM)	6.62
Resorts International	(RTA)	6.50
Showboat, Inc.	(SBO)	1.19

The symbol for the Gaming/Hotel Index is XGH. Note that Holiday Inns and Hilton Hotel Corporation account for over 56 percent of the market value of the index. Initially, position limits are 4,000 contracts on the same side of the market.

The Toronto Futures and Stock Exchange Indexes

The Toronto Futures and Stock Exchanges, Toronto, Canada, will be the first non-U.S. exchanges to trade index futures and index option contracts. The index will be known as the "TSE 300 Composite Index." The TSE 300 is a market-weighted index composed of 300 securities of representative Canadian companies. All issues are listed on the Toronto Stock Exchange (TSE). The index will allow investors to hedge price risks associated with the ownership of Canadian securities. The TSE 300 contains both common and preferred issues of Canadian companies. Both the futures and option contracts require cash settlement.

The Ontario Securities Commission is the Canadian Regulatory authority that monitors trading activities for the Toronto futures and securities markets. Unlike U.S. federal regulatory authorities, Canadian investment contracts must be submitted to and approved for trading by each of the 10 provincial authorities. U.S. citizens can only trade these contracts after they have been approved by the Commodity Futures Trading Commission (CFTC) and the Securities and Exchange Commission.

The TSE 300 Composite Index is composed of 14 group indexes and 43 subgroup indexes. Table 17–1 outlines the categories of group indexes with the number of companies of each in parentheses and the relative weight on the composite.

Table 17–1

As of August 31, 1983

		Number of Companies	Relative Weight
1	Metals and minerals	(32)	14.20%
2	Golds	(18)	4.20
3	Oil and gas	(63)	14.96
4	Paper and forest products	(10)	1.63
5	Consumer products	(23)	8.77
6	Industrial products	(35)	11.35
7	Real estate and construction	(8)	1.27
8	Transportation	(7)	4.49
9	Pipelines	(7)	3.07
10	Utilities	(11)	9.52
11	Communications and media	(16)	2.91
12	Merchandising	(30)	3.66
13	Financial services	(27)	14.71
14	Management companies	(13)	5.24
	Totals	300	100.00%

See Figure 17–3 for a 10-year price chart of the TSE 300 Index. The companies with the highest relative weight on the TSE 300 Composite Index are:

Bell Canada	(BCA)	6.68%
Alcan	(AL)	5.06
Canadian Pacific, Ltd.	(CP)	3.93
Royal Bank	(RY)	3.12
Northern Telecom	(NT)	2.96

Computation of Index Values

The prices of the index are quoted in Canadian dollars, not U.S. dollars. To determine the strike prices of the TSE 300 Index option, the present value of the index is divided by 10 and rounded to the highest number. The value of the TSE 300 Index futures is calculated by multiplying the index by 10. The following examples illustrate these points. Assume the TSE 300 closed at 2,370.50.

Strike prices × $100 =	Value
26.00	$26,000 Canadian
25.00	25,000
24.00	24,000
23.00	23,000
22.00	22,000

Index futures × $10 =	Value
2,450.50	$24,505 Canadian
2,369.30	23,693
2,250.80	22,508

To obtain the U.S. dollar equivalent of the TSE 300 Index, one must take the foreign exchange rate times the value of the index in Canadian dollars. For example, if the current exchange rate is

Figure 17–3

TSE 300 Composite

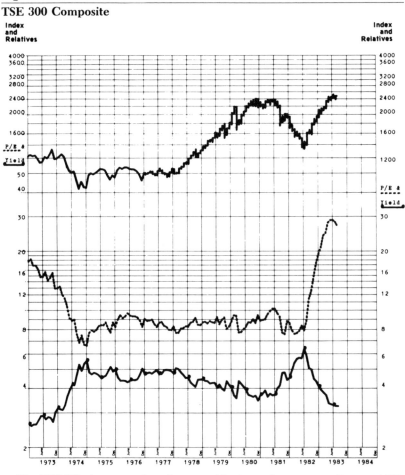

The TSE 300 charts are plotted on monthly closing basis prior to January 1977 and on monthly range basis thereafter. All other values are plotted on monthly closing basis. Relative strength values are plotted on basis of 1,000.

1.25 Canadian dollars to 1.0 U.S. dollar, the TSE 300 Index value in U.S. Dollars can be computed as follows:

2,450.50 × $10 = $24,505 Canadian ÷ 1.25 = $19,604 U.S.

In conclusion, the authors believe that other foreign exchanges will establish stock index futures and index option markets representative of their securities markets. The next five wears promise to be an exciting era in development of new financial markets.

A

List of Addresses for Commodities and Securities Exchanges

The following commodity futures and securities exchanges will provide information upon request to their marketing departments on their stock index products and services. Information ranging from promotional literature to detailed statistical data are available. This list only includes those exchanges that currently have or will have stock index products available. It is expected that both U.S. and foreign exchanges will add index products in the future.

Commodity Futures Exchanges

Chicago Board of Trade
LaSalle at Jackson
Chicago, IL 60604

Index and Option Market
Division of Chicago Mercantile Exchange
444 West Jackson Blvd.
Chicago, IL 60606

Kansas City Board of Trade
4800 Main, Suite 274
Kansas City, MO 64112

New York Futures Exchange
20 Broad Street
New York, NY 10005

Securities Exchanges

American Stock Exchange
86 Trinity Place
New York, NY 10006

Chicago Board Options Exchange
141 West Jackson Blvd.
Chicago, IL 60604

New York Stock Exchange
11 Wall Street
New York, NY 10005

Pacific Stock Exchange
301 Pine St.
San Francisco, CA 94104

Philadelphia Stock Exchange
1900 Market St.
Philadelphia, PA 19103

Toronto Stock Exchange
The Exchange Tower
2 First Canadia Place
Toronto, Canada

B

Contract Specifications

Value Line Composite Index Futures

EXCHANGE:	Kansas City Board of Trade
TRADING HOURS:	10:00 A.M. to 4:15 P.M. (New York)
TICKER SYMBOL:	KV
PRICE QUOTATIONS:	Futures price is based on the Value Line Composite Index. Value is 500 times the futures price. Example: Futures price is 200.00. Contract value is 500 × 200.00 = $100,000.
MINIMUM FLUCTUATION:	.05 (5 points), $25.00/tick
DAILY LIMITS:	None
DELIVERY MONTHS:	March, June, September, and December cycle for six forward months. Other months may be added.
EXPIRATION:	Last business day of contract month.
SETTLEMENT:	*Cash settlement.* On the last trading day of the expiration month, all contracts are marked to the market, and open contracts will be settled with the Clearing Company in U.S. funds based on the Value Line Index as of the close on the last trading day.

Mini-Value Line Composite Index Futures

EXCHANGE:	Kansas City Board of Trade
TRADING HOURS:	10:00 A.M. to 4:15 P.M. (New York)
TICKER SYMBOL:	MV
PRICE QUOTATIONS:	Futures price is based on the Value Composite Index. Value is 100 times the futures price. Example: Futures price is 200.00. Contract value is 100 × 200.00 = $20,000.
MINIMUM FLUCTUATION:	.05 (5 points), $5.00/tick
DAILY LIMITS:	None
DELIVERY MONTHS:	March, June, September, and December cycle for six forward months. Other months may be added.
EXPIRATION:	Last business day of contract month.
SETTLEMENT:	*Cash settlement.* On the last trading day of the expiration month, all contracts are marked to the market, and open contracts will be settled with the Clearing Company in U.S. funds based on the Value Line Index as of the close on the last trading day.

Standard & Poor's 500 Index Futures

EXCHANGE:
Index and Option Market, a division of the Chicago Mercantile Exchange

TRADING HOURS:
10:00 A.M. to 4:15 P.M. (New York)

TICKER SYMBOL:
SP

PRICE QUOTATIONS:
Futures price is based on the S&P 500 Composite Index. Value is 500 times the futures price. Example: Futures price is 150.00. Contract value is 500 × 150.00 = $75,000.

MINIMUM FLUCTUATION:
.05 (5 points), $25,00/tick

DAILY LIMITS:
None

DELIVERY MONTHS:
March, June, September, and December cycle.

EXPIRATION:
Third Thursday of contract month.

SETTLEMENT:
Cash settlement. On the last trading day of the expiration month, all contracts are marked to the market, and open contracts will be settled with the Clearing Company in U.S. funds based on the S&P 500 Index as of 4 P.M. on the last trading day.

Standard & Poor's 100 Index Futures

EXCHANGE: Index and Option Market, a division of
                                   the Chicago Mercantile Exchange

TRADING HOURS: 10:00 A.M. to 4:15 P.M. (New York)

TICKER SYMBOL: SX

PRICE QUOTATIONS: Futures price is based on the S&P 100
                                   Composite Index. Value is 200 times
                                   the futures price. Example: Futures
                                   price is 150.00. Contract value is 200 ×
                                   150.00 = $30,000.

MINIMUM FLUCTUATION: .05 (5 points), $10.00/tick

DAILY LIMITS: None

DELIVERY MONTHS: March, June, September, and December
                                   cycle.

EXPIRATION: Third Friday of contract month.

SETTLEMENT: *Cash settlement.*   On the last trading
                                   day of the expiration month, all contracts
                                   are marked to the market, and open
                                   contracts will be settled with the
                                   Clearing Company in U.S. funds based
                                   on the S&P 100 Index as of 4 P.M. on
                                   the last trading day.

New York Stock Exchange Composite Index Futures

EXCHANGE:	New York Futures Exchange
TRADING HOURS:	10:00 A.M. to 4:15 P.M. (New York)
TICKER SYMBOL:	YX
PRICE QUOTATIONS:	Futures price is based on the NYSE Composite Index. Value is 500 times the futures price. Example: Futures price is 100.00. Contract value is 500 × 100.00 = $50,000.
MINIMUM FLUCTUATION:	.05 (5 points), $25.00/tick
DAILY LIMITS:	None
DELIVERY MONTHS:	March, June, September, and December cycle.
EXPIRATION:	Business day prior to last business day in the contract month.
SETTLEMENT:	*Cash settlement.* On the last trading day of the expiration month, all contracts are marked to the market, and open contracts will be settled with the Clearing Company in U.S. funds based on the NYSE Index as of the close on the last trading day.

New York Stock Exchange Composite Futures-Options

EXCHANGE:	New York Futures Exchange
TRADING HOURS:	10:00 A.M. to 4:15 P.M. (New York)
TICKER SYMBOL:	YX
PRICE QUOTATIONS:	Options price is based on the NYSE Composite futures. Value is 500 times the futures price. Example: Futures price is 100.00. Contract value is 500 × 100.00 = $50,000.
MINIMUM FLUCTUATION:	.05 (5 points), $25.00/tick
DAILY LIMITS:	None
DELIVERY MONTHS:	March, June, September, and December cycle.
STRIKE PRICE INTERVALS:	2.00 point intervals, e.g., 96, 98, 100.
EXPIRATION:	Business day prior to last business day in the contract month.
SETTLEMENT:	*Cash settlement.* On the last trading day of the expiration month, all contracts are marked to the market, and open contracts will be settled with the Clearing Company in U.S. funds based on the NYSE Index as of the close on the last trading day.

Standard & Poor's 500 Futures-Options

EXCHANGE:	Index and Option Market, a division of the Chicago Mercantile Exchange
TRADING HOURS:	10:00 A.M. to 4:15 P.M. (New York)
TICKER SYMBOL:	CS—calls; PS—puts
PRICE QUOTATIONS:	Futures price is based on the S&P 500 Composite Index. Value is 500 times the futures price. Example: Futures price is 150.00. Contract value is 500 × 150.00 = $75,000.
MINIMUM FLUCTUATION:	.05 (5 points), $25.00/tick
DAILY LIMITS:	None
DELIVERY MONTHS:	March, June, September, and December cycle.
STRIKE PRICE INTERVALS:	5.00 point intervals, e.g., 160, 165, 170.
EXPIRATION:	Third thursday of expiration month.
SETTLEMENT:	*Cash settlement.* Settlement is based on the cash value of the difference between the strike price and the closing value of the index on the day the exercise notice is submitted to the Options Clearing Corporation.

Standard & Poor's 500 Index Options

EXCHANGE: Chicago Board Options Exchange

TRADING HOURS: 10:00 A.M. to 4:10 P.M. (New York)

TICKER SYMBOL: SPX

PRICE QUOTATIONS: Option price is based on the S&P 500
                                 Composite Index. Value is 100 times
                                 the index price. Example: Index price
                                 is 150.00. Contract value is 100 ×
                                 150.00 = $15,000.

MINIMUM FLUCTUATION: $\frac{1}{16}$ for option series trading below 3; $\frac{1}{8}$
                                 for all other series

DAILY LIMITS: None

DELIVERY MONTHS: March, June, September, and December
                                 cycle.

EXERCISE PRICES: 5.00 point intervals, e.g., 160, 165, 170.

EXPIRATION: Saturday following the 3d Friday of the
                                 contract month—same as for stock
                                 options.

SETTLEMENT: *Cash settlement.* Settlement is based on
                                 the cash value of the difference between
                                 the strike price and the closing value of
                                 the index on the day the exercise notice
                                 is submitted to the Options Clearing
                                 Corporation.

Note: Beginning in December 1983, this contract may begin trading in consecutive three-month cycles. For example, the first cycle would be January, February, and March. April would replace January after it expires. The farthest expiration date would be three months or 90 days.

Standard & Poor's 100 Index Options

EXCHANGE:	Chicago Board Options Exchange
TRADING HOURS:	10:00 A.M. to 4:10 P.M. (New York)
TICKER SYMBOL:	OEX
PRICE QUOTATIONS:	Option price is based on the S&P 100 Composite Index. Value is 100 times the index price. Example: Index price is 150.00. Contract value is 100 × 150.00 = $15,000.
MINIMUM FLUCTUATION:	$\frac{1}{16}$ for option series trading below 3; $\frac{1}{8}$ for all other series
DAILY LIMITS:	None
DELIVERY MONTHS:	March, June, September, and December cycle.
EXPIRATION:	Saturday following 3d Friday of contract month—same as for stock options.
SETTLEMENT:	*Cash settlement.* Settlement is based on the cash value of the difference between the strike price and the closing value of the index on the day the exercise notice is submitted to the Options Clearing Corporation.

Note: Beginning in December 1983, this contract may begin trading in consecutive three-month cycles. For example, the first cycle would be January, February, and March. April would replace January after it expires. The farthest expiration date would be three months or 90 days.

S&P International Oil Index Option

EXCHANGE:	Chicago Board Options Exchange
TRADING HOURS:	10:00 A.M. to 4:10 P.M. (New York)
TICKER SYMBOL:	OIO
PRICE QUOTATIONS:	Option price is based on the S&P Integrated International Oil Index. Value is 100 times the index price. Example: Index price is 120.00. Contract value is $100 \times 120.00 = \$12,000$.
MINIMUM FLUCTUATION:	$\frac{1}{16}$ for option series trading below 3; $\frac{1}{8}$ for all other series
DAILY LIMITS:	None
DELIVERY MONTHS:	March, June, September, and December cycle.
EXPIRATION:	Saturday following 3d Friday of contract month—same as for stock options.
SETTLEMENT:	*Cash settlement.* Settlement is based on the cash value of the difference between the strike price and the closing value of the index on the day the exercise notice is submitted to the Options Clearing Corporation.

S&P Computer and Business Equipment Index Option

EXCHANGE:	Chicago Board Options Exchange
TRADING HOURS:	10:00 A.M. to 4:10 P.M. (New York)
TICKER SYMBOL:	OBE
PRICE QUOTATIONS:	Option price is based on the S&P Computer and Business Equipment Index. Value is 100 times the index price. Example: Index price is 195.00. Contract value is $100 \times 195.00 = \$19,500$.
MINIMUM FLUCTUATION:	$\frac{1}{16}$ for option series trading below 3; $\frac{1}{8}$ for all other series
DAILY LIMITS:	None
DELIVERY MONTHS:	March, June, September, and December cycle.
EXPIRATION:	Saturday following 3d Friday of contract month—same as for stock options.
SETTLEMENT:	*Cash settlement.* Settlement is based on the cash value of the difference between the strike price and the closing value of the index on the day the exercise notice is submitted to the Options Clearing Corporation.

AMEX Major Market Index Option

EXCHANGE:	American Stock Exchange
TRADING HOURS:	10:00 A.M. to 4:10 P.M. (New York)
TICKER SYMBOL:	XMI
PRICE QUOTATIONS:	Option price is based on the AMEX Major Market Index. Value is 100 times the index price. Example: Index price is 2½. Contract value is 100 × 2½ = $250.00.
MINIMUM FLUCTUATION:	$\frac{1}{16}$ for option series trading below 3; ⅛ for all other series
DAILY LIMITS:	None
DELIVERY MONTHS:	January, April, July, and October cycle with three months traded at any one time.
EXPIRATION:	Saturday following 3d Friday of contract month—same as for stock options.
SETTLEMENT:	*Cash settlement.* Settlement is based on the cash value of the difference between the strike price and the closing value of the index on the day the exercise notice is submitted to the Options Clearing Corporation.

Note: Beginning in December 1983, this contract may begin trading in consecutive three-month cycles. For example, the first cycle would be January, February, and March. April would replace January after it expires. The farthest expiration date would be three months or 90 days.

AMEX Market Value Index Option

EXCHANGE:	American Stock Exchange
TRADING HOURS:	10:00 A.M. to 4:10 P.M. (New York)
TICKER SYMBOL:	XAM
PRICE QUOTATIONS:	Option price is based on the AMEX Market Value Index. Value is 100 times the index price. Example: Index price is 220.00. Contract value is 100 × 220.00 = $22,000.
MINIMUM FLUCTUATION:	$\frac{1}{16}$ for option series trading below 3; $\frac{1}{8}$ for all other series
DAILY LIMITS:	None
DELIVERY MONTHS:	March, June, September, and December cycle with three months traded at any one time
EXPIRATION:	Saturday following 3d Friday of contract month—same as for stock options.
SETTLEMENT:	*Cash settlement.* Settlement is based on the cash value of the difference between the strike price and the closing value of the index on the day the exercise notice is submitted to the Options Clearing Corporation.

Note: Beginning in December 1983, this contract may begin trading in consecutive three-month cycles. For example, the first cycle would be January, February, and March. April would replace January after it expires. The farthest expiration date would be three months or 90 days.

AMEX Computer Technology Index Option

EXCHANGE:	American Stock Exchange
TRADING HOURS:	10:00 A.M. to 4:10 P.M. (New York)
TICKER SYMBOL:	XCI
PRICE QUOTATIONS:	Option price is based on the AMEX Computer Technology Index. Value is 100 times the index price. Example: Index price is 110.00. Contract value is $100 \times 110.00 = \$11,000$.
MINIMUM FLUCTUATION:	$\frac{1}{16}$ for option series trading below 3; $\frac{1}{8}$ for all other series
DAILY LIMITS:	None
DELIVERY MONTHS:	March, June, September, and December cycle with two months traded at any one time.
EXPIRATION:	Saturday following 3d Friday of contract month—same as for stock options.
SETTLEMENT:	*Cash settlement.* Settlement is based on the cash value of the difference between the strike price and the closing value of the index on the day the exercise notice is submitted to the Options Clearing Corporation.

AMEX Oil and Gas Index Option

EXCHANGE:	American Stock Exchange
TRADING HOURS:	10:00 A.M. to 4:10 P.M. (New York)
TICKER SYMBOL:	XOI
PRICE QUOTATIONS:	Option price is based on the AMEX Oil and Gas Index. Value is 100 times the index price. Example: Index price is 100.00. Contract value is 100 × 100.00 = $10,000.
MINIMUM FLUCTUATION:	$\frac{1}{16}$ for option series trading below 3; $\frac{1}{8}$ for all other series
DAILY LIMITS:	None
DELIVERY MONTHS:	March, June, September, and December cycle with two months traded at any one time.
EXPIRATION:	Saturday following 3d Friday of contract month—same as for stock options.
SETTLEMENT:	*Cash settlement.* Settlement is based on the cash value of the difference between the strike price and the closing value of the index on the day the exercise notice is submitted to the Options Clearing Corporation.

New York Stock Exchange 1500 Composite Index Option

EXCHANGE:	New York Stock Exchange
TRADING HOURS:	10:00 A.M. to 4:10 P.M. (New York)
TICKER SYMBOL:	NYA
PRICE QUOTATIONS:	Option price is based on the NYSE 1500 Composite Index. Value is 100 times the index price. Example: Index price is 100.00. Contract value is 100 × 100.00 = $10,000.
MINIMUM FLUCTUATION:	$\frac{1}{16}$ for option series trading below 3; $\frac{1}{8}$ for all other series
DAILY LIMITS:	None
DELIVERY MONTHS:	February, May, August, and November cycle.
EXPIRATION:	Saturday following 3d Friday of contract month—same as for stock options.
SETTLEMENT:	*Cash settlement.* Settlement is based on the cash value of the difference between the strike price and the closing value of the index on the day the exercise notice is submitted to the Options Clearing Corporation.

Note: Beginning in December 1983, this contract may begin trading in consecutive three-month cycles. For example, the first cycle would be January, February, and March. April would replace January after it expires. The farthest expiration date would be three months or 90 days.

Appendix

C

Correlation Table

	S&P 500	KV	NYSE	DJIA	MMI	MVI
S&P 500	1.000*	—	—	—		
KV	.882*	1.000	—	—		
NYSE	.989*	.928	1.000	—		
DJIA	.729*	.507	.644	1.000		
MMI	.9496†	—	.9467	.9705	1.000	—
MVI	.6286‡	—	.7076	.7435	.6113	1.000

* Covers the period February 1, 1971–March 31, 1982 (p. 6, "Inside S&P 500 Stock Index Futures," Index and Option Market, a division of the Chicago Mercantile Exchange).

† Covers the period March 1982.

‡ Covers the period 1982.

D

Description and Evaluation of Computer Software

The following is a brief description of computer software packages designed to assist private investors, professional money managers, institutional investors, bank trust officers, pension fund managers, and strategic planners in accessing financial information and making investment decisions. These software packages permit user access to a large volume of technical and fundamental information on common stocks, options, bonds, and Treasuries. The cost of accessing computer time-sharing services has declined dramatically as the number of users has increased during the past five years.

Dow Jones & Company has developed software packages for use on several models of personal computers. The Dow Jones Data Base of common stocks includes nearly all of the stocks in the general market and industry indexes. The *Dow Jones Software* packages described as follows require the user to have the following hardware components: an Apple II, Apple II Plus, Apple III or IBM PC computer with two disk drives, monitor, printer, RS-232 communications board, and modem. *Prospective customers should check their hardware compatibility before purchasing software packages to ensure that all programs run properly.* Each of the packages comes with an instruction manual and a registration card with a full-year warranty. A customer-service hotline is available if a user is experiencing problems or needs to ask questions. A *Dow Jones News/Retrieval* membership is required to access data bases of fundamental and technical information.

Dow Jones Connector

The *Connector* includes a user identification (ID) number and secret *password* that allows a customer access to the *Dow Jones*

News/Retrieval Service. The purchaser receives a Directory of Symbols, a user agreement and a specification sheet, and one hour of free nonrestricted usage. A program disk that allows a personal computer to emulate a terminal is not included in this package. It must be purchased separately and be compatible with the model of computer used.

Dow Jones Market Analyzer

This package provides updated technical analysis via the *Dow Jones News/Retrieval Service.* Its charting capabilities include (1) relative strength and comparison charts and (2) individual price and volume charts with moving averages, straight-line constructions, price/volume indicators, and oscillator charts.

Dow Jones Market Microscope

This package provides updated fundamental information on 3,200 companies and 180 industries. Its capabilities include a (1) Screening Routine and (2) Price Alert Routine. It can select and store 20 fundamental indicators from a list of 68 that can be used as screens. In addition, it can set and store user-determined support and resistance levels. The *Microscope* can print out complete or summary ranking reports of selected securities.

The Corporate Earnings Estimator includes consensus forecasts of earnings per share for 2,400 companies based on estimates provided by analysts at major brokerage firms. Media General provides data on NYSE, AMEX, and selected OTC stocks. Fundamental indicators include earnings, dividends, price/earnings ratios, revenues, shareholdings, ratios, and stock price performance relative to market indicators.

Dow Jones Market Manager

This package is used for portfolio management by investors who require an accounting and control system for maintaining one or more portfolios. The program can control up to 26 different portfolios with a maximum of 150 tax lots. It can enter securities transactions for stocks, options, bonds, mutual funds, and Treasuries. It can enter buys, sells, short sells, and buy to cover transactions.

The *Market Manager* can generate system reports with regard to (1) valued security holdings by portfolio, (2) valued security holdings by security, (3) realized gain/loss report by portfolio—a record of long- or short-term capital transactions, and (4) year-to-date transactions—an audit trail of all entries made to a portfolio.

Stockpak

Stockpak is a software package offered by Standard & Poor's Corporation compatible with Radio Shack's TRS-80 32K Business System line of microcomputers. The package provides 30 key facts for each of the 900 most actively traded common stocks. The common stocks that comprise the S&P 500 and S&P 100 Indexes are included in this group. These facts are updated monthly by S&P. *Stockpak* comes in two parts: (1) the actual system software and (2) the annual subscription service. The system software includes four parts: (1) Portfolio Management system, (2) Screen and Select software, (3) Report Writer programs, and (4) a sample data base of 900 companies with 30 data items per company. The annual subscription service entitles a subscriber to receive a new disk with updated information each month and issues of *Investor's Newsletter.*

The Portfolio Management system can be helpful in the (1) preparation of tax returns, (2) tracking dividend payments, (3) analyzing portfolio performance, (4) identifying dates that issues are eligible for long-term capital gains, and (5) comparing performance of your portfolio of stocks to stocks in the *Stockpak* data base.

Registered Trademarks

Apple II, Apple II Plus, Apple III are registered trademarks of the Apple Computer Corporation.

Dow Jones Connector, Market Analyzer, Market Microscope, Market Manager, News/Retrieval Service are registered trademarks of Dow Jones & Company.

IBM PC is a registered trademark of International Business Machines, Inc.

Radio Shack and TRS-80 are registered trademarks of the Tandy Corporation.

Stockpak is a registered trademark of the Standard & Poor's Corporation.

Glossary

AMERICAN DEPOSITORY RECEIPTS (ADRs):   The equivalent of underlying shares of stock of foreign-based companies. Issued by New York banks at the behest of the foreign company.

ANNUAL TOTAL RETURN: The capital gain or loss plus the sum of dividend disbursements expected over the next three to five years, all divided by the recent price and expressed as an average annual rate of return.

ARBITRAGE: The simultaneous purchase and sale of similar index instruments in order to benefit from an anticipated change in their price relationships.

BANK RESERVES: The balances set aside by banks to meet reserve requirements. For member banks balances are held in the form of vault cash and deposits at the Federal Reserve banks.

BASIS: The difference between the price of the spot index and the price of a designated futures contract.

BASIS POINT: When discussing interest rates, one basis point equals one hundredth of 1 percentage point.

BEAR MARKET: A market in which index prices are declining.

BID: An offer to purchase at a specified price.

BONA FIDE HEDGER: A classification or definition that may be established by the Commodity Futures Trading Commission for regulation purposes. The definition typically includes the industries that are viewed as having a bona fide hedging potential in their use of futures contracts; the users of futures contracts that can be classified as bona fide hedging by some or all of those industries; and the size or degree of such industries. All market positions except those falling under the definition of bona fide hedging are classified as speculative and are subject to margins and position limits established by the CFTC and the exchange.

BOND: A long-term debt instrument that is typically characterized by fixed semiannual interest payments and a specified maturity date.

BOOK VALUE PER SHARE: The net worth of a company less preferred stock at liquidating or redemption value divided by common shares outstanding. Includes intangible assets.

BREAK: A rapid and sharp price decline.

BROKER: (1) A person paid a fee or commission for acting as an agent in making sales or purchases. (2) When used as floor broker, it means a person who actually executes someone else's trading orders on the trading floor of an exchange. (3) When used to mean account executive, it means the person who deals with customers and their orders in commission house offices. See also Registered Commodity Representative.

BULL MARKET: A market in which index prices are rising.

BUY IN: To cover at the end of the trading session at a price within the closing range.

CALL: An option to buy an index futures or security.

CAPITAL GAINS PAID PER SHARE (Investment Companies): Profits paid to shareholders from the sale of securities. Generally taxable as a long-term capital gain in the year received.

CAPITAL GAINS REALIZED PER SHARE (Dual Funds): The net appreciation realized on investments during the year expressed in terms of the number of common or capital shares outstanding at year-end.

CAPITAL STRUCTURE: Statement of the components of long-term capital (long-term debt and preferred equity) plus the number of common shares and warrants currently outstanding, including pension liability and leases.

CFTC: The Commodity Futures Trading Commission is the independent federal agency created by Congress to regulate futures trading. The CFTC Act of 1974 became effective April 21, 1975.

CHARTING: The use of graphs and charts in analysis of market behavior so as to plot trends of price movements, average movements of price, volume, and open interest, in the hope that such graphs and charts will help one anticipate and profit from price trends.

COMMON SHARES OUTSTANDING: The number of shares of common stock actually outstanding at the end of the calendar or fiscal year, excluding shares held in the company's treasury. Figures for previous years are adjusted for stock splits and stock dividends.

COMPOSITE STATISTICS: For Value Line, the composite statistics shown for each industry are derived by summing up the figures published in stockholder reports for the individual companies comprising the industry.

CONVERSION PRICE: The price paid for common stock when the stock is obtained by converting either convertible preferred stock or convertible bonds.

CONVERSION RATIO OR RATE: The number of shares of common stock that may be obtained by converting either a convertible bond or a share of convertible preferred stock.

CONVERTIBLE DEBENTURES: Long-term unsecured debt instruments that may be converted into a specified number of shares of common stock.

CONVERTIBLE PREFERRED STOCK: Preferred stock that may be converted into a specified number of shares of common stock.

CURRENT ASSETS: Assets that may reasonably be expected to be converted into cash, sold, or consumed during the normal operating cycle of the business, usually 12 months or less. These include cash, U.S. government bonds, receivables, and inventories.

CURRENT LIABILITIES: Liabilities that will have to be satisfied within the next 12 months. These include accounts payable, taxes, wage accruals, current installments on long-term debt, and notes payable.

CURRENT PRICE/EARNINGS (P/E) RATIO: The price of the stock divided by the sum of reported earnings for the past six months and estimated earnings for the next six months.

CURRENT RATIO: The sum of current assets divided by the sum of current liabilities.

DELIVERY: This common word has unique connotations when used in connection with futures contracts. Basically, in such usage, delivery refers to the changing of ownership or control of a commodity under very specific terms and procedures established by the exchange upon which the contract is traded. However, in the stock index futures markets, there is no actual delivery of stock certificates. All settlement is for *cash only.*

DEMAND DEPOSITS: Deposits that a depositor may withdraw from his account at a bank or savings and loan association by writing a check.

DIVIDEND YIELD: The year-ahead estimated dividend yield is the estimated total of cash dividends to be declared over the next 12 months, divided by the recent price.

DIVIDENDS DECLARED PER SHARE: The common dividends per share declared (but not necessarily paid) during the company's fiscal year.

DIVIDENDS PAID PER SHARE: The common dividends per share paid (but necessarily declared) during the calendar year.

EARNINGS PER SHARE: The net income less preferred dividends divided by the number of shares of common stock outstanding.

EARNINGS YIELD: Twelve-month earnings (last six months' actual plus next six months' estimated) divided by the recent stock price; the reciprocal of the price/earnings ratio in the annual array. A measure used to aid the comparison between stocks and bonds.

EX-DIVIDEND DATE: The date by which an investor must have purchased a stock in order to receive announced dividends or stock distributions.

FEDERAL FUNDS: Historically, reserve balances that member banks lend each other, usually on an overnight basis. Federal funds now include certain other kinds of borrowing by commercial banks from other types of depository institutions and federal agencies.

FEDERAL RESERVE SYSTEM: The central bank of the United States created by Congress and consisting of seven Boards of Governors, 12 Regional Reserve banks, and about 5,600 member commercial banks.

FUNDAMENTAL ANALYSIS: An approach to market behavior that stresses the study of underlying factors of supply and demand in the commodity or stock in the belief that such analysis will enable one to profit from being able to anticipate price trends.

FUTURES CONTRACT: A transferable agreement to make or take delivery of a standardized amount of a commodity, of standardized minimum quality grades, during a specific month, under terms and conditions established by the federally designated contract market upon which trading is conducted.

GOVERNMENT SECURITIES: Fixed-income debt obligations of the U.S. government and federal agencies, held as assets.

HEDGING: The initiation of a position in a futures market that is intended as a temporary substitute for the sale or purchase of the actual securities.

INCOME TAX RATE: Federal, foreign, and state income taxes (including deferred taxes) reported to stockholders.

INSIDER DECISIONS: The number of decisions to buy or sell a company's shares by officers and directors shown by month for a 15-month period.

INTRINSIC VALUE: For call options, the amount that the market is above the strike price. For put options, the amount that the market price is below the strike price. Put or call options with intrinsic value are in-the-money options.

MARGIN: An amount of money deposited by both buyers and sellers of futures contracts to ensure performance of the terms of the contract, that is, the delivery or taking of delivery of the futures or the cancellation of the position by a subsequent offsetting trade at such price as can be attained. Margin in futures is not a payment of equity or a downpayment on the futures contract itself but rather is in the nature of a performance bond or security deposit. In equity markets, margin operates as a downpayment with interest charged on the balance due.

MONETARY POLICY: Federal Reserve actions to influence the cost and availability of money and credit as a means of helping to promote high employment, economic growth, price stability, and international stability.

MONEY STOCK: Includes the monetary aggregates of M1, M2, and M3.

NET WORTH: All the assets shown on the balance sheet including any intangible assets (i.e., goodwill, debt discount, deferred charges) less current liabilities, long-term debt, and all other noncurrent liabilities.

OFFSET: The liquidation of a purchase of futures or options contracts through sale of an equal number of contracts of the same delivery month. Either action cancels the obligation to make or take delivery of the commodity.

OPEN INTEREST: The total number of futures contracts of a given commodity that have not yet been offset by opposite futures transactions or fulfilled by delivery of the commodity; the total number of open transactions. Each open transaction has a buyer and a seller, but for calculation of open interest, only one side of the contract is counted.

OPTION: The right to buy a stock or an index futures during a specified period at a specified price.

OPTION WRITER: An investor who sells (writes) options against futures contracts or against commodity inventories and is paid a premium by an option buyer.

P/E RATIO: The price of the stock divided by earnings for a 12-month period.

POSITION LIMIT: The maximum number of speculative futures or options contracts a person (or group of persons under certain circumstances) can hold as determined by the CFTC or the SEC.

POSITION TRADING: An approach to trading in which the trader either buys or sells contracts and holds them for an extended period of time, as distinguished from the day trader, who will normally initiate and offset his or her position within a single trading session.

PREFERRED STOCK: A security that represents ownership interest in a corporation and gives its owner a prior claim over common stock with regard to dividend payments and any distribution of assets should the firm be liquidated.

PREMIUM: The price of the option minus its intrinsic value.

PRESENT VALUE: The amount that, if paid today, would be the equivalent of a future payment, under specified investment assumptions.

PRICE STABILITY INDEX: A measure of the stability of a stock's price. It includes sensitivity to the market as well as the stock's inherent volatility. Stability indexes range from 100 (highest) to 5 (lowest).

PUT OPTION: The right, but not the obligation, to sell a futures contract through exercising an option at its strike price.

REALIZED GAINS (LOSSES):   Profits or losses made from the sale of specific holdings, such as index futures, stocks, and long options.

REGISTERED COMMODITY REPRESENTATIVE (RCR):   A member or nonmember of an exchange who is registered with the exchange to solicit and handle commodity customer business for a firm.

RELATIVE PRICE STRENGTH: The stock's price over time divided by an index over the same time span. A rising relative strength line means the stock has been outperforming the market, regardless of the market's direction.

REPORTING LIMIT, REPORTABLE POSITION: The number of futures contracts, as determined by the exchange and/or the Commodity Futures Trading Commission, above which one must report to the exchange and/or the CFTC with regard to the size of one's position by commodity, by delivery month, and by purpose of the trading (that is, bona fide hedging or speculating).

SAFETY: A measurement of potential risk associated with individual common stocks rather than large diversified portfolios (for which the beta is a good risk measurement).

SCALPER: A speculator who trades a large volume of contracts at small price differences in the hope of being able to earn an acceptable overall profit at minimal risk.

SETTLEMENT PRICE: The price established by a clearing house at the close of each trading session as the official price to be used in determining net gains or losses, margin requirements, and the next day's price limits, and for other purposes. The term *settlement price* is also often used as an approximate equivalent to the term *closing price.*

SPECULATOR: One who attempts to anticipate commodity price changes and to profit through the sale and purchase or purchase and sale of commodity futures contracts or of the physical commodity.

SPREADING: The simultaneous purchase of one futures contract and sale of another in the expectation that the price relationships between the two will change, at which time one can sell the first and buy back the second at a profit. Examples include the purchase of one delivery month and the sale of another in the same commodity on the same exchange, or the purchase and sale of the same delivery month and the same commodity but on different exchanges.

STOCK DIVIDEND: The issuance of additional common shares to common stockholders, with no change in total common equity.

STOCK SPLIT: An increase in the number of common shares outstanding by a fixed ratio, say 2 to 1 or 3 to 1, with proportionate allocation of underlying common equity.

STRADDLE: A combination of put and call options on the same commodity with the same strike price and expiration date.

STRIKE PRICE: The price at which a put or call option can be exercised for a short or long futures contract.

TECHNICAL ANALYSIS: An approach to analysis of futures or stock markets and future trends of commodity or stock prices which examines patterns of price change, rates of change, and changes in volume of trading and open interest, often by charting, in the hope of being able to predict and profit from future trends.

TICK: Refers to a change in price, either up or down.

VARIATION CALL: A call for additional margin deposits made by a clearing house to a clearing member while trading is in progress when current price trends have substantially reduced the protective value of the clearing member's margin deposits. Variation calls are payable at the close of the business day.

VOLUME OF TRADING: Constitutes a simple addition of transactions in securities, index futures, or options during a specified period of time.

WARRANT: An option to buy a security, usually a common stock, at a set price over an established number of years. A warrant has no claim on either the equity or the profits of a company.

Bibliography

Books

Arms, R. W. *Volume Cycles in the Stock Market.* Homewood, Ill.: Dow Jones-Irwin, 1983.

Bernstein, J. *The Handbook of Commodity Cycles.* New York: John Wiley & Sons, 1982.

Brealey, R. A. *An Introduction to Risk and Return from Common Stocks.* Cambridge, Mass.: MIT Press, 1983.

Coopers and Lybrand. *Strategies: Tax and Financial Planning.* New York: Coopers and Lybrand, 1981.

Edwards, R. D., and Magee, J. *Technical Analysis of Stock Trends.* Springfield, Mass.: John Magee, 1966.

Lorie, J. H., and Hamilton, M. J. *The Stock Market: Theories and Evidence.* Homewood, Ill.: Dow Jones-Irwin, 1973.

McMillan, L. G. *Options as a Strategic Investment.* New York: The New York Institute of Finance, 1980.

Power, M. J., and Vogel, D. J. *Inside the Financial Futures Markets.* New York: John Wiley & Sons, 1981.

Pring, M. J. *How to Forecast Interest Rates.* New York: McGraw-Hill, 1981.

Rudd, A., and Clasing, H. K. *Modern Portfolio Theory.* Homewood, Ill.: Dow Jones-Irwin, 1982.

Schmeltz, L. R. *Playing the Stock and Bond Markets with Your Personal Computer.* Blue Ridge Summit, Pa.: Tab Books, 1981.

Wilder, J. W. *New Concepts in Technical Trading Systems.* Greensboro, N.C.: Trend Research, 1978.

Woodwell, D. R. *Automating Your Financial Portfolio.* Homewood, Ill.: Dow Jones-Irwin, 1983.

Zieg, K., and Nix, W. *The Commodity Options Market.* Homewood, Ill.: Dow Jones-Irwin, 1978.

252

Articles and Pamphlets

Angle, E. W. "Keys for Business Forecasting." *Federal Reserve Bank of Richmond*, April 1980.

Board of Governors of the Federal Reserve. "The Federal Reserve System." *Federal Reserve*, Washington, D.C., September 1974.

Cook, T. Q., and B. J. Summers, ed. "Instruments of the Money Market." *Federal Reserve Bank of Richmond*, 1981.

Figlewski, S., and S. Kon. "Portfolio Management with Stock Index Futures." *Financial Analysts Journal*, January–February 1982.

Grant, D. "How to Optimize with Stock Index Futures." *Journal of Portfolio Management*, spring 1982.

McGraw-Hill. *120 Years of Preserving the Right to Know*. Booklet published by the Standard & Poor's Corporation.

Moore, R. J. "Turn to the Index." *Registered Representative*, September 1983, pp 39–44.

Paris, A. "Stock Index Futures." *Illinois Banker*, August 1982, pp. 19–32.

Thayer, P. W. "Stock Index Futures Key to Above-Market Return." *Pensions and Investments*, February 7, 1983.

Weiner, N. "The Hedging Rational for a Stock Index Futures Contract." *The Journal of Futures Markets* 1, no 1 (1981).

West, S., and N. Miller. "Why the New NYSE Common Stock Indexes?" *Financial Analysts Journal*, May–June 1967, pp 1–6.

Index

Account executive/Brokerage firm, selection, 16
Accounts, how to open, 18–19
Arbitrage, 146

Basis
defined, 68, 135–36
graphs, 68–69
risk, 166–67
Bearish opinion
defined, 151
fundamentals, 155
strategies, 160–62
technicals, 156
Beta
coefficient, 168
defined, 168
formula for adjusting, 41–42
Black and Scholes model, 83–84
Broker loan rate, 23
Bullish opinion
defined, 151
fundamentals, 154
strategies, 158–60
technicals, 155
Business cycle
defined, 53, 89
effects of the Federal Reserve on, 53
indicators, 89–92
peaks, 53
troughs, 53–55

Capital Asset Pricing Model (CAPM)
defined, 29
terms, 37–38
Capital gains, 200
Carrying charge, 135
Cash settlement, 10, 106
Charting services, 208
Computer Technology Index, 125–26

Computerized trading systems, 16
Contrary opinion, 71
Cyclical analysis, 71–72

Deltas, 84, 152
Disinflation, 52
Dow Theory, 72–77

Economic Recovery Act of 1981, 193
Exchanges, addresses, 208

Federal Reserve
credit policies, 50
credit regulation, 51
defined, 47
discount rate, 50
effects on stock index prices, 55–56
Federal Open Market Committee
(FOMC), 43
functions of, 43, 49
monetary policies, 44
security transaction regulations, 44, 47
structure of, 44
Fundamental factors, 87–88
Futures brokers, categories of, 16–17

Hedge ratio, 84–86
Hedging
defined, 149
IRC definition, 196–97
strategies, 166
taxation, 195, 197

Index options
advantages of, 5
compared, 5, 78–79, 106–7
defined, 12
taxation of, 196

253